I Hate Old Music, Too

I Hate Old Music, Too

How Familiarity & Overuse
Killed Our Favorite Music

Dave Thompson

Backbeat
Books

Essex, Connecticut

 **Backbeat Books**

An imprint of Globe Pequot, the trade division of
The Rowman & Littlefield Publishing Group, Inc.
4501 Forbes Blvd., Ste. 200
Lanham, MD 20706
www.rowman.com

Distributed by NATIONAL BOOK NETWORK

Library of Congress Cataloging-in-Publication Data available

ISBN 978-1-4930-7351-1 (pbk. : alk. paper)
ISBN 978-1-4930-7352-8 (electronic)

♾™ The paper used in this publication meets the minimum requirements of
American National Standard for Information Sciences—Permanence of Paper
for Printed Library Materials, ANSI/NISO Z39.48-1992

To my father, Brynley Weightman (1933–2023)

CONTENTS

Twenty-Two
Twenty Totally Tubular Hits of the 1980s—
or, The Wrong Box
178

Twenty-Three
First Time Ever in Limited Edition "Distressed"
(Scratchy Warped) Dirty Off-Black Vinyl—
or, In Praise of Rip-Off Store Day
184

Twenty-Four
The Sound of Tomorrow's Yesterdays Today—
or, The Wonder of Eurovision
189

Twenty-Five
In Which We Thank the Stars of the Past for Their Service
. . . and Tell Them It's Time to Let Go
201

FOREWORD

Brushing My Teeth with Robert Plant—
or, Dave Thompson Rules, Okay?

Mike Edison

Sacred cows make the tastiest meat. Dave Thompson knows this as much as anyone, hence his book of a few years back, *I Hate New Music: The Classic Rock Manifesto*, which was not so much published as it was deployed, and for which I was the gleeful editor.

I have now been demoted to writing the foreword of the putative follow-up, *I Hate Old Music, Too*, a job once held by the distinguished writer and mensch Richard Meltzer, who called the previous book "the flying fucking shit!" He meant that in a good way. I think that is a good descriptor for this book, too.

You might think that now that with this new screed, Dave has finally gone around the bend and hates *all* music, but that wouldn't be the case. No one loves music more than Dave, which is why he wrote this book—he is like the patriot who loves his country so much he is willing to do the jobs no one else is willing to do.

The ideas in this book are way above the pay grade of politicians: too risky even for the jerks on television who make ends meet by bloviating extremist positions, and too dangerous even for the best trained, best equipped fighting force in the world to tangle with. It's a zero-sum game, no prisoners are taken, and only Dave has the brass to take on the demigods of rock's zombie nation, armed solely with a writing machine, a grizzled smile on his face, a few cats in the garden who may or may not care, and a wife who is all too used to rolling her eyes and saying, "Well, that's just Dave being Dave."

And aren't we lucky to have him! Dave is also the most prolific writer in the history of rock, and deserves his own wing in the so-called Rock and Roll Hall of Fame, which, frankly, I don't like to even discuss, because that just gives some legitimacy to their creep capitalist crypt when all it really is, is a wax museum for people who don't like wax.

But while we're speaking of Ye Olde Mausoleum, I have a confession to make (and no better place to do it than in the preamble to Dave's highly enlightened takedown of classic rock fetishism)—when Jeff Beck died, it affected me far more than I ever would have imagined.

I didn't cry or nuthin', because here's the thing: I'm no Jeff Beck fan. To my mind, he's played maybe two dozen interesting notes among the four hundred billion he's peeled off in the last fifty years. There were a couple of cool things with the Yardbirds—we all know which ones—and about an album-and-a-half's worth of flashy hard rock with Rod Stewart that was exciting, but overrated by the same sort of people who are easily distracted by bright shiny objects (it was not in any way in the same class as Led Zeppelin for any number of reasons, not least of all that guitar players and bass players are not interchangeable). But after that, what? He seemed to pervert the simplicity tacit to playing the blues and spun it into a sort of aural pornography turning a perfectly good guitar into a gigantic spizz nozzle.

I'm sure you'll tell me I'm wrong. The guy could play the guitar, no doubt about it; Beck was a virtuoso guitar player. But as discussed elsewhere, virtuosity is not really a yardstick good for much; just look at the world's holiest cows, the Beatles. I'm pretty sure Sir Paul is the only one in that group that qualifies as "virtuoso" as generally understood by the hoi polloi, but more important, he had great taste; in fact, sometimes too good. You could never accuse him of playing too many notes; the worst crime he could be convicted of is laying the frosting on a bit thick. Such a romantic, that Paul.

When Beck died, the caterwauling and rending of garments came from many directions, but most surprising, from the coterie of boomers and entry-level Gen Xers who had always self-described as "punks," badging themselves with Ramones T-shirts and who were now wailing as if the guitar itself had actually passed away. My social media feed was jammed with gooey goodbyes from the same people whom (I thought) had dedicated their lives, as artists and consumers, to the eradication of marathon guitar solos, frilly fusion, and all manner of self-indulgent, gee-whiz circus tricks. *"He inspired me . . . the guitar will never be the same,"* and my favorite, *"Why are all the great ones being taken away from us?"*

Love him or whatever, the dude was seventy-eight, and given the high-risk profession he was in, that's a hell of a good run by any standard, or maybe you didn't get the memo: No One Here Gets Out Alive.

But we live in a world where reality bends in the digital breeze of the hive mind. The same lot was stricken with grief when David Crosby checked out, as if he had been snatched from the womb, and I tell ya, I never thought I'd see the day when the guys who used to elbow me in the mosh pit at CBGB would be weeping openly over David Fucking Crosby.

Nostalgia, as it turns out, is a disease. Maybe the folks who write the next edish of *The Diagnostic and Statistical Manual of Mental Disorders* should take a closer look at it. Sure, there are benign forms—sharing memories is supposed to bring us all together. But then, so does cancer.

Never mind that. If you find joy in the blurps and bleeps of Beck's guitar supernova *Blow by Blow* somehow appealing, well, God bless you; you'll probably inherit the earth.

But when punk rockers started rending their garments over Jeff Beck's body, the classic rock reach around had gone too far. Wasn't all that frilly fusion and gee-whiz look at me "I Am a Great Rock God" puffery the reason punk rock was invented in the first place? It's as if the Sex Pistols and the Ramones never happened, never mind hip-hop. Or the Residents. Or Captain Beefheart. And on and on.

Sid Vicious died when he was twenty-one years old. Of course, he didn't play as many notes as Jeff Beck, and the ones he did play weren't extraordinary in and of themselves, but as a place where pathos met bathos, where rock still meant revolution, he had a much sexier career than Jeff Beck, at least as far as creating durable art goes. I still get excited when I hear the Sex Pistols. Hell, I get excited just seeing the record cover; whereas, I spend very little time missing Beck, Bogert, and Appice, or the second Jeff Beck Group, whose influence, I am sure, is felt nowhere.

I remember once upon a time when Pink Floyd was frowned upon by nascent punks, and why not? The awesome inflatable pig aside, who needed to pay money to go to a hockey arena to listen to all of that contrived angst when you could just go to the local pub and get the real thing for free? All of a sudden, the same guys who formed bands precisely to reject the concept of overproduced concepts were going on and on about how much they loved Yes, Jethro Tull, and Jeff Beck, never mind the Beatles, who, in the sacred cow department, play in the same league as the Dalai Lama.

When the Beatles' *Get Back* documentary came out, the canonization of the group hit an all-time high (low?)—no criticism would be tolerated!! No wisecracks, no commentary that might alter the narrative . . . *Nein!!*

I genuinely enjoyed it, and in a well-meaning and casual post to a thing called Facebook, I suggested they sounded like a confused country band—even through all of their well-established Fab Fourisms, didn't George's telecaster solo on the title track seem to come straight outta Nashville? How come every time they had a moment they were hacking through songs by Hank Williams and Buck Owens and Doc Pomus and Eddie Cochran and Bob Dylan, and on and on? Wasn't "Let It Be" a legit stab at Southern gospel, or at the very least a Protestant hymn warmed up with a bit of orange corduroy soul? Weren't "Two of Us," "One after 909," and "For You Blue" *actual goddam country songs?*

And for this I was ripped apart as a know-nothing, a contrarian, an ill-educated punk, but most of all a troll, because obviously the Beatles were not confused, I was. Also, I should shut my fucking mouth because blah, blah, blah . . . Anyway, what began as a fan club had turned into a cult, and the long knives were out for any blasphemers.

I wonder whatever happened to all the people who burned Bob Dylan's records when he started to play the electric guitar.

But speaking of sacred cows, back to the abattoir. So Jeff Beck died, and for a moment the world seemed to stop. If you saw my social media feed, you would have thought that he had died and come back—which, admittedly, would have been something.

But this was it for me, the straw that broke my rainbow bridge to the past. The autofellation of the military industrial music industry had become so effortless that . . . well, as remarked before . . . it was as if the Sex Pistols and the Ramones had never happened, never mind hip-hop. Or the Residents. Or Captain Beefheart. And so on.

Rock'n'roll was no longer a sexy, existential threat. It was now, as Dave says in this wonderful book, just "a grotesque recycling plant." That is the story of twentieth-century rock in the twenty-first century. It is exactly what Thomas Pynchon defined as late-stage capitalism: "a pyramid racket on a global scale . . . getting the suckers to believe it's all gonna go on forever."

The highlight of the summer season at my local shed this year is an edition of the Grateful Dead so faded you can actually see through them. It sold out in moments. Also appearing are an animatronic version of

Journey, and Chicago, who have zero original members and claim to be the very best version of the band, ever, which is very likely true.

It's a good thing the Sex Pistols only made one record. It's a great one, and as self-destruction myths go, they're tippity-top. A second go would have knocked the shine off of the entire experience. But even they couldn't resist the siren call of freshly minted merch. And for all the hype and excitement surrounding that first comeback tour, it must be said that pound-for-pound those were among the least inspired performances I've ever suffered.

Maybe they deserve extra credit for crass cynicism, or maybe for being honest—they said right up front they were doing it for the money. Except in the end, I found out it was my money. So I've got no one to blame but myself, but fuck me, I thought I was in on the joke. Sadly, there's not a lot of irony in the rock'n'roll nostalgia racket. At least Jeff Beck, for all of his narcissistic noodlings and whammy bar shenanigans, went out there and gave his fans what they paid for. In fact, amortized as notes per dollar, a Jeff Beck concert ticket was probably the last best deal left in the free market of septuagenarian classic rockers, if you were into that sort of thing.

But now he's dead.

So where does that leave us? What is the shortest distance between fashion and fusion? Between classic rock and the Sex Pistols, from "Won't Get Fooled Again" to "Ever get the feeling you've been cheated?"

It's a trick question, because the show doesn't always have to go on, and the customer is not always right. Go, have your fun. But first, read this book. You've got 282 pages to decide if you are going to be part of the problem, or if you are going to be part of the solution. Or, as Jeff Beck once said, "Bleep blop bloop whannnnng splung ptaaang!"

Mike Edison
Barryille, New York

Mike Edison is an award-winning saboteur whose books include *I Have Fun Everywhere I Go: Savage Tales of Pot, Porn, Punk Rock, Pro Wrestling, Talking Apes, Evil Bosses, Dirty Blues, American Heroes, and the Most Notorious Magazines in the World*; and *Sympathy for the Drummer: Why Charlie Watts Matters.*

ABOUT THIS BOOK

When Backbeat Books published *I Hate New Music* in 2008, the book did not so much divide its audience as spike its drink with asparagus. Reviewers and readers alike either celebrated it ("A sometimes mystifying, often hilarious journey through 'rock'n'roll'"—*Under the Radar*) or tore it to shreds ("Horrific! Unreadable!"—online review).

Some regarded the book as a call to arms ("Bringing on the debate and urging the 18–35 demographic to create a golden age of their own and leave [the author's] the hell alone"—the *Agit Reader*). Others saw it as parody ("This book has to be a satire of all those middle-aged doofuses who sit around in a room with headphones on listening to the same 5 records until the day they die"—another online review). And some went full-bore Edgar Allan Poe on it, echoing his immortal declaration that "we shall take the liberty of throwing [it] unopened out of the window. Our pigs are not all of the description called 'Learned,' but they will have more leisure for its perusal than we." [1]

I Hate New Music sparked arguments, frustrated debates, and received the strongest reader response of any book I've written. It still raises its tousled little head in interviews today.

Fifteen-plus years later, much has changed. New music, of course, remains hateful. In places. Even then, however, I didn't claim to have discovered *nothing* of value in the world of modern popular music. Just not as much as I hoped I might.

But old music has also lost a lot of its bite, and we're not even looking for the orthodontist who will perform the *coup de grâce*. The teeth fell out years ago. Now, it's the gums that are the problem.

I Hate Old Music, Too is the story of twentieth-century rock in the twenty-first century, and the grotesque recycling plant that it has become. And why the focus on rock? Because of the manifold genres that constitute "popular music" today, rock is the only one that is constantly droning on about its past, to the expense of anyone who tries to put that behind them.

---

1. Poe, reviewing William Harrison Ainsworth's novel *Guy Fawkes* for *Graham's Magazine*, 1841.

Of course, arriving at an absolute definition of the term *rock* itself is no easy thing. Even *Encyclopedia Britannica* acknowledges that "There is basic agreement that rock 'is a form of music with a strong beat . . . but there are so many exceptions to this description that it is practically useless.'"

Let the following, then, be our guide.

It is a music in which the principal instruments are a combination of electric, but also acoustic and semi-acoustic guitar, electric bass, drums, and keyboards, but not necessarily all at once.

A music which Jerry Rubin described as "Hard animal . . . energy beat / surg[ing] hot through us, the driving rhythm arousing repressed emotions."[2]

A music which, through the heyday of the British and American music press (1966–1990), received the lion's share of coverage, far beyond the specialist corners into which were shunted "R&B," "hip-hop," "reggae," "country," "folk," "jazz," etc. Unless, in the latter three instances, there lurked the dread suffix "-rock."

A music which, even today, is primarily white, and in terms of coverage and international renown, largely Anglo-American. Prior to the mid- to late 1970s, the majority of its headlined practitioners were also male.

A music which tends to take itself very seriously, and has been prone to marry itself to other more "respected" genres (see above) in a bid to prove its worth to those that would otherwise dismiss it as childish, primitive, and crude.

The only major art form in musical history that has transformed itself into a verb. And the only one that eats its own offspring via a cottage industry that would enjoy nothing so much as to cut the tongue from every yowling beast that is currently described as a pop star, and replace them with sixties sludge, seventies sick bags, eighties enemas . . . and even the nineties don't get much respect.

If you doubt that, look at the waiting lists indie hopefuls have to swallow because the pressing plants are too busy turning out super deluxe boxed dinosaurs. Listen to the radio stations that focus their output on rock and pop oldies, rather than taking a chance on anything fresh. Read the critics who've abandoned reviewing anything that's not either

2. Jerry Rubin, *Do It!* (Simon and Schuster, 1970).

a reissue of a "classic" album, or the latest by someone who might have made one once.

And why? Dylan Thomas put it best. "Do not go gently into that good night." Which is fair enough. No former multi-million-dollar enterprise ever wants to admit that its time has come.

Sometimes, though, it has no choice. What could never have been predicted was the confluence of so many other disparate, but ultimately damaging, currents that would emerge to assist it through its death throes.

Electronic music, emerging in the 1970s and taking precedence in the 1980s, was already regarded as the icicle-fingered assassin of rock's hitherto skeuomorphic hegemony. By the late 1990s, however, the survivors were confronted with a generation of musicians who *grew up* on electronic music. Who knew little and cared less for all that had unfolded beforehand, and who now controlled technology that rendered most every other instrument surplus to requirements.

Some areas, punk and metal among them, were able to adapt, shifting their own sonic parameters to embrace these new expectations. But classic rock was neither willing, nor capable, of doing likewise, and why? Because if you change what classic rock sounds and feels like, you are no longer playing classic rock. You dead end. You're finished.

Another fatal wound was dealt by the final subversion of rock's hitherto secure role as the *lingua franca* of youth. A state of affairs that remains equally true today, so much so that it is scarcely even mentioned any longer. How long ago indeed were those days when rock and its rockers were the first to register complaints and concerns; the first to point out injustice and wrong; the first to face down prejudice and discrimination. The first to stage massive festivals to raise funds against disaster and starvation. The first to see their art as a force for good.

As Jerry Rubin, again, put it, "The New Left sprang, a predestined pissed-off child, from Elvis's gyrating pelvis."[3]

But that was then. This is now, and today when there is protest to be sounded, although there are still occasional outliers, we instinctively look to hip-hop to most vociferously voice a generation's discontent, and we have done so for the best part of the last thirty years.

---

3. Rubin, *Do It!*

Banned for their opinions, jailed for their convictions, Pussy Riot are the loudest sound of protest that rock has ever heard. ИГОРЬ МУХИН AT RUSSIAN WIKIPEDIA, CC BY-SA 3.0.

Wherefore the Fugs of the twenty-first century? Wherefore the "'F.I.S.H.' chant"? Wherefore "Volunteers," "Ohio," and "Out Demons Out"?

They're still around. They're just voiced as raps today.

Likewise, when there is celebrity to be feted by the mass media, again we look to the superstars of rap to promote new sneakers or launch their own range of scents. "Rock stars" barely get a look any longer.[4]

Add to this the final demise of the aforementioned music press (see chapter 14), and the emergence of the echo chambers that replaced serious commentary on the internet with nitpicking one-upmanship.

Then consider the passing, as a musical force, of the last generations to witness (or at least be aware of) how hard the likes of Paul McCartney, Bruce Springsteen, and the Rolling Stones worked to attain the omni-sponsored superstardom that was taken for granted in the eighties and beyond.

---

4. Although U2 did have an iPod named after them—see chapter 10.

It was the ultimate perfect storm, and if rock was to maintain its cultural role as the number one form in popular music, it had a serious fight on its hands.

How did it respond?

By reminding us of what it *used* to be, and how "superior" that was to what was happening now. By lionizing the past and belittling the present. By surrendering the high ground and becoming, instead, an internet troll with nothing more to say then a squealed "remember meeeeeee," because memories were suddenly all it felt it had to offer.

A scrapyard in which a major release is a modern remix of a fifty-year-old LP. A charnel house in which no artist is so decrepit (or deceased) that they cannot be resuscitated for one last hologram. A backyard barbecue for which even the most sanctimonious veteran will happily hand out napkins and slip into an apron. A financial model in which you are expected to pay in the region of a grand for a couple of hours in the company of its most sainted practitioners, because heaven forfend they should be confronted with an audience that still believes gigs should be a cheap night out.

And what does their audience receive for their investment? The marketing men insist we're attending a personal concert experience. In fact, we're the same abused cattle that we always were; only now we pay the rental on the stun guns.[5]

That's what this book is about. Partly.

But it's also concerned with comebacks and reunions, most of which involve half (or less) of the best-known members. The "vinyl revival" . . . Record Store Day . . . the continued cult of the Name Your Sacred Cow . . . tribute acts . . . modern marketing and the language thereof. "Kids today" who—we are led to believe—see nothing wrong with liking the music that their parents (or even grandparents) used to groove to.[6] And "super deluxe" reissues that expand an original album to Brobdingnagian proportions by adding multiple near-identical versions of the songs you

---

5. It's not only the hoariest veterans whose fans are fleeced. In March 2023, Ticketmaster hit headlines when their "service fees" and "facility charges" came close to doubling the cost of tickets to see the Cure's latest US tour. Ironically, the move came just two days after the mega-company was sued by upward of three hundred fans for antitrust violations and fraud after chaos erupted around Taylor Swift tickets earlier in the year.

6. If you'd done that in 1977, you'd have been telling everyone that you were an Ethel Waters fan ("and Dick Powell's amazing, too"), and let's guess how many friends you'd have been left with.

liked least of all, plus a brand-new superfluous remix, and one cannot help but nod in agreement, remembering what *Private Eye* magazine remarked when the Beatles' final LP release was given the once over in 2021. "Let It Fucking Be."[7]

And more besides.

That is what this book is about, and you know what? You don't even have to read the chapters in order. Think of it, instead, as a simple playlist. You can listen in order, you can open at random, you can shuffle to your heart's content. And the only apology that needs to be made is to any readers disappointed by such a narrow view, who were hoping to see the likes of Celine Dion, James Brown, Bob Marley, Public Enemy, and Tammy Wynette skewered with the same intensity as their favorite classic rockers.

Because they simply don't deserve it.

---

7. *Private Eye Annual*, 2022.

A FEW WORDS ON TERMINOLOGY

One of the most unexpected comments I read concerning this book's predecessor (albeit delivered several years after it was published) actually had nothing to do with either new music or old. It had to do with the use of the word "hate" in the title, and the brutal negativity that it thus apparently connoted.

It was a fair point. The dictionary definition of the word *hate* is quite simple: "An emotion of extreme dislike or aversion," says the *Oxford English Dictionary*. Johnny extremely dislikes brussels sprout enemas. Janet extremely dislikes the bright pink dress she was given for Christmas. That particular book extremely disliked new music.

Language changes, however, and meanings morph, and that's how it should be. Unless a tongue is already dead, it has no choice but to evolve—otherwise, we'd still be walking around saying "verily and forsooth" to one another. Our need for certain words develops likewise, and our interpretations of them also. We'll get deeper into that subject later, but suffice for now to say, if changing the meaning of a word means clickbait headline writers no longer need to repeat themselves so often, it can only be a good thing. Right?

Close to thirty years of internet convenience have gifted us with an entire new dictionary of altered meanings, abbreviated terms, acronyms, and emojis. Trying to reverse that flow is akin to trying to get a straight answer from a crooked politician. You can argue until you are blue in the face, but it won't make an iota of difference.

Our understanding of the word *hate* has not changed so drastically as some terms. But its adoption to define concepts of considerably more importance than one's feelings toward new music and brussels sprouts—hate speech, for example, or hate crimes—does convey considerably more weight to its usage than was the case in 2008.

Doggedly, however, this book adheres to an older, and perhaps more innocent definition of the word, intending no offense and certainly no criminality in its determined insistence to reiterate the flow of its predecessor's title. Yes, words have meaning. But sometimes, they have several.

Another area in which *I Hate New Music* caused occasionally unintended offense was in its apparent condemnation of certain artists, old and new, when in fact the book's intention was to cite them merely as an example of how things can go sadly awry within even the most well-managed and much-beloved of musical careers.

Not always. To state, for example, that the Beatles' *Sergeant Pepper's Lonely Hearts Club Band* stands among the most influential albums of 1967, but that not all of its progeny can be regarded with the same respect, is to merely echo a fact remarked upon by a myriad of critics, musicians, and fans throughout the last near-sixty years.

To then gleefully name and shame those progeny, however, could be construed as mean-hearted and spiteful. Besides, opinions are like adolescent pubic hairs. It doesn't matter how many you have, there's always more on the way. My bad.

It's a difficult issue to surmount, however, all the more so since facts are themselves now, apparently, as pliable as plasticine. As Prince Harry remarks in his bestselling memoir *Spare*, "There's just as much truth in what I remember and how I remember it as there is in so-called objective facts."[8] Meaning, if an individual recalls such-and-such a performer releasing such-and-such a record on such-and-such a date, then that statement should be accepted as readily as any historical document that argues otherwise.

How can one argue with that logic?

By cheating. Throughout this book, the goal is to adhere to the facts as history has thus far recorded them, regardless of whether some other estranged member of the royal family should come along and say, "Actually, it was the Stones who did *Sgt Pepper* and it came out in 1973. And this is true because I remember it."

There will be occasions, however, where I am searching for an exemplar as opposed to making a specific point, but intend no malice toward any particular artist. So what did I do? I invented an entire alternate history of rock, in which many of the artists and albums that we remember are supplanted by others which . . . well, I think I made them up. But, these days, how can anyone be sure of that?[9]

---

8. Prince Harry, *Spare* (Bantam Books, 2023).
9. For established precedents to this, witness the careers—real and imaginary—of Bad News, Llewyn Davis, the Folksmen, Jim MacLean and the Stray Cats, the Rutles, Billy Shears, Spinal Tap, and the Turds.

Appendix A offers an index of these acts, together with pertinent career details. However, and it cannot be stressed often enough, any similarity between these acts and any person, performer, or talentless loser, living or dead, is wholly coincidental. Even when you think it might not be.

INTRODUCTION

As Easy as Falling Off a Logarithm

First things first. The future of popular music is assured. It's the past that is unpredictable, and I'll level with you now. Do I hate old music? No. Do I even extremely dislike it? No, not particularly. As I wrote this book, I listened to everything from the hits from the Ziegfeld Follies (1908–1931) to a Tanita Tikaram bootleg (late 1990s); from Alan Lomax's sacred harp recordings (1950s) to a heap of scratchy Wings 45s (1970s). And let's not forget that ecstatic afternoon when Bonnie Tyler's "Total Eclipse of the Heart" (1983) was repeated seventeen times until I got up to take the single off the changer. Plus, a lot more besides.

No, what I extremely dislike (it's okay, I'll get bored with that term shortly) about old music . . . which, perhaps, it would be more accurate to describe as *vintage* music . . . is not what it was, but what it has become.

I extremely dislike vintage music radio because if I wanted to hear the same three songs about that damned dead dog eleven times a day, I'd have made a cassette tape.

I ~~extremely dis~~ hate vintage music awards ceremonies because there can surely be only so many times Billy Big Bananas[10] can collect another Lifetime Bereavement trophy before even he begs to be overlooked next time.

I hate vintage music forums where the faithful live only to mock whichever unfortunate modern artist was most recently compared to one of the sacred cows of their past ("not only is Jennifer Dingleberry[11] not the new Etta James, but I've heard throat polyps that can sing better than her").

I hate curated streaming services where you dial up one act and get a dozen others besides, because some algorithm you'll never understand thinks Bobby Goldsboro sounds like Christian Death.

I hate the modern media's pathological fear of contradicting what it regards as "common knowledge"—that *Dark Side of the Moon* must be Pink Floyd's greatest album because it sold more than any of their others,

---

10. See appendix A: An Index of Wholly Imaginary Artists.
11. See appendix A.

and remained on the chart for five thousand years or some such. That "Start Me Up" and "Satisfaction" are the Stones' finest recordings because they're the ones that everyone knows; and that anything by Queen that isn't "Bohemian Rhapsody" is automatically a "deep cut."

I hate "deep cuts."

I hate what Frank Zappa described as "the machinery that takes anything and exaggerates it to the point where it's blown out of proportion and the public believes the inflated version of what the reality is."[12]

But, most of all, I hate hearing that rock'n'roll is dead (it isn't), that nobody's writing music that matters any longer (they are), and that most young musicians are more interested in collecting social media likes than they are in actually writing and playing songs (they may be, but not for the reasons that are implied).

In fact, the past almost-quarter of a century has arguably seen at least as much "great" music produced, and "great" artists emerge, as any similar period in the history of rock'n'roll—which, for the sake of argument, this book pegs at beginning circa 1955, with the first great burst of rocking rolling talent emerging into the mainstream. Elvis Presley! Little Richard! Buddy Holly! Eddie Cochran! Rocky Biceps!![13]

This book is *not* a history of twenty-first-century rock. In fact, long passages, even chapters, will elapse without any reference whatsoever to the music that has made toes tap throughout the past quarter-century. What it explores is the manner in which certain performers, certain records, certain *beliefs*, have placed the past upon such a towering pedestal that it's sometimes difficult to believe we are not still living sixty years go, and gee-whizz, I just cannot wait to hear the latest fab waxing by the Rub-Outs.[14]

Sometimes one wonders whether any future act will ever truly displace the legends of yester-decade, no matter what they achieve.

For example.

For almost sixty years, the record for the most songs by an individual act on the *Billboard* Top Ten was the five that the Beatles rocked up in April 1964. That achievement, however, was shattered in September

12. John Swenson, "Frank Zappa Talks Music, Money and Steve Vai," *Guitar World*, March 1982.
13. See appendix A.
14. See appendix A.

2021, when Drake devoured nine of the places and again, little more than a year later, in October 2022, when Taylor Swift *was* singlehandedly the entire Top Ten. But did the Beatles' fans concede defeat graciously? Did they hell. To quote several dozen internet forum users, Drake's and Swift's successes were "just further evidence of how meaningless the charts are."

For fifty years, Don McLean's "American Pie" was the longest song ever to top the *Billboard* chart, clocking in at eight minutes. In 2022 (again), Taylor Swift's "All Too Well" set a new record of ten minutes. Doesn't count. Meaningless.

For a little over fifty years, the Beatles held the record for having the most UK number ones on Christmas Day—four. In 2022, LadBaby snatched the honor away from them by scoring five. Doesn't count. Meaningless.

And so on. No matter what record is shattered, no matter which top dog is suddenly relegated to second place, there is *always* a reason, *always* an excuse, *always* a gray man with a thoughtful beard to tell you why it doesn't count.

Because Elvis is King, The Beatles are God, and there is not a single artist out there today who couldn't be outperformed by a fingernail full of Jim Morrison's earwax.

Okay, then.

In fact, there has never been a point where one specific musical form, or even artist, was the *only* one that people were buying. Even at the heights of Presley- or Beatle- or even Rollermania, there has *always* been background noise, the records made that appealed to people who *didn't* want to go to San Francisco with flowers in their hair, or visit the Kings Road to pick up a safety-pin cheek piercing. And it's the background noise that is what popular music is *really* about—that has sustained it not only in the rock age, but before that.

Yet here we are, about to celebrate the seventieth anniversary of "Rock Around the Clock"—popularly, if not forensically, regarded as the song that kickstarted the entire rock'n'roll epoch—and there is an entire industry for whom the clock stopped ticking years ago; and who are devoted now to dismissing more or less any artist, or any form of music, that doesn't match its own definition of what the music should be. And how do they achieve that? Mindless repetition, cultural assimilation, and a seemingly pathological need to suck the last vestiges of freshness, rebellion, and excitement out of the *very music it claims to be championing*. While, again, dismissing anything that looks like it might displace it.

This record is crap because it was obviously composed on a laptop in ten minutes, and still required seventeen people to write it. It is true that songwriting credits do now feel a little like the closing credits in movies, where everybody down to the body doubles' dog walkers seem to get a name check. But so what?

This one is rubbish because it's clearly identical to an unreleased song by a band that never escaped the drummer's parents' basement in 1973—and this is possible because, after all, there are only so many combinations of notes and chords out there, and there can't be many left that nobody has hit upon. But again, so what?

And *that* is a heap of steaming armadillo turds because it wasn't made during what *everyone knows* was the golden age of rock'n'roll music, which itself is whichever arbitrary date the speaker deigns to saddle it with.

A lot of these arguments are circular, much like those people who find themselves sacrificing their health to the demands of a job they only have because they need the health insurance to take care of the body that is being ground into the dirt by their job. Circular and inescapable.

It is fortunate, then, that the records I happen to like or dislike are not of concern here. What we're far more interested in is the avaricious anaconda that "vintage music" has become, and how that has besmirched and even disgraced the memory of music that really doesn't deserve such a fate.

When Queen wrote "Bohemian Rhapsody," did they really expect it to become the most streamed classic rock song of all time?[15]

No. In fact, according to Freddie Mercury biographer Lesley-Ann Jones,[16] bassist John Deacon wasn't even sure about releasing it as a 45, fearing it "would prove the greatest error of judgment of Queen's career." Furthermore, both Queen's record label EMI and "the industry in general voiced misgivings. Radio stations wondered what the hell they were supposed to do with a six-minute single."

---

15. Aisha Hassan, "Queen's 'Bohemian Rhapsody' Is the Most-Streamed Classic Rock Song of All Time," *Quartz*, December 11, 2018, https://qz.com/quartzy/1491751/queens-bohemian-rhapsody-most-streamed-classic-rock-song-ever.

16. Lesley-Ann Jones, *Mercury: An Intimate Biography of Freddie Mercury* (Touchstone reprint edition, 2012).

When Keith Richards came up with the "Start Me Up" riff in the mid-1970s, did it ever cross his mind that he'd still be playing it into his own mid-seventies and beyond? No, because according to producer Chris Kimsey, Keith saw it as a reggae song. "Then, one evening, suddenly [he] started to play it as a full-on rock song. They only did two takes [before] Keith came into the control room, listen[ed] to it . . . and [said] 'Wipe that. I don't like it. Get rid of it.' Of course, I didn't do that."[17]

Keith would be justified if he'd cursed him every day since then.

There are countless similar examples, and in (almost) every case, the song and the songwriter are the most innocent parties of all. Yes, there are composers who seem able to write "hits to order"—Burt Bacharach, Carole King, Lennon-McCartney, Desmond Child, Björn Ulvaeus and Benny Andersson, Carole Bayer Sager—but even they can be taken by surprise when *this* song proves the all-time monster; whereas *that* one doesn't even make it onto deep-cut oldies radio.[18]

And let's not even mention "Ob-La-Di, Ob-La-Da."[19]

If the songs are the innocents, however, and the artists merely bystanders, then who are the guilty ones?

Well, there's you and me. There's radio programmers and record store buyers. There's music critics and record company promo people. There's the guy who has spent the last fifteen years whistling "Love Is a Cattle Truck" every time he walks past your house, and the ring tone that plays favorite hair metal anthems.

We are all to blame, every time we click on a link or purchase a product and—"hold right there," as Ellen Foley so memorably told Meat Loaf.[20] If you want any indication of how precipitously rock has fallen into the maw of corporate doublethink, then consider the ease with which the music industry's native tongue has so readily slipped into trendy business-style buzz speak.

How artists no longer release records, their "brand" now "shares product"; and when, by the way, did art of any kind (and rock music is

---

17. In the book accompanying *Tattoo You 40th Anniversary Super Deluxe Edition,* Rolling Stones records, 2021.
18. You know that's next. Random cuts from the last three Dave Clarke 5 albums, Poppy Family B sides and just-uncovered Cowsills outtakes.
19. Actually, we will. But not yet.
20. "Paradise by the Dashboard Light," from Meat Loaf's *Bat Out of Hell.* Obviously.

art, no matter what your high school classics professor said) begin to be described as "product"? Or its creators as a "brand"?

Around the same time as potholes in the street began to be referred to as "serviceable defects within the public road envelope," probably, or "Plug and Play" became "Plug and Fuck Around with It for a Few Hours," which was shortly before we stopped listening to albums and embarked instead upon "personal musical journeys," but after . . . need we go on?

Rather, let's clamber on board the time machine and ponder how the modern tongue might have treated the superstars of the past.

"Hey, Da Vinci! Daub us some product, will ya? It'll do wonders for your brand."

"Hey, Shakespeare, could you make the next one the powerful and captivating story of a family torn apart by circumstance and the heartbreaking secrets that are the price of reunion?"

"Oi, Mendelssohn! Could you bang out something a little more demographic-friendly next time? We need to increase your clicks."

Deary me, it was bad enough when advertisers thought of everybody as a number, but at least numbers are unique. Now, we're not even individuals, we're just a single homogenous demographic, and it doesn't matter what the criteria might be . . . age, race, creed, sex, favorite tree . . . because somewhere, even as you read these words, there's an algorithm measuring up your last ten social media posts to ascertain whether or not you're in the correct demographic to be offered a free week's trial to a podcast about vinyl siding.

Beyond those artists who have stepped into so many other arenas of merchandising that making music is simply one business interest among a myriad of others (sneakers, perfume, liquor, hoodies, condoms, whatever), artists do not have a "brand."

They have a reputation, a history, and an ethos. True, some acts' music can be dismissed for being as meaningful as an oven chip bag, and it's better to be branded than simply generic.

But what was David Bowie's "brand" as he journeyed from hippie-haired folkie to flame-headed spaceman, from sixties revivalist to future city stalker, from Philly-style soul boy to Thin White Duke? Imagine a can of baked beans doing that, changing flavor every time you bought one. A brand is something you rely upon to deliver the exact same experience every time. A *band*, on the other hand, might get away with repeating itself for an album or two, but that's not what careers are made of.

The medium in which the music is sold—CD, vinyl, cassette, whatever—yes, technically that *is* product, and the issuing label *is* a brand. But that is not what the artist is "sharing"—primarily because they're not actually sharing anything. They're telling you that something is available in the hope that you will buy it. Big difference. Johnny shares his sweets with Jocasta. Adele sells her latest album to people who liked the last one and/or will hopefully be interested in the new one.

To pretend it's anything else is as dishonest as those medical establishments that describe their patients as "customers." Because, seriously, how many customers are rushed to their destination in a siren-squealing ambulance?

It's as if, after decades spent by corporations trying to humanize their industries, they're now trying to corporate-ize their humans. And so brilliantly have they succeeded in this that artists, too, will now muse on the need to get some new "product" out there, at the same time hiring a college intern to keep their "brand" relevant by posting further "shares" on social media.

In other words, they are behaving no differently than any other megacorp CEO looking at the latest spreadsheet and deciding it's time to unveil the super updated Version 14.3 of a thingamajig that doesn't do anything different than Version 4.8. It's just a little bigger now, and it comes in different colors, it folds in unexpected places, and it doesn't do half the things you liked about the previous model because it has been determined that too many features "confuse" the "consumer." Don't you *love* the way our best interests are always the first thing that comes to the corporate mind?

Back to product. Music is not product. But if you flip the coin and step back from the romantic image of the rock star laboring on the cliff of inspiration, hewing out shimmering slithers of indefinable genius and brilliance, it *is* product. Because, and this is where we came in, it's not actually the music that we're talking about, is it?

It's the marketing, the hype, the all-consuming media circus that springs into action every time the Dental Assassins[21] hire their producer's nephew's chiropodist to remaster and remix another of their sixty-year-old outpourings, then sling in a disc of outtakes and a Dolby Atmos megamix in the hope that, because they ran the ancient tapes through some kind of newfangled process, nobody will notice that it's the same tired tat that grandma was listening to on her wedding day. With a few extra bits that the artists didn't intend for us to hear in the first place but which will give the consumer "an exclusive bird's-eye glimpse into the original recording sessions."

Because there is nothing better than spending twenty minutes listening to them get the hi-hat sound right. That's my favorite track.

That's what this book hates most of all. The fact that the most vital, creative, and rebellious art form of the twentieth century (© *Every Book of Lousy Musical Clichés That Are Past Their Time*) is now packaged, sold, and consumed like breakfast cereal . . . and, worse than that, *healthy* breakfast cereal.

Less sugar, less gluten, less high fructose corn syrup . . . remember those Parental Warning stickers that used to turn up on albums that possibly included a veiled reference to suicide, Satan, or sex? Let's play Twenty-First-Century Health Warnings.

Important warning! This product was manufactured in a facility that once permitted drug abuse, smoking, and casual sex.[22]

This product contains language and/or concepts that might cause offense to the sensitive.[23]

If you or anyone you know is affected by any issues addressed on this album, please contact [insert helpline number here].

Do not use this product while under the influence of alcohol.

---

21. See appendix A.
22. But it doesn't anymore because we've airbrushed all the album covers.
23. But it doesn't anymore because we had the singer rerecord the rude bits.

The Surgeon General of that Big State in the Middle has determined that using this product at high volume may result in elevated blood pressure, tinnitus, and serious injury including ~~Death~~ Deafness.

So this is what we'll do. Little by little, chapter by chapter, *I Hate Old Music, Too* investigates and explains how we arrived in the position where we are today, leading us from the neoreligious codification of rock, as solemnly ritualized by its most humorless acolytes, to the ultimate expressions of freedom that so garishly buck against ossification. If that is what we want it to.

But it can also be treated as a mixtape, to be dipped in and out of; or placed on "shuffle," its chapters to be perused at random. In its ordered form, the book tells the story as I see it. On random play, who knows?

But if, when you reach the end, you still disagree with the title of this book, you can pretend that it, like the modern music that you dismiss with such erudition, simply doesn't exist. Easy.

Now, get back to your corporate wallpaper and leave the rest of us to listen to music that they *didn't* pipe into Noah's Ark.

Chapter One

We Built This City on Landfill, Mud, and Shifting Sands. Rock'n'Roll Had Nothing to Do with It—or, If You Can't Spell It, Don't Sell It

Rock 'n' roll was very simple music. All that mattered was the noise it made, its drive, its aggression, its newness. All that was taboo was boredom.

—Nik Cohn, *Awopbopaloobop Alopbamboom: The Golden Age of Rock*

You could hear the joint creaking long before it collapsed—the groans that echoed from the attic at night, the bangs in the basement, the scratching in the scullery. The sense that the very floors and walls were alive, but decaying all the same, exhausted from decades of holding everything in place, and tired, so tired, of doing the same thing over again and again, day in, day out, world without end . . . until it ended.

Sex Pistols' drummer Paul Cook modeling bandmate Johnny Rotten's infamous "I Hate Pink Floyd" T-shirt. FINE LINE/PHOTOFEST ©FINE LINE.

Afterward, well-intentioned souls stepped forward to say they'd seen it coming, but they never could agree on the cause. Or, as others preferred to put it, the curse.

To a few, it was punk rock and its wholesale extermination not of rock itself (and that despite the best efforts of Johnny Rotten's "I Hate Pink Floyd" T-shirt), but of the blues-based formulae that had once been integral to the sound.

To some, it was the day when Music Television was born, and suddenly visuals became more important than sound.

Others pointed to the early 1980s emergence of electronics and synthesizers, how they were transformed overnight from hulking monsters the size of small cars into briefcase-sized boxes filled with vague approximations of every musical instrument you could dream of. And, if you pursue that line of reasoning, there is a lot to be said in favor of that one. (See chapter 9.)

But most of all, it was the fact that nothing lasts forever. Evolve or die. Popular music chose to evolve. But there's a lot of people who would appear to have been happier if it had chosen the alternative option.

And a considerable number more who ignored the imperative altogether.

The edifice was still sound, after all. For every lurching zombie supergroup or preening muppet pantomiming passion; for every cloying, half-speed power ballad, or overbuoyant affirmation of the strength of rock'n'roll; for every paint by numbers synthesizer preset or overwrought paean to the healing powers of luuuuuuurve . . . for every onstage recreation of Théodore Géricault's *The Raft of the Medusa*, a doomed vessel overcrowded with castaways, clinging on for one more number one, one more generation of listeners, one more twenty-minute *casserolade* . . . there was always the hope, the chance even, that some new kid might turn up on the block to stem the onrushing tide.

It was the hope that hurt the most.

Remember as the eighties and nineties rattled on, we were confronted with so many new contenders for the "future of rock'n'roll"; and so many new genres as well? Hands up if you remember when "new wave" was the next big thing? Or two tone, hardcore, straight edge, post punk, hair metal, synthipop, dark wave, cold wave, no wave, industrial, gothic rock, death rock, rave, crust, shoegazing, grunge, Americana, college rock, alternative rock . . . so many genres, so many directions in which to turn, so many bandwagons upon which to leap. And so many people to be leaping, which is why, when *Rolling Stone* published its 50 Genuinely Horrible Albums by Brilliant Artists,[24] more than a quarter of its contents dated from the 1980s, and occasionally, the 1990s.

Dylan, Bowie, Genesis, Beatles Paul and George, the Who, the Dead, the Clash, Kiss, the Allmans, Joni Mitchell, Cheap Trick, Lou Reed, CSN&Y, Elton John, the kings and queens of classic rock and thereabouts, all unleashing "epic duds" throughout that decade, and the most damning point is, very few readers could disagree. Unless it was to suggest another by the same act that was even worse.[25]

No wonder people got bored, no wonder they got confused. And think of the artists! They've just finished rehearsing themselves to the peak of what one genre would regard as perfection, and suddenly nobody's listening to it anymore. Back to the drawing board, kids.

Yes, most of these movements had their moments in the sun. That is all they were, though: mere moments—at best, a passingly popular cult; at worst, a fresh scapegoat for a nation to pin its latest ailments on. Why blame society for the last five years of cultural collapse? Obviously, it was those teenagers over there with the weird haircuts.

No. When new ideas arrived, they came from without. From genres that neither rocked particularly hard nor rolled especially convincingly, but nevertheless had the smarts to regularly rejuvenate, and constantly push forward. Country, hip-hop, dance music—*their* houses remained as stable as they always were, and maybe even stronger, too.

Rock's homestead, on the other hand . . . by the time most people realized that it had passed the point of no return, not only had the building fallen, but the land had been sold as well.

And guess what? They built a museum on it.

---

24. Andy Green, "50 Genuinely Horrible Albums by Brilliant Artists," *Rolling Stone,* February 15, 2023, https://www.rollingstone.com/music/music-lists/horrible-albums-by-brilliant-artists-1234672895/.

25. "50 Genuinely Horrible Albums by Brilliant Artists" caused such a delightful stir. "At last," agreed some readers, "a well-deserved pummeling for those artists who seldom get even a slap on the wrist."

"Damn you," bemoaned others. "That happens to be my favorite Dylan record."

And "the same old same old," grumbled the statisticians, as they reckoned up forty albums by old white guys, and just five apiece for women and nonwhite people. Kanye West's *Ye,* incidentally, was number one.

In pure chronological terms, if you really want to know when things went wrong, it was with the foundation of the Rock and Roll Hall of Fame.

The name itself should have tipped you off. Rock and Roll. With the "and" being the offending item.

Look at all the *great* records[26] that reference the music in the title: "Rock'n'Roll Music" by Chuck Berry, *Rock'n'Roll Animal* by Lou Reed, "It's Only Rock'n'Roll" by the Stones, *Long Live Rock'n'Roll* (Rainbow), "I Love Rock'n'Roll" (Joan Jett), "Rock'n'Roll Suicide" (David Bowie), "Rock'n'Roll Radio" (the Ramones), *The Great Rock'n'Roll Swindle* (the Sex Pistols), "Rock'n'Roll Train" (AC/DC), and plain ol' *Rock'n'Roll* by Motörhead, John Lennon, and plenty more besides.

Now, all the not-so-good records that call it rock *and* roll. *Rock and Roll Heart* by Lou Reed (this works, by the way; a secret code from Uncle Lou. *Rock'n'Roll Animal* was one of the best albums he ever recorded. *Rock and Roll Heart* was one of the worst). *I Dig Rock and Roll* by Peter, Paul and Mary; *Rock and Roll Outlaws* by Foghat; *Rock and Roll Machine* by Triumph; "It's Still Rock and Roll to Me" (Billy Joel); "Rock and Roll Hoochie Koo" (Rick Derringer); *Rock and Roll* by Vanilla Fudge.

Okay, this is totally unscientific because, when you think about it, there were some great records that threw the "and" in there as well. But basically, it's rock'n'roll, with or without the apostrophes, with or without a capital *N*. The "and" isn't simply extraneous, it's absolutely contradictory in a musical form where that word is traditionally reduced to a connective mumble. That's why nobody singing Ian Dury's "Sex and Drugs and Rock and Roll" has *ever* paid any attention to the title as written on the record sleeve. It's sex'n'drugs'n'rock'n'roll, in the same way as nobody singing their way through the Motown songbook ever added a "g" to "You Keep Me Hangin' On," or tried to address the spelling on an early seventies Slade album.

Nobody, that is, apart from SKOOL TEECHERS. Because that's who put the "and" in rock'n'roll, as well. School teachers, elocution coaches, and . . . oh yes, people who find a piece of garbage in the gutter and decide

---

26. "Great," in this context, is a subjective term, in that a surprising number of people have a distinct aversion to any song that is basically concerned with how well the singer does his day job. "Bang bang bang" sings the carpenter. "Drill drill drill" sings the oilman. "Plumb plumb plumb" sings the plumber. "I'm gonna rock you and roll you until you can't tell your roll from your rock and then I'm gonna do it again, yeah baby," sing ten thousand extraordinarily unimaginative lyricists. You don't hear country singers doing that, do you?

they're going to sell it as art. Which may or may not be dangerously close to what we're getting at here, but the point is worth making. Throughout the fifties, sixties, and seventies, in the eyes of polite society, rock'n'roll *was* garbage. And rightfully so. Rock'n'roll would not have had it any other way.

From Elvis grinding his hips and vicariously stimulating every impressionable female in the room, to Buddy Holly inverting forever the introverted intellectual imagery of spectacle-wearers; from the Rolling Stones pissing on a filling station wall, to Jim Morrison waving his willy around in Florida; from punk rockers drowning one another in phlegm, to the wholesale glorification of indeed sex and drugs; from antiwar protests to antigovernment rhetoric, rock'n'roll was everything that polite society hated. And the fact that its most garish practitioners were among the Western world's wealthiest artists only lashed the respectable buttocks even harder.

A backlash was inevitable—the only question was, from which of the music's most strident foes would it emanate?

Might it be America's Christian evangelists? They had been warning their flock for years about the dangers of Satanic influence on popular music and the ever-growing popularity of "backward masking"—basically, the art of disguising incendiary and/or blasphemous lyrics by recording them backwards.[27]

Might it be law enforcement, weary as it was of forever policing skate punks and surf punks and probably space-hopper punks as well?

Might it be concerned parents, mortified by the increasingly shocking language that was creeping into song?

Might it be President Ronald Reagan, whose administration canceled the Beach Boys' free July 4th concert on the grounds that rock music appealed to "the wrong element" and because the Reagan administration was "not going to encourage drug abuse and alcoholism as was done in past years"?[28]

Probably not. It turned out that Reagan liked the Beach Boys, and it was Secretary of the Interior James G. Watt who made the decision. But

---

27. Neither was this wholly an American phenomenon. Having grown up in a Christian household, British writer and folklorist Chris Lambert recalls, "My mum and I often listened to a tape of an American preacher urging us to burn our Queen and Led Zeppelin records due to all of the [backward masking]. My first experience of 'Stairway to Heaven' [one of the movement's most pronounced targets] was many years later (and it was a cover)."

28. Phil McCombs, "Watt Outlaws Rock on Mall for July 4," *Washington Post*, April 6, 1983.

still, there were dark forces gathering, and people like the Stones only made matters worse, with songs like "Respectable": "We're talking heroin with the president . . . You're the easiest lay on the White House lawn." Whoever could they have been singing about?

They never did say. But they made another point with that song title; the idea that even the scruffiest, hairiest, smelliest little rebel could pull itself up by the bootstraps and live the dream. And what do you get when you reach the top of the pile?

You get your name in the relevant Hall of Fame. Because then, *nobody* can say you're an undeserving jerk. Unless, of course, you've been inducted into the Undeserving Jerk Hall of Fame, but that's another discussion altogether.

In many ways, it was surprising it took as long as it did. Rock'n'roll has always had a gift for self-congratulation, most evident through the number of songs in which it references itself and its history—from "American Pie" ("the day the music died") to "I'm Gonna Rock and Roll Ya Till Yer Toes Turn Green All Night Long." Country singers don't make those kinds of promises, either.

It's also surprising because rock'n'roll has never felt ashamed of pickpocketing left, right, and center in its hunger for fresh ideas to say it invented. But the Country Hall of Fame had been around since 1967, building up a magnificent collection and a well-deserved reputation in the process. A Big Band and Jazz Hall of Fame followed in 1978, the same year as the Alabama Jazz Hall of Fame was launched. Outside of music, baseball could trace its Hall of Fame back to 1939, pro football launched in 1969, pro rodeo in 1979; while the Hall of Fame for Great Americans in New York City dates from 1901.

For perhaps the first time in its history, rock'n'roll was positively tardy in getting to the party. So come on. Put on your red shoes and let's be off. And we, too, can "Explore every Rock and Roll Hall of Fame Inductee," as the institution's website[29] so temptingly suggests. We can "Trace their signature." We can "Listen to their career defining playlist." We can even "Relive the best moments from their Induction Ceremony."

"Oh, yes please, yes please, yes please, can we, really??"

No.

---

29. https://www.rockhall.com/hall-of-fame.

Chapter Two

My Parents Went to Woodstock and All I Inherited Was Their Lousy Record Collection—or, Fear and Loathing in the Rock Hall of Fame

While they celebrate the past, the new lies dead on the shelves still-born, no chance of survival in the ever-decaying clamor to celebrate nostalgia, to promote the glorious past.

—Brian Bordello, Inthemindofabordello.com,
March 17, 2023

The dream is identical every time.

A guitar-draped dais, alive to the sound of the Stooges and the New York Dolls. A figure steps into the spotlight, her David Peel T-shirt

The Rock and Roll Hall of Fame. Really. JASON PRATT, PITTSBURGH, PA [FISH-SPEAKER]—FLICKR, CC BY 2.0.

tattered and joint-burned. The assembled crowd coughs its welcome, and she begins to speak.

"The winning nominations are . . . The Fugs." She pauses as fresh cheers erupt. "The Last Poets. Fanny. The Adverts. And . . . "

And there the dream dissolves and you stagger into wakefulness, just moments before the T-shirt is transformed into office casual standard; the speaker dons her finest clown makeup; and nobody even bothers reading out the list of inductees. Instead, they just screw it into a tight paper ball and toss it into the empty auditorium with a barely audible "the same old stuff."

Yes, it's Rock and Roll Hall of Fame induction time, and if there is any indication of the depths to which we will not sink in order to cannibalize the idols of our childhood, it is a fifty-five thousand square foot glass and concrete carbuncle on the shores of Lake Erie—one of the three most polluted lakes in the United States.[30] Although that latter was a nice touch.

It's not just curmudgeonly Dave Thompson who thinks so, either.

Back in 1997, shortly before original Alice Cooper guitarist Glen Buxton's death that October, drummer Neal Smith was shooting the breeze with his former bandmate when the subject of the Rock Hall, as it is most commonly known, arose.

Alice Cooper (the quintet as opposed to the solo singer) had been eligible for induction for three years at that point; the twenty-fifth anniversary of their late 1960s formation was celebrated in 1994, and the fact that the Rock Hall had not invited the Coopers into the club wasn't even inexplicable. For people who care for such honors, it was contemptible.

Buxton didn't care. "The Rock and Roll Hall of Fame," he declared, "can kiss my Rock and Roll Ass."

In theory, the Rock Hall is not a hideous idea. It's an opportunity for the pioneers and creators of the most vivacious art form of the late twentieth century to be acknowledged, and thanked, by their peers, for all they did to perpetuate the art form that we love, for advancing its frontiers and expanding its reach. For making a difference to the people who heard them.

---

30. "Great Lakes Pollution," Give Earth a Chance, https://michiganintheworld.his tory.lsa.umich.edu/environmentalism/exhibits/show/main_exhibit/pollution_politics /great-lakes-pollution.

Barrie Masters (of Eddie and the Hot Rods) backstage at the Marquee, London. This is what the true Hall of Fame should look like. DAVE THOMPSON.

At the same time, however, given the outlaw status that the music endured (or, more likely, *enjoyed*) for so much of its lifetime, isn't there something just a little (a lot) oxymoronic about star-studded galas, oddly shaped trophies, and lifetime free admission to the museum, when what really should have been constructed was a giant dressing-room wall upon which inductees can scrawl whatever slogan or imagery they like?

One recalls, after all, the Andrew Wood Memorial Wall that stared out onto a Seattle street for so many years, honoring one of the city's most beloved pregrunge fallen sons. How fans from around the world would come to add their own messages to the mass that were already there. How, until the corner on which it stood was repurposed for something that obscured it from view, that wall itself was a museum of all that made Seattle *Seattle*.

Or the backstage at venues like the Marquee in London, or Max's Kansas City in New York; from the Rat (Boston) to Rodney's English

Disco (Los Angeles); from the Fillmores (New York and San Francisco) to the Forty Watt (Athens, Georgia), entire volumes of irreplaceable rock history was written, sprayed, or even carved onto the walls with whatever implement came to hand. Those are the true halls of fame that rock'n'roll deserves, and the fact that none of them exist today says more for rock's true standing in societal eyes (and, perhaps, for its supposed supporters' own concern) than any number of exhibits on the riverfront in Cleveland.

Millionaires the world over, after all, have devoted immense funds to preserving, for posterity, this star's guitar, that star's stained T-shirt, this hero's gold records, that dude's last needle. Was there not even one who thought, "You know, a wall that celebrates ten years' worth of nightly gigs in a host of legendary acts' own handwriting might be worth saving from the wrecking ball?"

Instead, what do we get? A featureless wall of engraved gilt signatures. You've probably seen autograph books that are more impressive.

The story of the Rock Hall was traced in this book's predecessor, but for the benefit of those who may not have read (or remember) that, a brief summary.

It was Atlantic Records founder Ahmet Ertegun, himself one of popular music's most visionary figures, who established the Rock Hall on April 20, 1983, although it was 1986 before a suitable location was settled upon. The museum itself was finally dedicated in 1995, although the Rock Hall had been inducting members since 1986.

That first ceremony welcomed the cream of the very first wave of rock'n'rollers into its midst: Chuck Berry, Elvis Presley, Jerry Lee Lewis, and Buddy Holly. Bill Haley followed in 1987, alongside the formative pioneers of doo-wop and the early soul era; 1988 introduced the first suggestion of "modern" rock, as Bob Dylan, the Beatles, and the Beach Boys were ushered into the parlor. So far, so safe.

In the three-plus decades since then, however, induction has spread far and wide across the musical spectrum, although not so broadly that some artists are not now serial inductees. Indeed, Eric Clapton, uniquely for someone whose personal opinions are often seen as so diametrically opposed to the liberal tenets rock'n'roll holds closest, has been brought on board three times, as a Yardbird, for Cream, and as a solo artist.

Neither is induction awarded in an especially timely fashion. The aforementioned Glen Buxton was not the first artist to pass away prior to getting the nod, and he certainly wasn't the last. A decade later, in 2008, the Dave Clark Five's Mike Smith passed away on the eve of their induction—a full two decades after he became eligible. And no matter how loudly fans of the New York Dolls scream for their idols to be recognized by the Hall, nothing changes the fact that only one member of the original lineup remains alive. The band has been eligible since 1997.

Already then, we see that the flaws in the system are manifold and so blindingly obvious that it's astonishing that they weren't amended in the Hall's first few years of operation.

To Muse or Not to Muse

There's a great moment early on in *Daisy Jones and the Six*[31] where Daisy is talking with a male friend who, having applauded a particular comment she made, informs her that he might use it in a script one day.

"What makes you think that *I'm* not gonna use that in a something one day?" She asks.

"I meant it as a compliment," he responds, genuinely taken aback. "You'd be like my muse or something.." And he looks truly surprised when she gets up and walks away. "What did I say?"

"You said I'm your fucking muse. Like I'm the inspiration for your next great idea."

"Yeah," he replies. "What's wrong with that?"

Welcome to rock'n'roll, circa the early 1970s. Welcome to a world in which rock music isn't merely predominantly male, it's also predominantly up all night having a party while the ladies look pretty and do muse-y things.

You'd think the music would have grown out of that by now. You'd think wrong.

The Rock Hall prides itself on its diversity. Race, religion, musical background—all of these criteria are swept aside.

One scotoma, however, remains untouched. Up to and including 2023, some 374 acts have been inducted to the Rock Hall, including that charmed handful who have made two or more appearances.

Of these 374, approximately one-third are non-white—not great, but not bad. And a grand total of 52 are female. Fifty-two. That's about

31. See appendix A: An Index of Wholly Imaginary Artists.

14 percent of the overall total, and if we boil the numbers down even further, removing nonperforming songwriters and artists whose success lies in soul, pop, folk, R&B, blues, jazz, rap, singer-songwriters, and country . . . in other words, look for the "classic rockers" alone . . . we end up with (drum roll, please) 14 inductions and 18 women: Janis Joplin, Patti Smith, Chrissie Hynde (with the Pretenders), Joan Jett (but not her first band, the all-female Runaways), Pat Benatar (with Neil Giraldo), Stevie Nicks and Christine McVie (with Fleetwood Mac, and in Nicks's case, solo), Maureen Tucker (with the Velvet Underground), Tina Weymouth (with Talking Heads), Grace Slick (with Jefferson Airplane), Anne and Nancy Wilson (Heart), Debbie Harry (with Blondie), the Go-Gos, and Sheryl Crow.

Okay, you can add in Joni Mitchell, Carole King, Linda Ronstadt, and Bonnie Raitt because they do occasionally turn up on your favorite classic rock radio station. Kate Bush and Cyndi Lauper, too. But we still have just enough players to field two soccer teams, and let's hope there's no call for more than a couple of substitutions.

Does that strike anybody else as weird?

It is true that female contributions to what we think of today as classic rock were, certainly into the mid-1970s, scarcely overwhelming in number, although that in itself was primarily due to the culture of the day, and the ingrained belief that rock was a man's game; always had been, always would be. Women, it was snickered, just didn't get it. Unless they were muses, of course.

Except they did get it. It was the industry that didn't get the women. The industry that made such helpful suggestions as, "Could you ask her to look a little prettier?" Or, "Could she maybe smile a little more?" Or, best of all, "Does she really need her own dressing room and backstage bathroom?"

Which is better than the mostly male, probably drunk, and certainly not particularly well brought up audiences whose primary interaction with an onstage female was to bellow "get 'em off" and "show us your tits." But only by a few degrees.

Guitarist Lady Bo—Peggy Jones—was probably the first true female rock'n'roller, front and center alongside Bo Diddley beginning 1957. But when Bo was inducted to the Rock Hall in 1987, of Lady Bo there was not a trace. Nor was there any recognition for Norma-Jean Wofford, who replaced her in the lineup in 1962. We should have realized there was something wrong way back then.

The first band to truly buck the system was Fanny—not one, not two, but *four* young women, playing their own instruments, writing their own songs, singing their own observations, and—having landed a deal with major label Reprise—creating at least three of the best American rock albums of the first years of the seventies (*Fanny, Charity Ball, Fanny Hill*). And they were successful enough that they were eventually able to play gigs without being constantly barracked by the massed ranks of Neanderthal Man. They should be in the Rock Hall for that reason alone.

Then there are the women who fronted (and, in many respects, were widely viewed as the focal point of) otherwise male bands. They, too, made music that overcame the prejudices of period society; most enjoyed considerable success; all are at least as worthy of induction as the majority of male performers that have been given the nod. Move into the punk era, and the numbers swell further. Venture into the eighties and nineties and deserving candidates run neck and neck with their male contemporaries. Jann Wenner's ill-considered September 2023 remarks regarding the intellect of women (and Afro-Americans) notwithstanding.[32]

Where are they? What does rock—and, by extension, the powers that define its now-established continuum—have against women? They shouldn't all have stayed at home muse-ing, should they? Answers on a postcard please . . .

---

32. Sisario, Ben. "Jann Wenner's Rock Hall Reign Lasted Years. It Ended In 20 Minutes." *New York Times*, September 19, 2023, https://www.nytimes.com/2023/09/19/arts/music/jann-wenner-rock-and-roll-hall-of-fame.html.

An act becomes eligible for elevation to the self-proclaimed "Rock's Highest Honor" twenty-five years after their first steps—whether as a band or a solo artist—were taken, and that's fair enough. A quarter of a century is quite long enough in which to consider whether an act has made a lasting impact on the course of popular music or not.

So why do so many have to wait for years, if not decades, more? Why did it take the Moody Blues, whose first hits were scored in 1964, until 2018 to receive the nod? Why was Joan Baez, without whom second-year inductee Bob Dylan might never even have been noticed, left high and dry until 2017? Why are Jan and Dean, after more than forty years of patient eligibility, *still* on the outside? Why isn't Melanie in there yet?

Because the system is fucked, that's why.

If the Bleeding Goblins[33] were worthy of induction in 1997, then that is when they should have been inducted. What could they possibly have achieved in the quarter century since then, that they had not already done more successfully in the first twenty-five years? Surely, if they *weren't* considered worthy of induction in 1997, then case closed. Imagine if college graduation depended upon the same principle—"Yeah, you should have got your diploma when you were still young enough to do something with it. But never mind. It'll still look nice on the wall."

A band enters the Rock Hall on merit—or at least, that's what we're told. Pity should not enter into it. Neither should a few discontent comments on a Facebook page. Nor an upcoming record company reissue project. Not unless you really want every inexplicably delayed nomination to resemble a desperate attempt to maintain the interest of the older generation in an institution that, were it to actually be worth the land it's built upon, would now be inducting no act that was active prior to the very late 1990s.

The Rock Hall claims to represent, and honor, the *entire* expanse of popular music history. So—quick quiz time. Bearing in mind the twenty-five-year qualification period, and the fact that 1990 is already well over thirty years distant, how many acts that formed throughout that decade have so far been inducted?

2015 (for the class of 1990)—0/6
2016 (1991)—0/5
2017 (1992)—2/6 (Tupac Shakir, Pearl Jam)
2018 (1993)—0/5
2019 (1994)—0/7
2020 (1995)—2/6 (the Notorious B.I.G., Nine Inch Nails)
2021 (1996)—2/6 (Foo Fighters, Jay Z)
2022 (1997)—1/7 (Eminem)
2023 (1998)—1/8 (Missy Elliott)

With fifty-six places up for grabs, just nine went to newly qualified acts, and now you really have to wonder what is the Hall telling us?

That someone who has been inactive for thirty years, aside from occasional cruise ship tours and a couple of box sets, is worth more than

---

33. See appendix A.

someone who has been maintaining a constant stream of new releases since emerging from a Rhode Island basement in 1995?

That rock is dead, and with just three (three!) exceptions, rap is the only arena in which anything of note has taken place since the first George Bush was in the White House? And not much of that, either?

Or that (and here we go again) vintage music is worth more than "new"—even if "new" is now the same age as Elvis Presley's first army haircut when the Rock Hall first opened?

Yes, mistakes happen and worthy names can be overlooked. But that's what lifetime awards, long service medals, and senior citizen bus passes are for. Otherwise, until the Rock Hall acknowledges that just as many valuable, entertaining, and yes—influential—names have emerged across the last three decades as did in the thirty beforehand, then it's just another brick in the same sorry wall that should have been demolished long ago.

Not that everybody accepts the poisonous chalice, although their reasons do vary. In 1988, Paul McCartney refused to attend the Beatles' induction because, "After twenty years, the Beatles still have some business differences, which I had hoped would have been settled by now. Unfortunately, they haven't been, so I would feel like a complete hypocrite waving and smiling with them at a fake reunion."[34]

Grace Slick turned down a starring role at Jefferson Airplane's induction in 1996 because she believed that rock'n'roll was no place for a person her age—she was fifty-six at the time. "I'm not comfortable being an old person on stage," she told *Forbes* magazine twenty years on. "Rock is like sports. You have a certain run, then get out."[35] No doubt she, like many others, remembered the then-thirty-two-year-young Mick Jagger telling *People* magazine,[36] "'I'd rather be dead than sing 'Satisfaction' when I'm forty-five."[37] Try eighty (at the time of writing), Michael.

In 1999, it was Ozzy Osbourne's turn. "Just take [Black Sabbath's] name off the list. Save the ink. Forget about us. The nomination is meaningless, because it's not voted on by the fans. It's voted on by the supposed

---

34. Robert Hilburn, "McCartney's Absence Sparks Rancor at Rock Hall," *Los Angeles Times,* January 22, 1988, https://www.latimes.com/archives/la-xpm-1988-01-22-ca-25259 -story.html.

35. Jim Clash, "Grace Slick: 'Rock Is Like Sports—You Have a Certain Run, Then Get Out,'" Forbes.com, December 11, 2015, https://www.forbes.com/sites/jimclash/2015/12/11 /grace-slick-rock-is-like-sports-you-have-a-certain-run-then-get-out/?sh=45257f246dda.

36. June 9, 1975.

37. He didn't mean it. Touring his second solo album, *Primitive Cool*, in 1988, "Satisfaction" was one of around twenty-five Stones oldies than he performed throughout the year.

elite for the industry and the media, who've never bought an album or concert ticket in their lives, so their vote is irrelevant to me. Let's face it, Black Sabbath has never been media darlings. We're a people's band and that suits us just fine."[38]

He did, eventually, relent and Sabbath were duly inducted in 2006, when they should have been joined onstage by the Sex Pistols. Now, however, it was John Lydon's turn to be rotten.

"Next to the Sex Pistols, rock and roll and that hall of fame is a piss stain. Your museum. Urine in wine. [We're] not coming. [We're] not your monkey and so what? Fame at $25,000 if we paid for a table, or $15,000 to squeak up in the gallery, goes to a non-profit organization selling us a load of old famous."[39]

Regardless of Johnny's jaundice, the Pistols were inducted, and the Hall of Fame got what it thought was the last laugh when Rotten's refusal was read aloud onstage, to permit the audience a smug smile of grandmotherly indulgence and to say, "Oh, those Sexy Pistols. What impertinent imps they are."

In fact, the Sex Pistols, like Osbourne and Slick before them, crystallized what a lot of people thought, future inductees among them. When Guns N' Roses' turn came in 2012, Axl Rose was prominently absent, insisting, "I strongly request that I not be inducted in absentia and please know that no one is authorized nor may anyone be permitted to accept any induction for me or speak on my behalf."[40]

He also questioned the very process by which it is decided "who, out of all the artists in the world that have contributed to this genre, officially 'rock' enough to be in the Hall?"—a remark that foreshadowed the Hall's decision to begin asking the public for their opinions. In as much as they were graciously permitted to make their choice from a preselected list, of course, which is a little like the condemned man being told he can have whatever he chooses for his final meal, so long as it's lettuce. "Let's see. Do I want iceberg, butterhead, romaine, Batavia, arugula, coral . . . ?"

38. Jaan Uhelszki, "Ozzy Says 'No Thanks' to Hall of Fame. Osbourne Wants Sabbath Removed from Hall of Fame's List of Nominees," *Rolling Stone*, October 5, 1999, https://www.rollingstone.com/music/music-news/ozzy-says-no-thanks-to-hall-of-fame-79479/.

39. David Sprague, "Sex Pistols Flip Off Hall of Fame. Invited In after Five Snubs, the Original Brit-Punks Snub Back," *Rolling Stone*, February 24, 2006, https://www.rollingstone.com/music/music-news/sex-pistols-flip-off-hall-of-fame-78131/.

40. Sean Michaels, "Guns N' Roses Lead Rock and Roll Hall of Fame Inductions," *The Guardian*, April 16, 2012, https://www.theguardian.com/music/2012/apr/16/guns-n-roses-rock-roll-hall-fame.

Dolly Parton, meanwhile, highlighted what many onlookers felt was one of the Rock Hall's most pernicious habits—that of snatching its inductees from other halls altogether (she was inducted into the Country Hall in 1999) and claiming them for its own. Withdrawing her name from consideration for the 2022 event, she said simply, "I don't feel that I have earned the right."[41]

Parton did, ultimately, relent, conceivably after somebody played her the Sisters of Mercy's cover of "Jolene," to remind her of her seldom-remarked-upon status as the Godmother of Gothic Rock.

Her initial point, too, can be debated, in as much as rock'n'roll has *always* been a magpie, lifting both influence and practitioners from more or less every musical genre that has ever existed, be it classical, blues, jazz, soul, folk, rap (Grandmaster Flash and the Furious Five were inducted as long ago as 2007), or, indeed, country. Besides, if the Grammys could honor Jethro Tull with the Best Heavy Metal song,[42] then why shouldn't Dolly Parton be celebrated for her contributions to rock'n'roll? Jimmy Rodgers, Hank Williams, Johnny Cash, Floyd Cramer, and Bob Wills didn't complain.[43]

We praise her, however, for at least making the point.

So, the Rock Hall. Is it a gold-plated carriage clock graciously bestowed to mark decades of loyal and devoted semi-retirement?

Is it a popularity contest in which it doesn't matter what you actually contributed to music, so long as enough people remember liking it?

Or is it a well-aimed kick in the teeth for any performer with the temerity to have tried making a career in music in the years since President Reagan left office?

It depends upon who they induct over the next few years. The class of 2000 is already forming an orderly line.

---

41. Matthew Leimkuehler, "Dolly Parton Removes Herself from Rock & Roll Hall of Fame Consideration," *The Tennessean*, March 14, 2022, https://www.tennessean.com/story/entertainment/music/2022/03/14/dolly-parton-removes-herself-rock-hall-consideration/7034603001/.

42. In 1989, the fiddly flute-fronted prog-folkers pipped Metallica, Iggy Pop, and Jane's Addiction for the title.

43. At the time of writing (2023), fifteen performers have been inducted into both the Rock and Country Halls, the remainder being Bill Monroe, Chet Atkins, Brenda Lee, Elvis Presley, the Everly Brothers, Sun Records supremo Sam Phillips, fiddler Johnny Gimble, Ray Charles, and Jerry Lee Lewis.

Chapter Three

First World Problems—or, So You Think You Hate Old Music?

From now on frenzy, chaos—screams, shrieks and gestures![44]

—*Ed Sanders, 1964–1965*

Three chapters in and it's time we decide what, exactly, do we mean when we say "vintage music"—or "new music," come to that?

Theoretically, it should be self-evident. Vintage music is . . . well, it's old, isn't it? And new is . . . obviously, new.

But beyond that particular argument, precisely where does one end and the other begin? And what is the difference between them? So far, we've been using the turn of the last century as a dividing line, but, as the dendrochronologists among us will testify, a lot of that would now be considered "old," especially if you're reading this while still in your teens or early twenties.

Heavens, when I was seventeen, even college freshmen struck me as impossibly ancient. Twenty-five years old was positively Jurassic. And we all know that musical fashions and styles move even faster than life. This year's zippy wordsmiths are next year's pleonastics, and all that.

So a quick history lesson. Quick, because there's only a few points that need to be emphasized, and quick, too, because the last thing we require is another attempt at telling the Story of Rock, up to circa 1964 and the dawn of what we now call "classic rock."

And unto the blues was born R&B and unto R&B was born Bo Diddley; and Bo Diddley begat James Brown; and James Brown begat Little Richard; and Little Richard begat Elvis; and Elvis begat Eddie and Eddie begat Buddy and Buddy begat the Everlys. Then they all got together after a gig

---

44. From Sanders's handwritten notes for the hoped-for underground dance sensation, the Gobble, https://www.granarybooks.com/images/upload/edsandersarchive.pdf.

one night and simultaneously begat Rocky Biceps . . . and the record-buying
public saw that verily, daddy-o, rock'n'roll was groovy.

And why classic rock? Because, when we really sit down to look at the
most egregiously self-aggrandizing aspects of past pop, it's not the Elvis
and Eddie fans who are making all the fuss; it's not the punks and syn-
thipoppers who are bellowing "look at me!"; it's not soft rock hammering
hard on your head, or seventies art rockers graffiti-ing your granny.

It's classic rock bands. It's the generations that begin with the Beatles,
end with Boston, and who will maybe grant admission to a handful of
Johnny-come-latelies, provided they make the right noises. Which are . . .
much the same noises as everyone who came before them make.

No, we're not going to get into definitions now, and we're certainly not
going to try and out-pedant one another. Classic rock is a broad church,

Billy Joel. We know he didn't start the fire,
because he didn't use that song for kindling.
PHOTOFEST.

but you know it when you hear it. And you *will* hear it, every time you leave the house.

We should also consider what a crock the very term *classic rock* is, in that something like a decade's worth of earlier, and equally insistent, music is effectively left out in the cold. Even the Rock Hall acknowledges that there was life before the British Invasion, and that the prehistory of rock reaches back for as long as there have been gramophone records to record upon, be it Edwardian folksong, Prohibition-era jazz, post-Depression blues, dust-bowl balladeers, or 1940s bobby-soxers.

Classic rock, on the other hand, isn't really even a genre, just an apparently random smorgasbord whose extremes bookend a witch's brew of FM radio hits by yeah, yeah, yeah, predominantly white, predominantly male, and predominantly rockin' Anglo-American performers. And it's only been around since the end of the 1970s, when a handful of FM radio stations (Cleveland's M105 and Chicago's WMET, the Mighty Met, were among the first) chose to market their output as "classic rock."

Meaning, at that time, you could tune in and be reasonably secure in the knowledge that you would never be forced to endure the same era's other demon offspring, punk and disco.

They were demons, too. Punk was responsible for what remains the greatest ever schism in the once relatively united church of rock, by virtue of its dismissal as irrelevant anything that predated its own inception; and disco was disco, and we need say no more. Indeed, it was one of WMET's fellow Windy City broadcasters, WLUP, the Loop, that organized Chicago's legendary Disco Demolition Night in 1979, where a crate full of disco records (many supplied by the fifty thousand strong crowd) was blown up on the playing field.

Classic rock was, in these earliest years, an elastic concept. It had no choice. A lot of what we hear today on classic rock stations (yes, even those now-ancient Foreigner, Van Halen, and Bon Jovi foot-stompers) was still to be recorded at that time. And so new releases rubbed shoulders with golden oldies and, whether or not you actually liked "album-oriented rock" (as some stations still referred to it), there was at least the sense that the playlists were forever expanding.

Certainly, there was no danger of anybody confusing, say, the latest single by Toto with some twenty-year-old Kinks 45, and hearing the pair in the same block of songs could be regarded as much as an educational experience as a musical one. Because yes, at that time, a lot of new music really did stink.

The slide from such stations appearing at least partially contemporary (and classic rock is by no means the sole casualty in this regard) into monolithic, *neolithic,* slabs of carefully curated nostalgia, then, was a gradual process, largely precipitated by the same kind of corporate buy-outs that were bringing other forms of local media (television and newspapers) under the same roof as their counterparts in other towns and cities.

This streamlining of ownership inevitably led to a streamlining of content—centralized news sources for every paper to share; centralized playlists for every station to play. No longer could disc jockeys, once the heart and soul of a station's identity, simply play their show according to their own tastes. Now their programs were programmed, and the more stations that fell into the grasp of the corporations, the faster the process became the norm. By the mid-1990s, Clear Channel Communications controlled forty-three stations nationwide. Less than a decade later, they operated in excess of 1,200 across forty-nine states, with a listenership of one hundred million listeners.[45] And while "classic rock" was by no means a key concern in this new world, it was a reliable one.

Because who doesn't want to hear "Stairway to Heaven" five times a day?

By this point, what was regarded as classic rock was more or less codified . . . some might say "fossilized" . . . in the form that it remains to this day, and again it is not alone in this. Even the most widely disparate musical genre can, given time, be whittled down to a solid pack of audience favorites, and it would be unfair to rephrase that as "the lowest common denominator," although it would be no less accurate. Whether it's the reggae channel forever repeating Bob Marley's "Buffalo Soldier," or the all-eighties station endlessly assailing you with Billy Joel's "We Didn't Start the Fire" (and how brilliant was that? A political listicle set to music!), there will come a point when even the most casual listener will beg for mercy.

From a cultural standpoint, we should not be unduly surprised by any of this. Even in its most callow youth, rock'n'roll was always obsessed

---

45. "Gee, Thanks Dad," Forbes.com, October 18, 2004, https://www.forbes.com/forbes/2004/1018/106.html?sh=6d22aa8b496b.

with its own past; indeed, the music was still a toddler when the first dedicated "oldies" record store opened in New York City, to sell doo-wop records to fans who believed that the music was already past its prime. By the 1970s, artists the caliber of John Lennon, David Bowie, and Bryan Ferry were releasing albums dedicated wholly to favorite oldies, even though few of them were more than twenty years old. When the movie *American Graffiti* set out to recapture the "good old days," those days were barely fifteen years old.

So a degree of retrospection is not simply to be expected, it is to be demanded.

What is more pernicious, however, is the manner in which classic rock alone slipped away from its anointed role as purview of FM (and, more recently, satellite) radio and into so many other walks of life.

Radio, after all, you can turn off, or not even switch on to begin with. There was a record released by British easy-listeners Smokie back in the mid-1970s, titled *Don't Play Your Rock'n'Roll to Me* (note the spelling). At the time, it felt a bit daft, and deserving of a facetious rejoinder—"okay, I'll play you jazz fusion saxophone solos instead." Today, it could be the most heartfelt plea of anyone who has ever . . .

. . . encountered the greatest hits of Swampwitch[46] while waiting on hold for the service department. ("Your call is very important to us." How do you know? I might just be ringing to ask if your fridge is running . . . better go catch it then, haha.)

. . . had their evening's sitcom reruns interrupted by an especially insistent ad for adult diapers, artfully soundtracked with sixties psyche-delia. (Yes, I know; target audience and all that, but it doesn't make it any better.)

. . . curled up with their popcorn for a few hours of movie sequel silli-ness, only for the first five minutes to be lost beneath a needless remix of a 7 Deadly Synths'[47] B side.

And all that's before you even sat in the dentist's chair, let alone real-ized that, for the next forty minutes, you were going to be at the mercy of a satellite yacht rock station, when—until that very moment—you didn't know there was even something called yacht rock out there. Let alone the knowledge that someone, somewhere, had managed to track down

---

46. See appendix A: An Index of Wholly Imaginary Artists.
47. See appendix A.

every single song you most physically loathed while growing up and pro-grammed them into a brand-new pit of fire.

That, then, is vintage music. Music that is not only so far past its sell-by date that, were it any other consumer product, you'd be measuring it up for a museum case, but which has instead assumed a sempiternal half-life midway between a pernicious bank of fog and the ectoplasm of a ghostly Edwardian matriarch, not only leaking into every corner of your existence, but doing so purposefully, too.

Music whose ground rules were laid out so long ago that there are stone tablets being unearthed by archaeologists that feel fresher. Music that, if you're aged under thirty (and, in some cases, under fifty), you could probably talk to your parents about. And it's music that the last quarter of a century's worth of new rocking talent has devoted itself to attempting to overthrow, only to be knocked back at almost every turn *by the very people who ought to be supporting it.*

Chapter Four

The Top Ten Rock'n'Roll
Anatidaephobiacs—or, When Will
the Cloud Start Shouting Back?

Does anyone seriously believe that Beatles music will be an unthink-
ingly accepted part of daily life all over the world in the 2000s?

—Brian McGee, The Listener, *1967*

The elephant in the room throughout all of this chest-beating, of
course, is the fact that "adults" aren't supposed to like what "the
kids" are listening to today. That's not the point of music, and it's not the
point of adulthood, either.

There is no hard and fast law that says popular music—as in, the
records that are the most popular at any point in time—is strictly for "the
young." Indeed, it is quite possible for an individual listener to continue
engaging with what they would regard as "new" music until the bitter
end. However, and this is where it gets interesting, the caveat will often
be increasingly diminishing returns.

An exploratory exercise.

Take a look, should you be aged in your forties or beyond, at your
own record collection. Then, however you have it organized, reorganize
it according to each album's year of release. Now reckon up the totals.
How many albums by different artists do you own from your first years of
actively buying or listening to new releases, so that's probably your teens?
Now, discounting acts whose records were in the last count, how many
from your twenties . . . and how many for the decades thereafter?

The decline will likely startle you, but it ought not to. For the majority
of adults, their musical tastes were settled long ago, and their attitudes
toward it, likewise. Their interest in music itself persists, and perhaps
they do still buy occasional new releases by artists who weren't even born
when they picked up their first long-player.

"Pop stars today, what do they look like?" Sam Smith infuriates an entire internet's worth of seventies rock fans. DAVE J. HOGAN/GETTY IMAGES.

But if you delve deeper into your own listening habits and re-reorganize your albums, this time by the number of times you've actually played each one in the last few years . . . the average middle-aged (or older) music fan is probably wishing we'd change the subject around now. Or, contrarily, rejoicing in confirmation of what they've been saying for the past few decades. Vintage music is better than new, and Bob Seger was

"[It's] Extraordinary How Potent Cheap Music Is"

(Noel Coward, *Private Lives*)

When a man is tired of the Top 40, he is tired of living, Samuel Johnson most assuredly did not write. But if he had, he would not have been wrong.

Aging is responsible for a plethora of changes in both the human body and the human mind. Reflexes begin to slow, joints begin to ache, memories grow elusive, and we laugh at different things. But most pertinent from this book's perspective, we begin to lose interest in the weekly pop charts.

Hands down, the charts are *the* most accurate barometer of the state of music at any given time, and have been since the first ever listings of the bestselling, the most played, and the most hyped records in the land were published, in 1936 in the United States, and 1952 in the United Kingdom.

It is the charts that dictate whether a record is a deathless smash or a dismal flop. The charts tell us at a glance if a new musical movement is genuinely popular, or just a figment of some writer's imagination. But, most crucial of all, they tell us what we're spending our money on, and they are the greatest leveler, too. The "best album" polls that we will be looking at in chapter 7 inform us what the critics reckon we ought to be listening to. The charts are our way of telling them, "Well, thank you for your concern, but I think I prefer . . ."

And for a long time, on either side of adolescence and into adulthood too, for some people, the charts mattered.

You know what? They still do. You should give them a listen sometime.

---

bang on the money when he sang, "Today's music ain't got the same soul. I like that good old time rock'n'roll."[48]

A March 2023 article in *Neuroscience News*[49] declares that "until around the age of eleven, children are generally happy to engage with

---

48. "Old Time Rock and Roll," written by George Jackson and Thomas E. Jones III (1978).
49. "Why Do We Stop Exploring New Music as We Get Older?," *Neuroscience News*, March 5, 2023, https://neurosciencenews.com/music-aging-22716/.

unfamiliar music." Early adolescence, on the other hand, might see interest in music grow stronger, but also sees "a reduction in open-earedness."

Partially this is caused by shifting priorities and, perhaps, "less discretionary time" in which to explore new sounds. It's why you don't tape the Top 40 off the radio any longer. Heck, it's why you don't even know what's in the Top 40, or maybe even if they still compile one any longer.

But what if you'd been born ten years later and, instead of being brought up on the sultry R&B rhythms of Darkwater, the melodic riffery of Cat Sandwich, and the twisted folk of Skull Turnip, you were raised on the rock of the next generation? Would you *still* love the album-side-long Mellotronic meanderings of Matterhorn Slender's second album? Or would you instead be tied just as firmly to the sharp electro anthems of 7 Deadly Synths and Rhubarb?[50]

Advance another ten years . . . or ten after that . . . or retreat, it doesn't matter. On every occasion, it's the music that you grow up with that makes the greatest impact, together with the societal and cultural stimuli that is likewise at play upon your world.

The argument that aesthetics are largely the product of environment is scarcely a controversial one, and there is no need to render it so in these pages. Rap and hip-hop could never have developed, let alone become so popular, under any other circumstances than those in which it was formed—that is, the Black American experience of the 1960s and 1970s.

Punk rock might, for many people, have felt like waking up to discover they were trapped in a lousy movie, but the music grew out of a lousy movie of its own, namely, the teenaged wasteland of mid-seventies Britain, with unemployment, poverty, and the sense of government that had forgotten how to govern. Country and western could have blossomed out of nowhere *but* the American South; grunge could only ever have oozed from the Pacific Northwest.

Yes, all of these later found equally fertile territory elsewhere, because ultimately, they tapped into a universal mindset. But not at the outset, and it doesn't matter whether someone actually liked the music they grew up with or not. The sounds that surrounded them . . . the environment . . . made its mark, and the only key difference was whether they accepted what was taking place, or rejected it. For every yin there is a

---

50. For all artists in this paragraph, see appendix A: An Index of Wholly Imaginary Artists.

yang; for every hippie, there was an uptight straight. It is no coincidence whatsoever that the birth of British punk in the seventies was mirrored by a revival for the rock'n'roll–loving "Teddy Boys" of twenty years previous. Opposites can detract as well as attract.

What is important here is the fact that those influences likely still form a significant part of their owners' psyche today, decades after they filed away their final safety pin and cleaned that last gob of phlegm off their portrait of President Reagan.

No wonder, then, that when these people listen to the music of later years, particularly that made by generations whose closest connection with punk rock is their septuagenarian grandfather's memories of dying his hair with blue food coloring . . . of *course* there's no connection.

Neuroscientist Daniel J. Levitin confirms this when he writes, "When we love a piece of music, it reminds us of other music we have heard, and it activates traces of emotional times in our lives."[51]

Thus, *Neuroscience News* continued in March 2023, "What we think of as our 'taste' is simply a dopamine reaction arising from patterns our brain recognizes which create the expectation of pleasure based on pleasures past. When we stop actively listening to new or unfamiliar music, the link between the musical pattern and pleasure is severed.

"It may take a decade or two to get there, but the result is, eventually, 'young people's music' will alienate and bring no pleasure."[52]

Because that is how it *should* be. What possible interest could a person have, as they creak toward a well-earned retirement, in music that is targeted expressly for people who haven't even applied for their first job yet?

Probably the same amount as their own parents or grandparents had regarding whatever today's adults were listening to at a similar age. Which was likely similar to that which *their* parents, in turn, evinced. It is the nature of art to continue evolving, but nowhere in the contract into which it enters with its admirers is there any clause that states it needs to evolve in a manner that they will find forever palatable.

Here, from 1914, is the renowned Boston critic Louis Elson discussing the fourth symphony of Sibelius, one of the most renowned European composers of the late nineteenth and early twentieth centuries, but lucklessly almost twenty years the venerable observer's junior:

51. Daniel J. Levitin, *This Is Your Brain on Music: The Science of a Human Obsession* (Dutton, 2007).
52. "Why Do We Stop Exploring New Music as We Get Older?," *Neuroscience News.*

Instead of melody, there is dissonance, gloomy mutterings. There are some of the most bitter harmonies that we have ever heard, a mixture of musical quassia and wormwood. It is a composition that the earnest music lover will "first endure" and "then pity," but never embrace[53]

Here is actress Nell de Silva, passing judgment upon the flappers of 1920, at the ripe old age of thirty-one:

Girls with no aim in life but to walk up and down streets, satisfied if they can get enough money to take them to picture palaces and keep them supplied with high heeled shoes. These little girls, the type of womanhood known as flappers . . . [are] one of the saddest types this country has ever known. They do nothing and are of no use; on the contrary, they do incalculable harm. They do not qualify for mothers or for wives and there is nothing before them but disaster. Their idea of life is teas and lunches in hotels and smoking cigarettes. The latter of which, de Silva muses, perhaps misguidedly, "is not a harmful thing [in itself] . . . [but] when acquired as a female habit, it is a sign of general looseness."[54]

A flapper, smoking. RUSSELL PATTERSON / WIKIMEDIA COMMONS.

---

53. Boston *Daily Advertiser*, November 14, 1907.
54. *El Paso Herald* (Texas), May 8, 1920, home edition.

Time passes, but things don't change. Here's FBI agent L. B. Nichols discussing the adult reaction to the sight of Frank Sinatra's teenaged fans, lined up excitedly outside a Detroit theater in 1946:

> *There was widespread indignation on the part of numerous individuals that I came in contact with and a severe indictment of the parents of the girls. One individual went so far as to state that Sinatra should be lynched.*[55]

And here's Sinatra himself on rock'n'roll, a mere decade later: "[It] smells phony and false. It is sung, played, and written for the most part by cretinous goons and by means of its almost imbecilic reiteration, and sly, lewd, in plain fact, dirty lyrics . . . it manages to be the martial music of every side-burned delinquent on the face of the earth."

Ol' Blue Eyes singled Elvis Presley out for particular opprobrium: "His kind of music is deplorable, a rancid smelling aphrodisiac [which] fosters almost universally negative and destructive directions in young people."[56] And ten years on, when Elvis was asked if he wanted to spend time with the Beatles, he is said to have responded, "Hell, I don't want to meet those sons of bitches!"[57]

Here's guitarist Icarus Peel (the Honey Pot, Crystal Jacqueline) recalling his father's response to televised pop music in the English 1960s: "I can remember watching [him] turn some very interesting shades of purple when watching the Dave Clark Five performing 'Bits and Pieces' on TV. 'They're just stamping their bloody feet!'"

Or how about Noel Coward on the Beatles: "bad-mannered little shits."[58] Which is bad, but not as bad as novelist Anthony Burgess wishing, upon their arrival in a newly forged circle of hell, that the Fab Four be tied to "a white-hot turntable [and] stuck all over with blunt and rusty acoustic needles."[59]

Finally, here's Tipper Gore,[60] just fifteen when the British Invasion washed ashore in 1964, considering the music of two decades later:

---

55. Sinatra's FBI file was released to the public in December 1998.
56. Quoted in Peter Guralnick, *Last Train to Memphis—The Rise of Elvis Presley* (Little, Brown Book Group, 1994).
57. Gillian Garr, "Crossing Paths: When Elvis Met the Beatles," *Goldmine* magazine, 2009.
58. Craig Brown, *Here There and Everywhere, The Oldie*, Spring 2002.
59. Brown, *Here There and Everywhere*.
60. The wife of future Democratic vice president Al Gore, and cofounder of the Parents' Music Resource Center.

I grew up listening to rock music and loving it. . . . But something has hap-
pened since the days of "Twist and Shout." A small but immensely success-
ful minority of performers have pioneered the "porn rock" phenomenon. A
Judas Priest song about oral sex at gunpoint sold two million copies. So did
Mötley Crüe's album Shout at the Devil. . . . Sheena Easton's "Sugar Walls"
about female sexual arousal, was an even bigger hit on top forty radio
stations. And Prince peddled more than ten million copies of Purple Rain,
which included a song about a young girl masturbating in a hotel lobby.[61]

The Changing Face of Popular Music

If any hard evidence of the demise of rock's popularity is required, it is
to be found in the "bestselling albums of the decade" charts that bookend every ten-year cycle.

Where once Pink Floyd, Led Zeppelin, Fleetwood Mac, Boston, the Eagles, Meatloaf, and Van Halen (the 1970s); AC/DC, Bruce
Springsteen, Guns N' Roses, Prince, Dire Straits, and Bon Jovi (1980s);
Metallica, Alanis Morissette, Santana, Creed, Hootie & the Blowfish,
Nirvana, and Pearl Jam (1990s) cavorted so freely, the 2000s was the
first decade in which not one contemporary rocker made the top ten
bestsellers list—and that despite a compilation of the Beatles number
ones proving the bestselling record of the entire span.

A decade after that, it was not only the top ten that was all but
devoid of rock, it was the ten below that as well. Rather, the bestselling albums of the year were effectively shared between Adele, Taylor
Swift, Mumford and Sons, and Luke Bryan, who occupied ten of the
top twenty places between them, plus Eminem, Christophe Beck, Lady
Antebellum, Michael Bublé, Justin Bieber, Kate Perry, Jason Aldean,
Justin Timberlake, and Chris Stapleton. (Oh, and Imagine Dragons as
the exception to the rule.)

This is not the place to ask who, exactly, was buying these records,
although we will assume it was roughly the same age group that had
always pursued the biggest pop stars. The fact was, whoever they were,
they no longer had any interest in what an older generation would
describe as "rock."

---

61. Tipper Gore, *Raising PG Kids in an X-Rated Society* (Abingdon Press, 1987).

In other words, if you're over thirty or forty, it's your *job* to hate the music that the "kids" are listening to. More than that, it's your sworn duty as an adult. The slang they deploy, the hairstyles they sport, the clothes they wear, the jewelry they flash, the food they eat, the games they play, the inanimate objects that they adopt as pets, all are there to be dismissed, and it was surely coincidence alone that saw 2023 open with two incidents that placed what was once called "the generation gap," but is now better regarded as "old men shouting at clouds," firmly into the public view.

First, Harry Styles (age twenty-nine) being compared—and not by himself—to David Bowie, for the eye-catching outfit he wore to the Grammys. "From what I saw," veteran producer Tony Visconti (seventy-eight) responded, "[Harry Styles is] not worthy of shining [David Bowie's] shoes."[62]

Not to be outdone in the "outraging granddad" stakes, Sam Smith then stepped out at the Brit Awards wearing an inflatable black latex jumpsuit that, according to its designer, Harri, was intended to "celebrate the beauty of being one's self."[63]

True, it did make him look as though he was being consumed by an especially aggressive Naugahyde sofa. But it was also, in its marked uniqueness and unconventional style, precisely the kind of costuming that an internet's worth of probably-over-fifties had spent their teens fiercely defending against their own parents' scorn.

Only now, they had effectively become their own parents, tearing the outfit and its wearer to cyber-shreds, and who's the "stodgy square who needs to get with it" now?

As William Shakespeare had Hamlet declare, "Tis the sport to have the engineer hoist with his own petard."

62. Lizzie May, "David Bowie's Producing Partner Tony Visconti Hits Out at Claims That Harry Styles Is the 'New Bowie' after Winning Album of the Year at the Grammys," Mail Online, February 7, 2023, https://www.dailymail.co.uk/tvshowbiz/article-11721801 /David-Bowies-producing-partner-Tony-Visconti-hits-claims-Harry-Styles-new-Bowie .html.
63. "Sam Smith's Latex Suit at Brit Awards Gets Trolled by Netizens," TRSTDLY, February 14, 2023, https://www.trstdly.com/news/read/493286/sam-smiths-latex-suit-at -brit-awards-gets-trolled-by-netizens.

Chapter Five

How to Dismantle an Atomic Eff-Bomb—or, The Rudest Words Are Rock'n'Roll

Rock music should be gross: that's the fun of it. It gets up and drops its trousers.

—Bruce Dickinson

"The past," declared author L. P. Hartley in 1953, "is a foreign country."[64] In musical terms, it is also a foreign language, and quite possibly, an alien one.

We will admit now, despite all past suggestions to the contrary, that not everything is groovy in the garden of modern pop music.

Ghastly records by grisly ghouls still overwhelm our ears when we misguidedly walk into a teenager's crash pad; posturing poseurs still broadcast their asinine assumptions about everything from vegan poetry to nuclear energy; and there are still performers out there who make the very worst behavior of eons past sound like postcoital pillow talk with the movie idol of your dreams.

But that's a blessing, too, because if there's nobody policing the barricades, then there's no one to stop you singing whatever you like. Social media might still suspend users who have the temerity to post, for example, the topless covers of Sky Ferreira's *Night Time, My Time* or Keelhaul's *Conspiracy*, but language flies free, no matter how "controversial" it might once have been regarded.

Which is fascinating because, for the longest time—and we're still talking about music, here—there were some very real, and apparently very powerful, forces ranged against freedom of expression in song, and the fact that you really don't hear much about that any longer is something for which we *can* thank the generations that came before us.

---

64. L. P. Hartley, *The Go-Between* (Hamish Hamilton, 1953).

For it was they who proved, once and for all, what an absurd waste of time and resources it was for the authorities to try and tell pop stars what they were allowed to sing about. The days when, as *Rolling Stone* put it in 1985, "a Senate committee which normally presides over such esoteric issues as trade reciprocity [is currently] interpreting the lyrics of Bitch's 'Be My Slave.'"[65] Or that moment in 1977 when the British legal system was faced with the burning question of whether an Anglo-Saxon word for a clergyman's penchant for speaking nonsense, "bollocks," was obscene a millennium later.

Or the day the FBI opened a file on "Take Me Home, Country Roads" singer John Denver because he performed at a 1971 antiwar benefit in Colorado.

Indeed, looking back on these, and a host of similar instances, it seems absurd that untold oodles of taxpayer resources could be lavished upon what can only be described as authoritarian overreach.

For really, what difference whatsoever did it make to society at large if, by playing a certain Swampwitch song backwards, you might hear a heavily distorted voice suggesting that you should spend your weekend having sex with a demon? Now, if they'd suggested everyone evade the draft by having powerful parents, bone spurs, educational deferments, and asthma, that *would* have been worth investigating. But sex with demons? You'd have to find one that even fancied you, first. And can you even imagine the first date?

"What do you do for a living?"

"I impale the damned on fiery pitchforks."

"How interesting. I'm an architect."

Furthermore, if anybody had truly been serious about clamping down on obscenity in popular music in general, and rock'n'roll in particular, they should have started at the very beginning, with the term *rock'n'roll* itself. It was, after all, applied to the sex act long before it was grafted onto a musical style, and longer still before the first long-haired louts turned their guitars up loud and declared they're "gonna rock'n'roll ya all night long." Yes, dear, of course you are.

---

65. David Zucchino, "Rock Censorship: Big Brother Meets Twisted Sister," *Rolling Stone*, November 7, 1985.

Colorful Characters from Rock's Rich Tapestry No. 1

The Trivia Fiend

The Trivia Fiend is utterly harmless but is, in too many ways to count, one of the most irritating of all our colorful characters.

It's the sheer pointless blandness of its questions that frustrates.

The Trivia Fiend is the one who will start what appears to be a harmless social media thread—"What was Tommy from Wasp Invasion's[66] favorite Zonk album?" Or, "Did Swampfox ever include raspberry ice cream on their concert riders?"—and then deploy up to half a dozen sock puppet aliases to keep the conversation going, regardless of how many other genuine users become involved . . . and how many of those that did want only to ask one question.

"Why do you care?"

---

66. See appendix A: An Index of Wholly Imaginary Artists.

As we will see in the next chapter, the 1980s were the moment that the present truly collided with the oncoming future, a potential Armageddon heralded by the convening of the first ever federal government–approved investigation into the influence of rock and pop music.

It was not, however, the first time a government agency had turned its attentions toward popular music. As far back as the 1940s, the FBI was keeping tabs on Frank Sinatra, in connection with his contacts with sundry subjects of separate racketeering investigations. By the 1950s, folk singer Pete Seeger and ethnographer Alan Lomax were under the microscope for alleged Communist sympathies; and into the 1960s and 1970s, acts as disparate as singer Buffy Sainte-Marie, the Grateful Dead, and funk overlord James Brown had files opened on them.

It tended to be an artist's ideology and/or activism that dominated the bureau's investigative agenda. Abbie Hoffman would probably have been scrutinized even if he *hadn't* encouraged the hippie hordes to form a circle around the Pentagon and perform a rite of exorcism in 1967.[67]

---

67. Did they succeed? According to official sources, the crowd simply stood around and made some noise, and then went its shiftless way. But according to some of the march's more volatile organizers, the Pentagon rose thirty feet into the air, turned orange, and vibrated. And if that seems a little hard to believe, future James Taylor sideman Danny

As acts of antiwar protest, levitating the Pentagon in October 1967 was definitely one of the most memorable—whether it actually worked or not.
US NATIONAL ARCHIVES AND RECORDS ADMINISTRATION / WIKIMEDIA COMMONS.

But Big Brother was watching Sainte-Marie because she was as vocal in her support for indigenous rights as Brown was regarding black rights. Jerry Garcia and the Grateful Dead were investigated for potential connections to LSD suppliers in the Bay Area; and we can only guess how Richie Havens, Sam Cooke, and Nina Simone strayed onto the bureau's radar, because their files were destroyed.

Even associating with known agitators or criminals was enough to put an agent on your trail, as the Monkees' Mickey Dolenz has lately discovered. Rarely, however, was an artist's actual musical output the primary

Kortchmar is adamant that the building shifted and rose, just as Hoffman had predicted it would. "Amazingly, the Pentagon *did* levitate about a foot off the ground. Only for a short time . . . most everyone missed it but me and [a] few others." But it did move.

object of attention, although Richard Berry's "Louie Louie" would be the subject of a two-year investigation after the bureau was alerted to the potential for vulgar language secreted within the Kingsmen's 1963 hit rendition.

Talking to NPR in 2015,[68] documentary maker Eric Predoehl explained, "Kids would hear [improvised schoolyard] versions of the song, and they would pass around these written notes of what they thought were the lyrics. And parents were concerned, and they figured 'my gosh, this sounds like a dirty song, I don't understand it—maybe we should have an investigation of this sort of thing.'"

The investigation never did unearth any concrete evidence against the song, and when Iggy Pop and the Stooges recorded an unambiguously filthy version of the song[69] a little over a decade later, the FBI ignored it altogether.

Nevertheless, language, and the use (or misuse) of it in popular song, has always been a problem for those who would act as society's watchdogs. Slang itself has long been frowned upon in polite circles; somewhat huffily, the *Oxford English Dictionary* defines it as "the special vocabulary used by any set of persons of low or disreputable character." Indeed, a full century before Cardi B and Megan Thee Stallion sent parents thumbing frantically through the latest edition of *Commonly Used Net Terms* in the hope of deciphering "WAP," there was growing concern over the popularity of jazz, with its own secret language of, potentially . . . well, they could be singing *anything*!

The great thing is, they *were*. Jazz slang was developed *specifically* to allow performers to voice sentiments, terms, and themes that could not be broached in "polite company," and so effectively did it work that many of the words that were familiar to performers of the 1920s continue to be used today, often with the very same meanings.

Some terms were themselves adapted from earlier usages by these early pioneers of linguistic camouflage. The word *gig*, so commonly used for live performances (and, latterly, a form of generally usurious employment), is in fact a seventeenth-century word for "vulva." But it is the

---

68. "'Louie Louie': Indecipherable, or Indecent? An FBI Investigation," NPR.com, May 2, 2015, https://www.npr.org/2015/05/02/403623915/louie-louie-indecipherable-or-indecent-an-fbi-investigation.

69. Find it on the live album *Metallic KO*.

liquidity of certain words that can render any song a confusing morass for those listeners who like to *understand* the words they are singing along to.

Sometimes, context alone aids comprehension. When Peter Hammill declares, in Van Der Graaf Generator's 1970 song "Killer," that "you can't have two killers living in the same pad," it is fairly obvious that he is deploying what is now an archaic term for "home," no matter how clumsy the phrase sounds today. But always there are others where, the more you encounter them, the murkier they become.

More than any era since the original jazz age, the late 1960s were a crucial time for slang, as both existing and newly coined words and phrases fell into common usage.

It is said that the native people of the Arctic regions[70] have fifty words for snow. The summer of love probably had as many words for *good*, of which "cool," "groovy," "right on," and "far out" are just the tip of a happening iceberg. Antonyms include "bummer," "bad trip," and "drag," with the former, in British terms, also being a crude term for anal sex practitioners.

Yet there are nuances to almost every one of these. Simon and Garfunkel "feeling groovy" in their "59th Street Bridge Song" are not necessarily undergoing the same experience as the Young Rascals "grooving on a Sunday afternoon." P. P. Arnold demanding "If You Think You're Groovy" does not necessarily assign the same meaning to the word as the Small Faces, as they sing of feeding buns to the ducks "who all come out to groove about" in "Itchycoo Park."

Indeed, *groove* is among the most versatile words in the entire lexicon of pop slang. It can mean that moment when a band, or a musician, finds that special place in a musical passage—"hitting the perfect groove." It can be a sense of inner harmony ("I've got my groove on"). It can mean to understand ("you groove?", in which instance it is interchangeable with both *grok*[71] and *dig*, even as the latter equates also to an expression of approval: "I dig that crazy beat").

It can refer to an integral part of a gramophone record, it can be an invitation to a fight, and once again, it can refer to the female genitalia

---

70. Not to mention Kate Bush's ninth all-new album.
71. A term lifted wholesale from Robert Heinlein's novel *Stranger in a Strange Land*.

(with sexual gyrations thus referred to as "shaking that groove thang"), in which instance rocking'n'rolling is the same thing as grooving, and the corresponding male organ becomes the groove bone.

Be aware, too, that *jazz*, and *swing*, were slang terms for copulation some years before they were applied to music; just as *boogie-woogie* was once a sexually transmitted disease. Even something as innocent as a jukebox owes its name to the kind of establishment in which such devices were originally installed—a juke joint, or a brothel.

The attempts by one generation to actually understand the language of another can, of course, lead to some delightful misunderstandings. Few researchers, now or then, would dispute the overall veracity of jazzman Cab Calloway's *Hepster's Dictionary*, published in 1938 and destined to become the *OED* of jazz-age slang.

Other such publications abound, from sundry period translations of sixties hippie speak, designed to ensure that even the most unfashionable moms and dads might learn to dig their long-haired offspring's rap; to some positively gallant attempts to wrangle meaning from the twisted torrents of punk-era verbiage.

Few, however, will ever top the glossary of grunge published by the *New York Times* on November 15, 1992, as compiled from a phone conversation with Sub Pop label associate Megan Jasper. Unfortunately, it did not occur to her hapless interrogator, journalist Rick Marin, that Jasper might have been making things up as she went along.

Faithfully, then, did he introduce his readership to such decidedly nonwords as "lamestain" (an uncool person), "swingin' on the flippity-flop" (hanging out), "cob nobbler" (a loser), "harsh realm" (a bummer), and "tom-tom club" (uncool outsiders).

A drunk, he was informed, was a "bloated, big bag of blotation." Staying home on a weekend evening meant you had been "bound and hagged," and the regulation grunge uniform comprised "fuzz," "wack slacks," and "kickers" (heavy boots). Unless you were into hair metal, in which case you might still be wearing "plats" (platform boots).

"All subcultures speak in code," the *New York Times* article proclaimed, and the following terms would be "coming soon to a high school or mall near you." Which they were, although probably not in the manner the newspaper believed. Instead, the Seattle record label C/Z

Records launched a line of T-shirts reproducing choice selections from the glossary.

One term that few would-be lexicographers ever came to grips with was that which sprang to prominence during the early to mid-1970s, and was derived, apparently, from Hell's Angel culture's habit of referring to girlfriends as "mama." And in that cultural context, it worked. Where things went askew was when less Hellishly Angelic characters chose to adopt it for their own musical vocabularies. It was never difficult to figure out what was going on. It was just that the term felt so bizarre, even out of place, in its new surroundings.

Mama, one does not need to explain, is a corruption of the word *mother*. What conclusion, then, can be drawn from Led Zeppelin's insistence that the way "mama" moves makes them want to see her "groove"?[72] Precisely what is on the Eagles' mind when they declare their intention to discover what turns on "mama's lights?"[73] Are they really helping a parent find the lamp switch?

Or there is the "pretty mama" who is taking the Doobie Brothers by the hand in "Black Water" immediately prior to dancing with her daddy, presumably the singer's grandfather, "all night long."

Which is all very confusing because, just as you're thinking this whole thing is stupid, and *of course* they're deploying the word in its original Angel sense, along comes Heart's "Magic Man," and mama is telling her daughter "to come on home." Which, one might be tempted to remark, is what any decent mother should have been doing all along.

Indeedio, cats and kittens, it's an alien language, made all the more confusing by the fact that even as we understand the words, we falter at what they mean. Even Quantum Jump's 1976 classic "Lone Ranger," with its opening lyric of "Taumatawhakatangihangakoauauotamateapokai-whenuakitanatahu," is at least familiar to visitors to the hill of that name in New Zealand. All this other stuff about rock'n'rolling your mama's groove thang because she forgot to pay the electric bill, however, is mega uncool.

If the above strikes the reader as a somewhat puerile attempt at juvenile humor, the fact is—it is. Its purpose, however, is to disguise a more

---

72. "Black Dog," from *Led Zeppelin IV*.
73. "One of Those Nights," from the album of the same name.

sinister problem lurking for the unsuspecting listener, in the form of the now critically outdated motifs and themes with which the past is so virulently seeded.

From the Beatles proudly declaring that the object of their affections was "just seventeen" ("I Saw Her Standing There") to Johnny Burnette championing the ten-year age difference between himself and the object of his affections ("You're Sixteen"), and on to Iggy Pop's insistence that "my girlfriend . . . she's just fourteen" ("Dogfood"), one begins to comprehend the aforementioned Tipper Gore's outrage over the concept of what she described as "the 'porn rock' phenomenon." Except for the realization that two of those songs, by the Beatles and Burnette, were both roughly contemporary with the age of innocence to which she hankered to return.

Statutory rape is not a subject to make light of, and it is not this book's intention to do so. Nor is the standard response that the songs simply reflect the culture of the time acceptable as an excuse, any more than if one were discussing songs that traded upon racism, xenophobia, misogyny, homophobia, ableism, or personal prejudice of any sort.

Rather, we can expand the condemnation past both the artists and the industry that allowed such concepts to spring freely onto the record racks, and turn our attention to the one nationally recognized body to proclaim itself a campaigner against all the ills that were, by the mid-1980s, endemic in the rock'n'roll vocabulary.

Forget trying to figure out how to turn on mama's light. We should talk about what a brilliant idea parental guidance stickers turned out to be. They made it so much easier to decide which new records to purchase. The rude ones, of course.

Chapter Six

Sdrawkcab Siht Etirw em Edam Lived Eht—or, Satanic Messages in Reverse

The Sex Pistols would be vastly improved by sudden death. I would like to see someone dig a huge hole and bury the lot of them in it.

—Bernard Brook Partridge, Greater London Council, 1977

In November 1983, a new British band called Frankie Goes to Hollywood released their debut single, "Relax." It didn't do much . . . hung around the bottom of the UK chart on the strength of the handfuls who bought a copy after hearing it in a club, picked up a little airplay and a few more sales from that, but when the Top 40 chart was published on January 3, 1984, "Relax" was number thirty-five, and didn't look like climbing much further.

And then a BBC disc jockey went to play it on his show and announced he would never air it again, so suggestive was its sleeve and so obscene was its lyric. Two days later, the BBC as a whole banned the song from their airwaves, and when the following week's chart was published, "Relax" had positively soared to number six. Two weeks later, it was number one.

Why? Because the more you tell people they shouldn't listen to something, the more they'll go out of their way to do so.

Another decade, another continent. In 1992, rapper Ice T's heavy metal alter-ego Bodycount recorded "Cop Killer," an explosive response to recent cases of police violence. Ultimately, the song would be withdrawn from the band's album following condemnation from as high up as then President George H. W. Bush, VP Dan "don't ask me to spell potato" Quayle, Charlton Heston ("catchy little number, isn't it?"), and law enforcement agencies across the country. Before that, however, but with the controversy mounting, a Texan news report declared, "sales of [Bodycount's] album have tripled in Houston and doubled in three other cities."[74]

---

74. Excerpted in *Fight the Power: How Hip-Hop Changed the World,* episode 3, PBS TV.

Protecting 1980s youth from the foul and profane—the PMRC's greatest sticker. AUTHOR'S COLLECTION.

Stick it to the man.

Art cannot be banned. It cannot be controlled, it cannot be suppressed, it cannot be told what to do. Or it can, and it has been (Nazi Germany's prohibition on what the authorities termed "degenerate art" is a case in point), but you have to goosestep down some pretty dangerous roads in order to get to a place where such injunctions will be obeyed, and there's going to be a lot of kickback while you're doing it.

Sensibly, then, Western governments have seldom had the appetite to confront popular music head on. Individual figures might, as we saw in the last chapter, be challenged, and even harassed. But, as an industry as a whole, popular music is more or less left to the whim of the marketplace.

If a controversy is aroused, either it will burn out when people get bored, or it won't. And every time it burns out, it's taken for granted that the basic laws of wedge theory[75] will promptly come into play—art-

---

75. Wedge theory is the scientific term for what was once (and may still be) the popular canard, "Give them an inch, and they'll take a mile," meaning, once you grant someone permission to break one unwritten rule, they'll continue to shatter more and more, until the rule itself has been entirely forgotten.

The latter expression has been around since the late 1800s, although it is certainly far older than that; the similarly intended "Give him an inch and he'll take an ell" (an archaic measurement used by cloth merchants, equivalent to forty-five inches) was included as long ago as 1546 in John Heywood's *A Dialogue Conteinyng the Number in Effect of All the Prouerbes in the Englishe Tongue.*

ists who had hitherto been given an inch and then took a mile will step forward and take another mile. Only now, nobody will raise an eyebrow. Problem solved.

Twice, however, forces within the US government have felt sufficiently concerned to actually convene hearings upon what the now-defunct British newspaper the *Sunday People* once termed "the filth [that we] fling at our pop kids."[76]

The article itself was actually concerned with the "foul words and phrases" that an eagle-eyed someone had spotted "crop[ping] up in almost every issue" of the weekly *New Musical Express* music paper. "In one recent article alone, the four-letter word for sexual relations appeared no fewer than seven times."

Eek.

How many times it turned up in the music that the paper wrote about, of course, is another matter. Folk singer Al Stewart is generally credited as the first performer to include the word *fucking* in a song (the title track of 1968's *Love Chronicles* LP), and Beatle John Lennon fired off two "fucks" in a single number, 1970's "Working Class Hero."

The Jefferson Airplane uncorked "motherfucker" during "We Can Be Together," from 1970's *Volunteers*; Fanny mumbled "it's so fucking hard" in their "Rock Bottom Blues" (1972). The Sex Pistols were credited with unleashing such a shitload of filth every time they opened their mouths that, when they finally released a single that British radio agreed to play, there were still ears out there that misheard the pronunciation and emphasis of the last syllable in "Pretty Vacant." Naughty!

On every occasion, eyebrows may have been elevated, tuts may have been tutted. But it would be 1985 before the first genuinely meaningful

---

Wedge theory, on the other hand, is of somewhat more recent coinage, and is applied in the main to any deliberate undermining of convention or law, to cause existing prohibitions to fall into disarray. Initially, and most potently, applied to the more slippery machinations of the political class, it has since broadened to encompass any practice, whether by an individual or a group, an industry or an ideology, that incrementally erodes the standards of the day, with the aim of replacing them with a situation that the perpetrator prefers.

For example. A builder is granted permission to erect a four-story building in an otherwise low-rise neighborhood, before then successfully pleading to be allowed to add a fifth floor for whatever reason. A year or two later, a second builder is permitted to build five floors, and then negotiates a sixth. And so on. Before the townspeople know it, the entire area is bristling with multifloor tower blocks, and the older residents can still remember saying: "I told you at the time, didn't I? You give them an inch . . .

That is wedge theory.

76. No author credited. *Sunday People*, November 14, 1976.

conversation on the corrupting energies of popular music was heard in the corridors of power, at the urging of a small but determined lobby whom the media swiftly (but accurately) termed the Washington Wives.

The old men had had their chance to shout at clouds. Now it was time for the middle-aged women to have a go.

It was early 1985 when Tipper Gore, Susan Baker, and Pam Howar—respectively, the wives of Tennessee senator (and future vice president) Al Gore; President Reagan's treasury secretary, James Baker; and the owner of a major Washington construction company, James Howar—independently found themselves being exposed to song lyrics to which they took exception, but which were apparently being enjoyed by their children, their friends, and—in Howar's case—their aerobics instructors. Rude lyrics, shocking lyrics, coarse lyrics.

"We got together," Mrs. Gore explained, "and said, 'these things were happening to us in our homes.'"

Most parents who consider the music blasting from an offspring's bedroom to be a little off-color would tell them to turn it off, or at least turn it down. The Washington Wives, however, had other remedies at their disposal. They wrote a letter to multifarious friends and associates, many of whom were as well-connected as they were, and invited them to discuss the matter at a Washington church the following month.

The Washington Wives made no bones about their shocking discoveries. "Some rock groups," the invitation declared, "advocate Satanic rituals . . . others sing of killing babies." Alice Cooper, hang your head in shame.

Other songs recommended "open rebellion against parental . . . authority," as though rebellion were not one of the very pillars upon which rock'n'roll was built, even back in Mrs. Baker's teenage years, when this self-described "golden oldie" was happily listening to her Chuck Berry records—presumably unaware that her idol served eighteen months in prison after being found guilty of violating the Mann Act.

Their friends shared their outrage. Swiftly, an action group—the Parents Music Resource Center (PMRC)—was launched, seemingly unaware that its clunky name made it sound more like a leisure facility for moms and dads who wanted to read books about pianos.

But the PMRC had teeth. Lobbying the Recording Industry Association of America (RIAA), the umbrella organization that represented the nation's major record labels, the PMRC demanded that all albums that could be considered "objectionable" should be prominently labeled according to the offense, in the same manner as movies and video games.

"X" would indicate explicit sexual or violent content, "O" condemned occultist material, "D/A" warned of songs that glorified drugs and alcohol—and so on until Frank Zappa, one of the PMRC's most vociferous critics, asked whether "the next bunch" would include "a large yellow J on material written or performed by Jews?"

Its confidence boosted by the pulviscular willingness of several RIAA members to go along with a modified version of those demands, and campaigning now for this initial victory to become an industry standard, the PMRC next took the battle into its fast-swelling membership's own backyard, the halls of government.

In mid-September 1985, the Senate Committee on Commerce, Science and Transportation sat to consider the PMRC's requests. Of its august members, *Rolling Stone* was not alone in noting, "The wife of its chairman, Senator John Danforth, is affiliated with [the PMRC]. So, too, is the wife of Senator Hollings."[77]

The PMRC's basic argument was that a parent had a discretionary right over the music their children listened to, and they should be afforded some means of personally checking the record prior to purchase. Fair enough. Indeed, this was never seriously challenged. Maybe other parents were fine with their child being exposed to the likes of Chicago's "Hard Habit to Break," or Toto's "Roseanna." The PMRC represented those that weren't.

We are speaking of a time before YouTube and the streaming services that made so much music, new and old, available to anyone who wanted to hear it. In 1985, as we will see in chapter 11, broadcast music was still strictly controlled by the broadcasters, who resolutely upheld certain prohibitions on language and context.

This gave rise to such now-amusing anomalies as Chuck Berry being prohibited from performing his hit "My Ding-a-Ling" on British television because the hand movements he made during the chorus were adjudged obscene; the Beatles' "Ballad of John and Yoko" being banned in Australia for blasphemy; and Serge Gainsbourg being invited onto every chat show

---

77. Zucchino, "Rock Censorship."

in France after he told Whitney Houston he'd like to fuck her on live late-night television.

Meaning (except in France, probably), if your children were listening, for example, to Patti Smith potty-mouthing through her version of the Who's "My Generation," you can bet your bottom dollar that *they were doing it deliberately*. And they also knew that you were listening.

Twisted Sister's colorful frontman Dee Snider sensibly suggested that listening booths be reinstalled in record stores[78] to enable concerned parents to actually listen to the record before it was purchased. But you can imagine how well that must have been received—oh no, we need someone else to tell us we're offended. Plus, who has either the patience or the willpower to listen to an entire album in search of a single veiled reference to having smacked-out oral sex with the entire cast of *Cats*? In costume.

Other suggestions, too, were somehow lacking. A printed lyric sheet on the back of every album cover might have worked, but who would have spent the most time reading them: worried moms? Or the same thrill-seeking children who used to pore through the library's dictionary in search of the rudest words?

And how would this apply, for example, to any all-instrumental albums that were deemed equally capable of causing offense? Frank Zappa's *Jazz from Hell* was slapped with a parental guidance sticker[79] despite being wholly vocal-free.

The Senate committee was granted no powers of legislation. However, sensing that something needed to be done, by November no less than twenty RIAA member labels had thought of something, and said they'd do it. They agreed to print warning labels to alert consumers to potentially controversial subject matter. In fact, only nineteen went ahead with it in the end, but it was a start.

Of course, it was not enough for the PMRC. Unless the warning labels became universal, "porn rock" could continue to assail what Senator Ernest Hollings described as "the tender young ears of this nation."

Stalemate.

Throughout the first year of the PMRC's existence, the group's prime target was the "Filthy 15," a clutch of predominantly heavy metal and dance

---

78. These were a common feature of many record stores at least into the 1970s.
79. By the Meyer Music Markets, a chain in the Pacific Northwest.

bands whose lyrics, as Mrs. Gore put it, represented "a sick new strain of rock music glorifying everything from forced sex to bondage to rape."

Looking closer at the songs, and the lyrics therein, however . . . Well, not to be judgmental, but hands up if you'd heard far worse on the oldies channel, and nobody was suggesting labeling any of that? The Rolling Stones salaciously suggested "let's spend the night together"; and the Beatles demanded to know "why don't we do it in the road," together with the reassurance that "no one will be watching us," and that was back in the sixties.

In 1970, Black Widow were inviting listeners to "come to the sabbat," because "Satan's there." In 1975, the Starland Vocal Band's "Afternoon Delight" was a barely disguised invitation to have sex after lunch. In 1977, Alberto y Los Trios threatened "to cut [my] liver out and nail it to your wall," while the Sex Pistols' "Bodies" described an abortion ("squirming bloody mess"). At the end of the decade, Marianne Faithfull's "Why D'You Do It?" demanded "why'd you let her suck your cock?"

Compared to any of that, AC/DC's suggestion that you allow them to "cut your cake with my knife, oh" was positively snow white.

Playlist-The PMRC's Filthy Fifteen

AC/DC, "Let Me Put My Love into You" ("Driving all night with my machinery.")

Black Sabbath, "Trashed" ("I drank a bottle of tequila.")

Cyndi Lauper—"She Bop" ("I want to go south and get me some more.")

Def Leppard—"High 'n' Dry (Saturday Night)" ("I've been drinking all day.")

Judas Priest—"Eat Me Alive" ("I'm gonna force you at gunpoint to eat me alive.")

Madonna—"Dress You Up" ("Gonna dress you up in my love.")

Mary Jane Girls—"In My House" ("When it comes down to makin' love / I'll satisfy . . . every fantasy you think up.")

Mercyful Fate—"Into the Coven" ("Come into my coven / And become Lucifer's child.")

Mötley Crüe—"Bastard" ("Out go the lights, in goes my knife.")

Prince—"Darling Nikki" ("I met her in a hotel lobby masturbating with a magazine.")

Sheena Easton—"Sugar Walls" ("Blood races to your private spots.")
Twisted Sister—"We're Not Gonna Take It" ("We'll fight the powers that be.")
Vanity—"Strap On 'Robbie Baby'" ("If you want to glide down my hallway, it's open.")
Venom—"Possessed" ("I drink the vomit of the priests.")
W.A.S.P.—"Animal (Fuck Like a Beast)" ("I fuck like a beast.")

Open to ridicule though they were, the Washington Wives were not to be deterred. Indeed, they were only further emboldened when a new menace lurched into harsh focus. Within hours of rioting at a Run DMC gig at Long Beach Arena in 1986, Tipper Gore added rap to her list of musical menaces.

"Angry, disillusioned kids unite behind . . . rap music and the music said it's okay to beat people up," she insisted. And she would be on the frontlines again in 1989, as state authorities set about purging local communities of 2 Live Crew's *As Nasty as They Wanna Be*. Soon, as journalist Ira Robbins put it, it would be "a crime to tell a dirty story with a beat," and in 1994 a new set of hearings unfolded on Capitol Hill as the Senate Juvenile Justice Subcommittee appeared to accept that as a call to action, and took on West Coast gangsta rap.

It was an event which the *Chicago Tribune* declared "began with the air of a political cocktail party, sprinkled with the obligatory stars— Dionne Warwick making nice with Sen. Carol Moseley-Braun. It evolved into a kind of tent revival, with people loudly voicing affirmation. And at times it sounded like a city street corner, with talk of 'bitches' and 'ho's.'"[80] And all this because "senators were trying to understand whether a form of popular music they have rarely heard is a cause or an effect of violence."

The hearings ultimately came to naught, just as the PMRC's attempts to "clean up" music were, ultimately, a failure. The parental warning stickers did linger on for several years, but not only was their usage haphazard in the extreme, they also became a promotional tool in their own right, as labels took to producing both "clean" and "uncensored" versions of potentially (or hopefully) controversial records, in the certain knowledge

---

80. Linda M. Harrington and Tribune staff writer, "On Capitol Hill, a Real Rap Session," *Chicago Tribune*, February 24, 1994.

that it was the uncensored ones that would sell the most, including to people who might not otherwise have looked at them.

Of course, they did! Ever since Elvis Presley's hips were banned from nationwide television in 1956, nothing short of death has boosted sales better than scandal, and the louder that scandal resonates, the more people want to know what it's all about.

The difference was, this time around, you didn't even need to know the names of the raunchiest, nastiest, ugliest songs around. They were signposted in the stores for you, with a federally approved marketing sticker.

More important, however, the hearings failed because freedom of speech and artistic expression were victorious. And today, thanks to those who fought so hard to preserve that freedom, not even the most insensitive singer-songwriter needs to coat their sugar walls in schoolyard cartoon violence and B-movie Satanism. They can just come out and WAP 'em.

Thank you, vintage music. Now, kindly #%^$&*% &^%) off.

Plus ça Change–Today's Sicko Seventeen

Akinyele—"Just Put It in My Mouth" ("In my motherfuckin' mouth.")

Cannibal Corpse—"Frantic Disembowelment" ("Intestines exposed by violent thrusts, the innards removed, dissecting the guts.")

Cardi B featuring Megan Thee Stallion—"WAP" ("Bring a bucket and a mop for this wet ass pussy.")

Dirty Sanchez—"Fucking on the Dancefloor" ("You got invisible fangs and Terri Nunn bangs.")

Electrocute—"Fun Is a Floppy Bitch" ("You can piss on my couch, I piss on your face.")

Fergie—"Fergalicious" ("Maybe then you'll get a taste of my tasty, tasty.")

Ghost—"Ritual" ("This chapel of ritual smells of dead human sacrifices.")

Jose Nunez featuring Taina—"Bilingual" ("You fucking me makes me bilingual.")

Larry Tree featuring Roxy Cottontail—"Let's Make Nasty" ("You got that nasty bounce so make my kitty pounce.")

Lil Nas X—"Montero" ("Shoot a child in your mouth while I'm riding.")

Niko B—"Who's That What's That" ("Fucking gherkin.")

Peaches—"Fuck the Pain Away" ("Suckin' on my titties like you wanted me.")

Sickotoy—"2 High 2 Care" ("Ninety-nine bitches all wanna fuck.")

Sky Ferreira—"Omanko" (The very title is obscene if you speak Japanese.)

Sunn O)))—"Báthory Erzsébet" ("She is the presence that is all that is un-named, for it is Her, the unbegotten Mistress of the eternal hunger, dwell forever in her great unholy stomach where the damned befoul themselves in the glory of her fecund and bloody history.")

TV Rock featuring Nancy Vice—"Bimbo Nation" ("Don't be fooled by the killer rack bitch.")

Watain—"Devil's Blood" ("I have swallowed the hanged man's semen with necrophageous delight.")

Chapter Seven

Ten Things You Didn't Know about Elvis Presley's Bottom—or, The Greatest Albums Ever Listed

[The Beatles'] Revolver *is . . . a moment in western culture as pivotal as Beethoven's* Eroica, *Presley with "Hound Dog," Stravinsky's* The Rite of Spring, *the ceiling of the Sistine Chapel.*

—*Dan Cairns*[81]

Rock'n'roll is one of the few arts in which it's the crap that is often the most enjoyable. Especially when it isn't actually crap. Even one hit wonders are great for one hit, and there are some—Question Mark and the Mysterions' "96 Tears"; M's "Pop Muzik"; Lipps Inc's "Funky Town"; Thelma Houston's "Don't Leave Me This Way"; even Right Said Fred's "I'm Too Sexy"—where the impact of that one hit was so transcendent that its memory dwarfs the entire output of countless "established" hit makers.

Others—Terry Jacks's "Seasons in the Sun" is a prime example—serve to introduce audiences to other talents altogether, in this instance the Belgian songwriting genius Jacques Brel. And we should remember, too, that a one hit wonder (OHW) in the United States might well have enjoyed a considerably grander career overseas (and vice versa). Gary Glitter, Soft Cell, Dexy's Midnight Runners, Suzi Quatro, Nena, A-ha, and Sinead O'Connor, denizens of every stateside list of OHWs, were serial chart-toppers elsewhere.

The singles market, however, is deceptive. There it takes just one song to make a mark, and a lot of artists have. Albums, we are led to believe, take considerably more work—even those, like the Beatles' *Please Please Me* debut, that were recorded in less than a day. As biographer Mark

---

81. Dan Cairns, "*Revolver:* The Inside Story of the Beatles' Greatest Album," *Sunday Times,* October 22, 2022.

Lewisohn later remarked, "There can scarcely have been 585 more productive minutes in the history of recorded music."[82]

Sometimes, however, an album is just an album, a collection cobbled together with the finesse of a drunken dowager digging a ditch, in the hope that whoever bought the single might buy the LP as well. And sometimes . . . well, sometimes, you'd rather get a tattoo on your tenderest part than be told, once again, how "great" a certain album is, on the assumption that, like 1950s Elvis fans, fifty million rock critics can't be wrong, even if they are clearly all suffering from acute cognitive dissonance.

Worse still, you know exactly who they are, as they publicly hamstring their own personal opinions ("the first Beat Lemurs album is the one of the worst records I've ever heard") so as to blend in more securely with their chosen peer group ("the first Beat Lemurs album is one of the best records ever made"). Because who wants to stand out from a crowd *that* wise?[83]

At least since the mid-1970s there has existed a hierarchy of those albums that, at least according to the received wisdom of the critical establishment, are regarded as untouchable. The Beatles' *Revolver, Sergeant Pepper*, and the so-called (but, in reality, titled simply *The Beatles*) White Album; the Beach Boys' *Pet Sounds*; the Rolling Stones' *Exile on Main Street*; Dylan's *Highway 61 Revisited, Blonde on Blonde*, and *Blood on the Tracks*; the first Velvet Underground album; Van Morrison's *Astral Weeks*; Joni Mitchell's *Blue*; Stevie Wonder's *Songs in the Key of Life*; Marvin Gaye's *What's Going On*; David Bowie's *Hunky Dory* and *The Rise and Fall of Ziggy Stardust and the Spiders from Mars*—a critically correct canon with which nobody dared disagree. And why?

Because what would be the point?

The criteria for inclusion in such lists was varied, but sales, critical response, and influence all played a major part, as indeed they needed to—anything else would have been so subjective as to be meaningless. But peer pressure, too, was essential. What did the last "best albums" chart rank, and shouldn't we just stick with that? Plus, if you publish the results with sufficient fanfare, the unassuming reader will feel compelled to agree with at least the majority of it.

---

82. Mark Lewisohn, *The Complete Beatles Recording Sessions* (Harmony Books, 1988).
83. For more on this phenomenon, see Mike Edison's foreword at the beginning of this book.

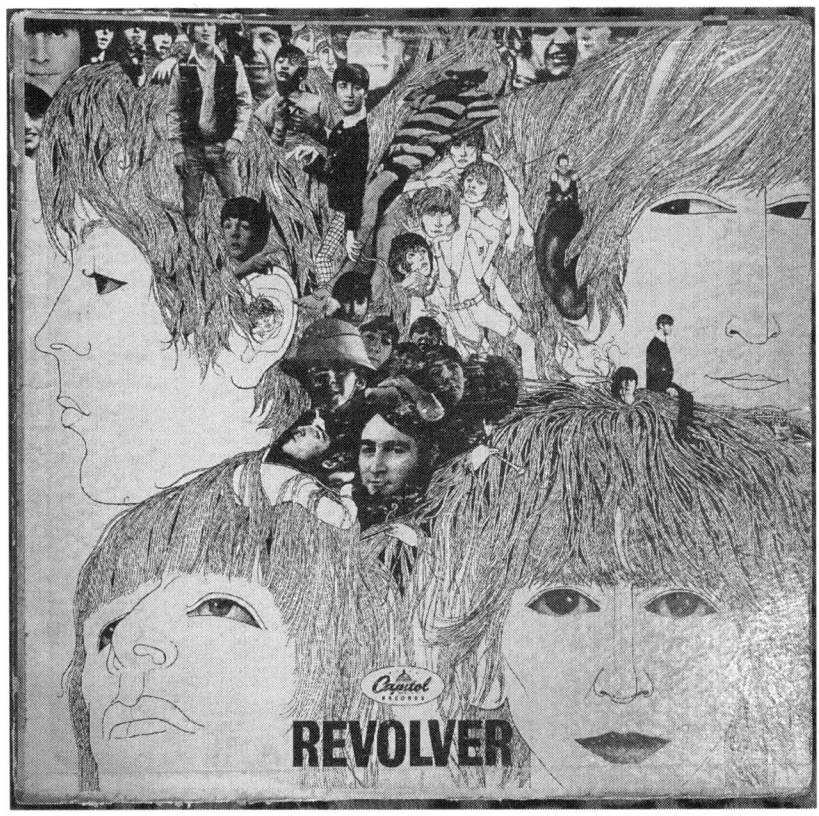

Yes, you could buy the snazzy box set full of outtakes, remixes, and so forth.
Or you could stick with the original popping, crackling, and jumping copy
that has served you so well for the past sixty years. AUTHOR'S COLLECTION.

"Of course, *Nico Teen & the Stains XI* is the seventeenth greatest LP
ever made. What else could it be?"

On the other hand, who are these lists really made for? Certainly not
you or me, because we already have our "best albums" lists wedged firmly
in our minds, and they probably don't include any of the clutch raised
so high by the critical establishment. Certainly not the artists, for they
are almost inevitably guaranteed to disagree. "Number twenty-three? It
should have been number nineteen *at least*."

And certainly not anybody whose faith in polls has been slipping
downhill ever since that peculiar moment on the eve of the 1948 presidential election, when Gallup placed Thomas E. Dewey five percentage

points ahead of incumbent Harry S. Truman. (Although at least they got the winning margin correct, even if they mixed up the names.)

Add to that the calumnious predictions that haunted such recent polls as the 2016 presidential election and that same year's Brexit referendum in the United Kingdom, and it's small wonder that polls elicit so little trust these days.

So we hate polls. But we love lists. And that's fortunate, because so do magazine editors and online content managers. In fact, lists provide such a foolproof means of attracting a multitude of readers for the minimum

Despite surely ranking among the most overrated album covers ever (now, there's a listicle I'd like to see), Lance Corporeal's Saladin's Beard *is synonymous with her early 1970s success.* AUTHOR'S COLLECTION.

of effort that it's surprising humankind ever bothered with books and magazines to begin with.

Famously, the very first thing Johannes Gutenberg did upon introducing the moveable type printing press into Europe, around 1448, was publish an edition of the Bible.

What he should have done, and what he would do were he in the same position today, is throw together "Ten Cool Things That God Did," and then sit back and watch the comments flow.

Not everybody agrees. There are those who will tell you that listicles are lazy; listicles are puerile; listicles are not only a waste of the reader's time reading them, but of the writer's time writing them. Indeed, by the time they're finished delineating every last thing that's wrong with listicles, they could have saved everybody a lot of time . . . and made a list.

The Top Five Diseases You Can Catch from Used Vinyl
The Ten Most Imaginative Soft Rock Suicides—Rated and Reviewed
Ten Surprising Ways in which Downloads Cause Obesity

Of course, disputes have always been at the heart of music's relationship with the printed word, and the listicle is simply the latest manifestation of this. Even more exciting, the author does not even need to be critical. A listicle claiming to rate "The Five Greatest Rocky Biceps B Sides" is as likely a candidate for castigation as one that denies the star ever made even one decent record.

Assail them as we wish, however, and batter them with indignant opprobrium, but still listicles are irresistible, just as books of lists were in the pre-internet era. *The Guinness Book of Records*—effectively a long list of stupid pet tricks as performed by humans—has been a perennial bestseller since 1955; while 1977 saw the publication of the very sensibly titled *Book of Lists*, compiled by David Wallechinsky, Irving Wallace, and Amy Wallace, which was so successful that it was quickly followed by two further, similarly sensibly titled, collections in 1980 and 1983.

Therein, the enterprising browser could discover everything from radio host Dr. Demento's ten worst song titles of all time—number one was "Mama Get Your Hammer (There's a Fly on Baby's Head)," by the Bobby Peterson Quintet)— to "Fifteen Unusual Stolen Objects." Indeed, this vigorous pantechnicon of trivia has led more than one online commentator to credit the book's authors with inventing the internet fifteen years too soon.

That may be hyperbole, but they certainly invented a large part of the internet's contents.

Ten Pictures of My Cat Eating My Breakfast That You'll Never Forget.

Music lists played only a small part in the *Book of Lists* series, but as other publishers boarded the bandwagon, the first books of Rock Lists soon followed (along with sports, sex, food, and more or less anything else you can think of); and while readers' commentary in those days was very much restricted to pen, paper, and a stamp, authors were doubtless kept busy reading their mail.

For all the controversy that they can arouse, however, listicles are essentially benign. Indeed, by inviting open debate and sharing opinions, they are as accurate a barometer of, for example, an artist's standing within a certain community (i.e., the regular readers of a magazine) than any article or picture spread.

Not everybody, after all, has time to read a seven-page interview with the surviving members of Skull Turnip. But give them a list of the Turnip's five best songs, and they will reply with the ten reasons you're wrong. It is fan interaction at its purest, both in its immediacy and also in its ability to shatter, at last, the eternal *hrönir* that is the greatest albums ever made.

It was Argentine writer Jorge Luis Borges (1899–1986) who introduced the concept of the *hrön* to the language in his short story *Tlön, Uqbar, Ortbis Tertius*. Published in 1940, it's the tale of a secret society of intellectuals who, having created the fictional country Uqbar (somewhere in Asia Minor), set about "proving" its existence by planting evidence throughout the real-life historical record, and thus creating a whole new reality—one in which Uqbar's existence becomes unquestioned.

Substitute Uqbar with . . . oh, I don't know, let's say "the ten greatest albums ever made," and then ask yourself this: "Are they *really*?" Or is their preeminence, too, the idle workings of some self-styled secret society of intellectuals trying to pull the wool over our eyes for whatever reasons you like to imagine?

What once were events are now everyday occurrences—from being a phenomenon during slow news months. If you enter "best albums of all time" into a search machine today, you'll have so many hits that it's amazing modern journalists have time to do anything but compile new lists of the things. Or maybe they don't actually compile them. Maybe they just heft the same heap of *hrönir* into a jar, and then pull each one out at random.

Although it was by no means the first of its kind, *Rolling Stone's* "500 Greatest Albums of All Time" list is generally regarded as the granddaddy of them all, despite appearing for the first time as recently as 2003. Compiled from the votes of 273 people drawn from across the music industry, each offering up their personal fifty favorites, the listing was topped by the Beatles' *Sergeant Pepper's Lonely Hearts Club Band*, with the Beach Boys' *Pet Sounds* in second place.

The list was not controversy-free, and not solely because it was so predictable. That was only to be expected. Artists of color accounted for less than 25 percent of the top fifty, women just 6 percent. The Beatles, on the other hand, occupied nine of the 500 rankings.

Did the magazine learn from those mistakes, however? Here's the same publication's offering from 2012: *Sergeant Pepper, Pet Sounds, Revolver, Highway 61, Rubber Soul, What's Going On, Exile on Main Street, London Calling* by the Clash, *Blonde on Blonde*, and *The Beatles*.[84] And from 2020, Marvin Gaye, the Beach Boys, Dylan, and the Beatles—but this time with *Abbey Road*, an insertion which, surely coincidentally, had enjoyed a much-trumpeted fiftieth anniversary reissue just months earlier.

And here, to save any further faffing about, is a Best Albums of All Time list compiled for rate-your-music.com from twenty-nine different lists published between 1995 (*Spin*) and 2011:[85] *Revolver, Pet Sounds, Sergeant Pepper*, the White Album, *Ziggy Stardust, Led Zeppelin IV, Nevermind, Never Mind the Bollocks, Rubber Soul*, and *Abbey Road.*

So that's settled. The greatest albums of all time are . . .

The entire Matterhorn Slender discography.

---

84. "The 500 Greatest Albums of All Time," *Rolling Stone*, May 31, 2012.

85. erikfish, "Best Albums of All Time—29 Lists Combined," Rate Your Music, updated July 2, 2012, https://rateyourmusic.com/list/erikfish/best_albums_of_all _time___29_lists_combined/.

Matterhorn Slender's proposed performance atop the mountain from which they took their name was ultimately canceled due to high winds. Instead, the concert—recorded for the band's first live album—took place at base camp. AUTHOR'S COLLECTION.

Now, maybe we are making something out of nothing here, and the reason why those same artists and albums keep appearing in every list is because they really are the greatest record ever made.

Indeed, one suspects that even the most benevolent attempt to alter this implacable hegemony with a smattering of records released in more recent times would be widely perceived as an act of heinous iconoclasm. Nirvana's *Nevermind*—a stripling at just thirty years of age—proves that chronology is no block to admission to this sainted company; entries for Joni Mitchell, Lauryn Hill, Stevie Wonder, and Prince prove that gender and race are no longer considered an impediment, either. And, if you dig deeper than the top ten, *Rolling Stone*'s last top 500 did acknowledge more recent history—twenty of the bottom 100 (plus a latter-day Bob Dylan album) hailed from the present century; nineteen from position 301 to 400; and then fourteen (201–300); ten (101–200); and thirteen in the top 100.

Is that truly correct? Of the 500 greatest albums ever made, the first fifty years of music history contributed 430 of them. The last quarter century delivered seventy. And, once again, most of those were from genres that would not be considered rock. Unlike the remaining 430, within which the majority would.

Which is fine. If kids today can't rock, then they can't rock. It's as simple as that. Or maybe they just don't bother because who's going to pay any attention if they do? But one final thought.

We should all dread the day when the aliens finally land on earth and demand humankind justify its continued existence by playing representative samples of the greatest albums ever made.

Well, here's "Lovely Rita." This is "The Continuing Story of Bungalow Bill," and this is "Maxwell's Silver Hammer." And that's just the Beatles. Wait till we play you Valerie Potsdam.[86]

Well, apologies if you love those songs, but you might as well prostrate yourself before the death rays now.

---

86. See appendix A: An Index of Wholly Imaginary Artists.

Chapter Eight

The Five Funniest Jokes Jim Morrison Ever Told—or, Quality versus Quantity

It's alright for them. They aren't the comics who have to get up on stage tonight and play at being Judy Garland for an hour. I've jumped through enough hoops and I've spent enough time locked up inside fucking planes and bathrooms trying to hide from the people I've made rich. . . . Sod the bastards.

—*Jim MacLaine,* Stardust[87]

We have, perhaps, arrived at a working hypothesis of what vintage music is. It is time now to pinpoint the precise moment when the two streams—vintage music and new—diverged.

Again, it is largely dependent upon genre. Metal and punk, for example, continue on today, with a very coherent line of succession running throughout, even if—to the unschooled ear—the modern style takes very different forms to its forefathers and responds to very different stimuli as well. To the average fan of Granny Massacre Syndrome,[88] the first Black Sabbath album doubtless sounds as archaic as Edison's pioneering recording of "Mary Had a Little Lamb" does to anyone with ears.

But if you follow the threads and ignore the manifold weasels dead-ending beneath the cocktail cabinet (sludge metal, hair metal, crust metal, Christian metal, screamo), the bloodline is pure.

Nevertheless, there are certain aspects of the twentieth-century music industry that hallmarked the nature of music back then, and are signally absent from that of today, beginning with the very nature of the industry.

We are not speaking only of rock, in all of its manifold guises, but rather, of popular music as a whole—that is, rock, pop, soul, R&B, hip-hop, country, fusion, dance, alternative, psychedelia, grime, grunge, electronic, J-pop, K-pop, Europop: any artist in any musical field who took

---

87. Ray Connolly, *Stardust* (Fontana Books, 1974).
88. See appendix A: An Index of Wholly Imaginary Artists.

their first steps into the limelight in the thirty-or-so years following the birth of rock'n'roll.

Peruse, if you will, the average discography from the 1950s and 1960s; for the sake of argument we will start with the legend that was Rocky Biceps. He would have a new single released every two to three months, a couple of albums a year, and a few extended plays (EPs) as well. Between 1956 and 1960, Biceps—like the majority of his peers—cut around a hundred different songs altogether, almost all of which were freshly recorded weeks, even days, before their release. Move into the 1960s and the Dental Assassins maintained a similar output between 1962 and 1966, when they cut back to one album (but still several singles) a year. That's over two hundred songs.

Ed Sheeran. Over 150 million album purchasers cannot be wrong. HARALD KRICHEL – CC BY-SA 3.0.

These numbers are not unique. "Real" artists worked to a similar schedule, so the Beatles and the Stones, Elvis and Buddy, Cochran and the Kinks all worked their butts off in the studio, and when they weren't recording, they were zipping around the country on tour, filming for TV, playing live on the radio, posing for pinups, answering questions for fan mags . . . ; a few of them even found the time to squeeze in a movie or (in Elvis Presley's case) thirty-one.

And why? Because the industry demanded it. First and foremost, being hired as a musician was the creative equivalent to being sentenced to hard labor, and not only because it kept the cash machines ringing. Equally crucial, and the point that a lot of exhausted musicians often failed to acknowledge, was the need to keep the fans loyal.

Think about it. It's the early to mid-1960s and what's your favorite act from back then? Let's say it's the aforementioned Dental Assassins— shaggy hair, shabby suits, loud guitars, lousy teeth (hence the group's name), English accents, and at least three of them are cute. You bought their last single; you saved up for their latest album; you saw them when they played the local drive-in; and you've taped all their photos to your bedroom wall.

Now what?

Easy. You wait a couple of months and then repeat the cycle over again. And again and again and again. Never get bored, never lose faith, never forget they're your favorit-est faves, even when others catch your ear in between times. Even when you sometimes wonder if that classmate you fancy might like you more if you changed your allegiance to Foxy and the Redcoats.[89] And even when, as was inevitable on a treadmill such as this, the Assassins' latest release was . . . well, pretty shit, actually.

Viewed through the rose-tinted sensory deprivation chamber that is the human memory, it is very easy to reflect upon an adolescence devoted to abject hero worship and remember every new release as the second coming of the Hittite sun goddess Hebat.

Yet when you actually sit back and play the things, and this was as true back then as it is today . . . before I finish this sentence, let's try an experiment. Or if this were a high school textbook, an exercise.

---

89. See appendix A.

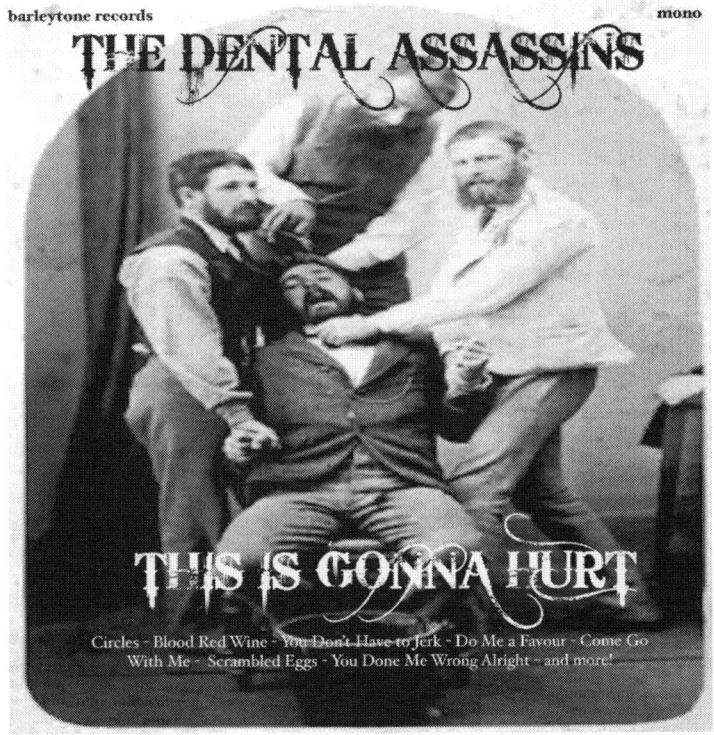

The artwork for the Dental Assassins' fifth LP in 1965 was pulled following complaints from across the dental profession. AUTHOR'S COLLECTION.

From a master list of every album and single your favorite act of that era recorded, compile a comprehensive list of songs *in order of personal preference.* No exceptions ("well, that was a cover version"), no excuses ("well, they were obviously stoned when they did it"), no second-guessing what they were *trying* to achieve, as opposed to what actually came out at the end. And see how many squabble for the honor of finishing in the bottom half of the list.

Because even the brightest star was ultimately responsible for an awful lot of filler. Off-piste meanderings, off-kilter wobblings, off moments that expanded to entire off days.

Only the studio staff, however, were privy to the musicians' own feelings about such excursions. The split-second glances that flashed between the players as they silently acknowledged, "Gee man, that was really bad." The embarrassed grin that the song's composer suppressed as he listened back to a ditty he penned in three minutes on the back of a discarded cigarette pack, and had only persuaded his colleagues to perform because he had multiple copies of *those* photographs. And the harsh, unforgiving laughter as the optimist in the group finally sighed, "Yeah, but the kids will love it regardless."

Which was true. Paul McCartney, composer of the Beatles' immortal "Ob-La-Di, Ob-La-Da" is said to have looked askance at the song once it was completed. Why, we cannot imagine. But his fellow Fabs hated it from the outset, as the authors of the book *The McCartney Legacy: Volume 1: 1969—73* make clear when discussing John Lennon's response to "a comment Paul had made, to the effect that [he] wasn't fond of the two songs that John particularly disdained," one of which was "Ob-La-Di, Ob-La-Da."[90] (The other, incredibly, was "Maxwell's Silver Hammer.")

Lennon explained, "It just struck me, when I was thinking it over, it would be mad for us to put a song on the album that nobody really dug, including the guy who wrote it, just because it was going to be popular." [91]

They did it, though, and it *was* popular, prompting a slew of cover versions, including one, by Scotland's the Marmalade, that topped the British chart for three weeks at the end of 1968.

But does that make it alright? Do popularity and success equate to quality every time? And if they do, why are there so few boy bands and/or teen idols in the Rock and Roll and Grammy Halls of Fame? The Spice Girls have been eligible for the former since 2020. *Where are they, then?*

We are not saying these records should not have been made. Some readers might even argue that one of the most vital components of the rock'n'roll experience is the ability to watch an artist "growing up in public" in real time, following their development, pursuing their musical trains of thought, and if that includes the occasional mistake, so be it.

It is true that, in these days of so-called super deluxe editions of so many classic albums, we get to hear far greater embarrassments than a single bad album track. There, however, is the key; those embarrassments tended to remain on the shelf, archived for what their creators hoped was eternity, even if it did turn out to be just a handful of decades. In the

---

90. Allan Kozinn and Adrian Sinclair, *The McCartney Legacy: Volume 1: 1969–73* (Day Street Books, 2022).
91. Kozinn, *The McCartney Legacy.*

event, most so-called super deluxe editions of favorite albums are akin to waking up to find a foie de gras skid mark across your most treasured musical memories.

Now compare the lot of that era's biggest names with the regime under which their modern equivalents labor. Cynics will point out, and they're not wrong about this, that it is quite feasible for the act you adore when you're fourteen to not release another album until you graduate high school, and by the time it makes the record after that, you'll be too busy juggling the children to care that much about it.

They point out that, back in the sixties, an artist would be drip fed into your consciousness, a constant reminder that they are a crucial component within your very existence. Whereas now, you get the occasional splash; and as for what goes on in the depths of the creative process, forget about the changes that three or four years can wreak upon your own life, what does the passage of time do to the musicians themselves?

It's a point that Ed Sheeran made, discussing the genesis of his third album—(*Subtract*), in March 2023. Two years had passed since his last LP, and he had amassed what he described as "hundreds" of songs from which to choose. All of which he scrapped as his life lurched into crisis followed by crisis—the death of a close friend, his wife being diagnosed with a tumor, and yet another lawsuit regarding the authorship of one of his past hits.

Together, those events "changed my life, my mental health, and ultimately the way I viewed music," he wrote on his Facebook page on March 1, "spiraling through fear, depression and anxiety. . . . And in just over a week, I replaced a decade's worth of work with my deepest, darkest thoughts. I wrote without thought of what the songs would be, I just wrote whatever tumbled out." And that became his new album.

Good for him. Regardless of your feelings about Sheeran and his music, for him to acknowledge that "for the first time I'm not trying to craft an album people will like," and admit to "putting something out that's honest and true to where I am in my adult life," completely shattered all perceptions of "how" modern music is "made," and "why."

Not that it really made a difference. Even at whatever point his audience describes as his peak, Sheeran was never the most deeply analytical writer, nor the least underwhelming. This is the man, after all, who once addressed the personally significant milestones of growing up and becoming a father by announcing, in "Tides, I have grown up, I am a father now." Wow.

Yes, it is true that if the Beatles had been working to the same schedule as the Arctic Monkeys of the 2010s, they'd have released *Please Please Me* in 1963, and nothing more until the White Album in 1968. That's a lot of music being left on the cutting room floor, and a lot of musical progress as well. Although it still might not have spared us "Ob-La-Di, Ob-La-Da."

Attach the same strictures to the Rolling Stones, and you leap from a debut album of R&B covers in 1964 to *Let It Bleed* in 1969. Bob Marley and the Wailers would have left behind no permanent record of their development between *Catch a Fire* (1973) and *Kaya* (1978); Marvin Gaye would have been silent between *That's the Way Love Is* (1969) and *Live* in 1974, which itself would have presented a very different track listing; and there'd be a gap at the top of the *Rolling Stone* best albums poll, too. *What's Going On* was released in 1971.

But you know what? Maybe that's a good thing. The great songs would have been saved for the album, if and when it was released; the filler would have been left on the shelf or, as Lennon continued, given away "to people who *like* music like that."

It's what CD bonus tracks are for, benefit albums, or giveaway downloads. Rather than cluttering up your fans' record collections with your cast-offs at the time and *hope* they'll like them enough to buy them, parcel them up for the archive anthology, where it doesn't matter what they think. Because they've already spent $300 on the box set.

That's what the current crop will be doing.

Chapter Nine

We're Just Not That Into You, Boomer —or, What Does This Button Do?

Every generation's the same—a load of crap and a few brilliant people!

—Arthur Askey[92]

The quality of a recording is not the only issue that was at stake in the pressure cooker of old-time pop creativity. Originality, too, took a beating. The story of sixties and seventies rock, in particular, is littered with records that, effectively, take somebody else's idea and "improve" upon it—"Oh, the Leccylite String Machine[93] have a bumbulum[94] on their new single. Quick, let's overdub three onto ours."

Sometimes such blatant copy-cat-ism would prove successful and open an entire new musical direction to all concerned—one need think only of the initially tentative arrival of the sitar on the British beat scene of the mid-1960s, and the bottomless well of not at all ham-fisted creativity that emerged thereafter.

Other times, however, it was as unsuccessful as any knee-jerk response to someone else's already half-baked stab at "doing something different" ought to be.

This particular process reached its nadir in the early to mid-1980s, although there were precedents aplenty, from the aforementioned sitar to Peter Frampton's 1976 hit "Show Me the Way," with its pioneering deployment of a robot trying to speak underwater, and onto the electronic percussion pads responsible for that "boo-boooo" sound that resonated through a plethora of late 1970s period disco records, before making its way into rock.

---

92. Quoted in "Sefton Writers Festival: Barry Cryer Talks to Jamie Bowman about His Newfound Fame Front of Stage," *Liverpool Echo*, October 28, 2010.
93. See appendix A: An Index of Wholly Imaginary Artists.
94. A medieval instrument which appears to have been named from its sonic resemblance to flatulence—*bumbulum* is Latin for "fart." The *Liber Feodorum* (The Book of Fiefs), published in 1302, describes a performer executing "*unum saltum et sifflettum et unum bumbulum*" ("one jump, one whistle, and one fart").

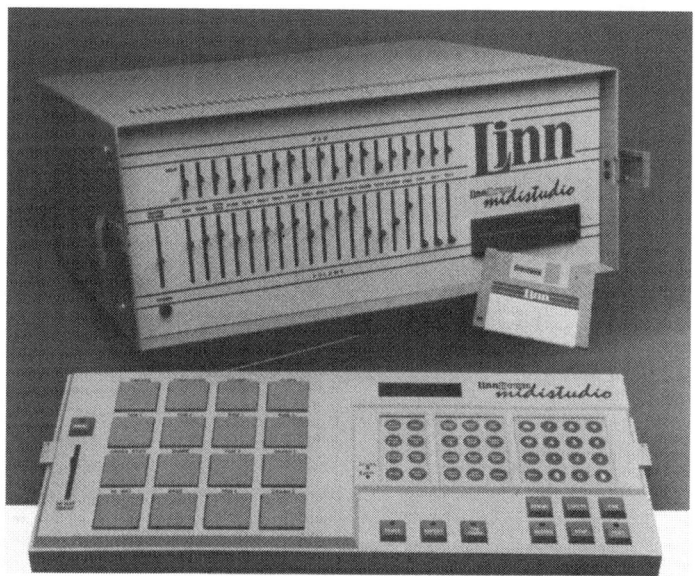

The mighty LinnDrum. Percussion would never sound the same again. FORAT ELECTRONICS, CC BY-SA 3.0.

It was the 1980s, however, when things really sped off the rails. That was when the swift advance of technology, coupled with the absurd amounts of cash that were sloshing around in the record biz kitty, saw a panoply of gimmicky new instruments conscripted into active service the moment they emerged (but usually before anyone had figured out how they worked), and then mimicked *ad nauseum* until the next one came along.

Indeed, arguably, the entire eighties began precisely three minutes and sixteen seconds into Phil Collins's debut solo single "In the Air Tonight," and the decade careened downhill from there. Created with "gated reverb," a percussive technique developed during the sessions for Peter Gabriel's eponymous third album (upon which Collins was a key player), it is astonishing how often you heard people attempt that record's most heart-stopping percussive moment on their own records, and how abjectly the vast majority failed to pull it off.

To that effect can be added the welter of new synthesizers and key-boards that were flooding onto the market and, at least in the realms of new music (as opposed to older acts doggedly sticking to formula), we were set for a decade during which, to paraphrase the Man Who Rejected the Beatles,[95] guitar groups were out. Or, if they weren't, they had no interest in guitars that sounded like guitars—unless, of course, the guitarist could shred nerves from a thousand paces. Or give the impression that he could. Sit back for a moment and recall all the ferocious axemen who emerged in the wake of Eddie Van Halen, before asking yourself whether even one of them could actually *play* the instrument? As opposed to making a lot of noise very quickly and describing it as a solo?

Between the guitar synthesizers and the effects pedals that so coolly castrated the sweat and blood that was the instrument's native preserve (and the add-ons and strap-ons that were transforming the meekest home laptop into a fully equipped cock rock extravaganza), even straightforward rock records were all but unrecognizable, and there were fewer and fewer artists who wanted to make them. Confront them with a big red button, however, and a lifetime of watching edgy science-fiction disaster movies went straight out of the window. Push it! Push it *real* good . . .

Colorful Characters from Rock's Rich Tapestry No. 2

The Blogger
Heard the band's name on Monday
Read the Wiki on Tuesday
Downloaded the discography on Wednesday
Listened to it on Thursday
Launched a website on Friday
Argued with the Expert on Saturday
Had the page closed down on Sunday

The 1980s *were* an era of staggering innovation, even if the vast majority of it turned out to be a one-way street. But it was also the decade when more or less every record you heard reminded you, in some way, of something else—whether it's the hook to "All by Myself" bleeding through Bon Jovi's "Never Say Goodbye"; Billy Squier's "The Stroke"

---

95. Decca A&R man Dick Rowe is the traditional bearer of this title, having auditioned and rejected the Fab Four in 1962. There is growing evidence, however, that at least some elements of the story may be apocryphal.

taking crowd control lessons from Queen's "We Will Rock You"; or his "Rock Me Tonight" from Foreigner's "Cold as Ice." Most insidious of all, however, must be the urge to sing the Sisters of Mercy's "This Corrosion" every time you heard Crowded House's "Don't Dream It's Over."

It was a time when every guitar solo (Van Halen's "Love Walks In" among them) resembled an especially sadistic dentist's drill; and there were those keyboards *shaped* like guitars that might not have contributed anything new to the sound but allowed an awful lot of hitherto seat-bound organists to cavort like the groin-thrusting axeman they had always dreamed of becoming. (And, on that subject, did you ever notice how many early eighties rock keyboard players took to mugging the camera whenever it came into view, rather than sitting quietly and practicing their scales like they were supposed to?)

It was the decade during which the human equivalent of a worn-out Xerox machine could get away with cutting such note-perfect replicas of forgotten sixties hits that you couldn't even say you preferred the original.

And, most chilling of them all, it was the age of the "electric piano" preset button on the newly launched Yamaha SX7 synthesizer. According to scholar Megan Lavengood, this particular sound was audible, if not predominant, "in up to 61% of #1 hits on the pop, country, and R&B *Billboard* charts in 1986."[96]

Imagine that! Almost two-thirds of the year's biggest records *all sounded very much the same.* Can you even guesstimate how many lesser records must have deployed it as well?

There are a multitude of similar examples. The Fantasia preset patch on the Roland D50 synthesizer went through its hour of overused glory; and the Oberheim OB-Xa synth, responsible for the intro to Van Halen's "Jump," would be guilty of a lot more in its wake. Another Roland innovation, the TB-303, without which acid house would have been a lot less acidic.

There was the ubiquitous Fairlight Computer Musical Instrument (commonly abbreviated CMI), with its unprecedented ability to "sample" and manipulate sound, and which sounded so unique when Peter Gabriel

---

96. Megan Lavengood, "What Makes It Sound '80s?: The Yamaha DX7 Electric Piano Sound," *Journal of Popular Music Studies* 31, no. 3: 73–94, https://online.ucpress.edu/jpms /article-abstract/31/3/73/105979/What-Makes-It-Sound-80s-The-Yamaha-DX7-Electric.

(him again) got his hands on one in the early 1980s but rapidly lost its sparkle once everyone else followed suit.

Of course, the same practices exist today, as technology continues to gallop merrily forward and everybody wants to get in on it. How many acts, for example, film their own videos on an iPhone? How many mix their songs so they'll sound good through the speakers on a laptop? And how many have deployed auto-tune technology in the years (now decades) since Cher introduced it to the world, thirty-six seconds into her 1998 hit "Believe"?

A lot. As *Pitchfork*'s Simon Reynolds noted, "MCs like Future, Chief Keef, and Quavo are almost literally cyborgs, inseparable from the vocal prosthetics that serve as their bionic superpowers. But we can also hear the long-term influence of Auto-Tune on singing styles on Top 40 radio."[97]

He notes, too, that "Rhianna is the dominant singer of our era, in no small part because the Barbados grain of her voice interacts well with Auto-Tune's nasal tinge, making for a sort of fire-and-ice combination."[98]

The process is definitely noticeable, then, and sometimes overly so. But the difference does not stamp its very identity across a performance, a lowest common denominator that can render the most original composition on earth sonically indistinguishable from the least.

The advent of auto-tune may, as many commentators have declared, mark the final triumph of technology over talent. But pop stars have been faking it for years. The annals of even beloved sixties and seventies pop are littered with hitmakers who never played (or sang) on the records that made them famous, while the rise in cheap synthesizers in the early 1980s meant the most untalented soul could suddenly sound like a multi-instrumentalist.

In fact, the ability to make a bad singer sound good, or a nonmusician sound like a virtuoso can surely only be to everyone's advantage. It is easy to mock such performers as the Monkees, the Sweet, and Milli Vanilli because their producers did not allow them to play (or, in the latter case, even sing) on the records released under their name.

---

97. Simon Reynolds, "How Auto-Tune Revolutionized the Sound of Popular Music," *Pitchfork*, September 17, 2018, https://pitchfork.com/features/article/how-auto -tune-revolutionized-the-sound-of-popular-music/.

98. Reynolds, "How Auto-Tune Revolutionized."

But why should eighties hitmakers 7 Deadly Synths have had their dreams of pop stardom crushed because not one of them could even spell *guitar*, let alone understand which way round to hold it? If there is a workaround that works, then work it, baby.

The other thing about auto-tune, of course, is that it takes one more step toward giving the public the very best-sounding vocal performance possible. As opposed to the discordant yowling of so many squabbling raccoon babies.[99]

In fact, if vintage records have any genuinely productive saving grace, it is as a teaching tool, with lesson number one being: absolutely nothing "dates" a record worse than being up-to-date with a distinctive new sound; and nothing leaves performers wider open to ridicule, and the disdain of future history books, than flying the flag for, say, the Robosonics Mark III Triangle Emulator (the trademark sound of the Bunglebears' 1987 smash "My Baby's Tattooed Toenails"[100]) when the Mark IV will be along in another couple of months.

Yes, artists should use every advantage that technology offers them. But they now understand that the traffic is strictly one way. Use it, but don't be used *by* it. And if they should find themselves seduced by the sounds of some great new musical breakthrough, the gaps that yawn between new releases ensure it is more likely to be left on the shelf, or at least given time in which the idea can mature. Everybody wins.

So, to answer (finally!) the question that was asked a while back. Vintage Music—records made by exhausted wage-slaves who made infinitely far too many, a lot of which were either rubbish or plagiaristic. New Music—the relaxed raconteurs who aren't simply *expected* to take a sensible break between new releases, they might even be contractually obliged to do so.

Of course, Prince did not write "slave" on his face for kicks, and there should be an option for ultra-prolific artists to follow their muse. But actually, being allowed the time to recharge one's batteries and get the creative juices flowing once more means we have also witnessed the near-total eradication of a disease that once killed, or seriously maimed,

---

99. Yes, we all know who this is an utterly unnecessary dig at. Get over it.
100. See appendix A.

untold hundreds of performers in the past, the dreaded Second Album Syndrome (SAS).

The symptoms were easy to spot. Mark Syllabub,[101] for example. There's probably not a soul on earth who did not rate his self-titled debut album as high as any other album you could name. But even as that first world tour shifted into its final phase, he seemed oddly hesitant about introducing new material into his live show.

And when, just nine months after its predecessor, his long-awaited sophomore set was released . . . it was awful. A bunch of half-formed ideas wrapped around tunes that weren't even vaguely memorable, and when the first single ailed and the second one died, that was the end of it. That was the end of Syllabub. Sometimes an act can recover from SAS. More likely, however, they are humanely put down, and we all pretend they never existed.

The problem was not a sudden draining of what had once promised to be a bottomless reservoir of talent. It was much crueler than that. It was the fact that Syllabub, and a host of artists like Syllabub, had devoted their entire life-so-far composing that all-important first album; had probably been thinking about it since their earliest teens. All the best songs, all the finest licks, all the smart-as-a-whip-est lyrics, everything was poured into the cauldron of their debut.

Unfortunately, there was nothing left to put on the follow-up, and thanks to incessant touring and promotion and so forth, no time to write and develop something new. So they threw together some untried songs, wrote a few in the studio, even strung words over jams. And that was it. Their next great statement, and it was the kind of runny, undercooked omelet they'd normally have abandoned in the notebook before they even booked the rehearsal studio.

It's why, although you often see lists of the greatest debut albums, you rarely see any for their follow-ups. Because, too often, that's what they were. Sloppy seconds.

It doesn't happen so often these days. Performers do get to relax, do get to rest, and recharge their batteries before starting again. Once, the only excuses for taking a few years away from the coalface were writer's block, rehab (and even that wasn't guaranteed to work), and getting

---

101. See appendix A.

dropped by your label. Today, yes—people can still release bad records. Some have even released appalling ones. But at least we know they had plenty of time in which they got some even worse material out of their systems.

Not that anything said thus far should be regarded as a hard and fast definition.

Even in the 1970s, there were artists who *did* take their time, who honed every edge and ironed every bump, and if Stevie Wonder made us wait two years before he uncaged *Songs in the Key of Life* (and three more for *The Secret Life of Plants*) and Emerson, Lake & Palmer left us hanging for four before they perfected *Works Volume One* (1977), then not only did they have good reason to do so, they clearly believed they were making the very best records they possibly could.

They knew what we all know. Art cannot be rushed, and artists should not be hurried. If Zonk[102] wanted to take three years to make their second album (in fact, it was closer to four), then three years was what they took. It is true that Mozart turned out the scores of his final three symphonies in six weeks. But, according to the *Encyclopedia Britannica*, "Beethoven's *Symphony No. 9* was ultimately more than three decades in the making."

Of course, he banged out a few other things in between—eight symphonies, eighteen concertos, and a mass of other material. He also went deaf, which was doubtless a ferocious impediment, as well.

But he took his time, and how was he thanked? Perhaps predicting the fate of the Beatles' similarly symphonic "Revolution #9,"[103] *Symphony No. 9* was, declared London magazine *The Harmonicon*, in April 1825, "precisely one hour and five minutes long, a fearful period which puts the muscles and lungs of the band, and the patience of the audience, to a severe trial."[104]

Even Beethoven's hearing loss was not sufficient to cage the tigers. Today, one trusts, a musician being suddenly stricken with a potentially career-ending ailment, but soldiering on regardless, would be the object of undying admiration, which in turn would leaven at least some sympathy from the chattering classes. "No, it's not very good, *but . . .* "

---

102. See appendix A.
103. From 1968's *The Beatles*, where it shared vinyl, ironically, with "Ob-La-Di, Ob-La-Da."
104. Quoted in Nicolas Slonimsky, *Lexicon of Musical Invective* (University of Washington Press, 1965).

Beethoven's deafness, on the other hand, was effectively blamed (by the Boston, Massachusetts, *Daily Atlas*[105]) for the fact that this new piece should be "an incomprehensible union of strange harmonies."

But again, Beethoven stuck to his guns, refused either to be rushed, or hamstrung by his frailties, and the soundtrack to the movie *A Clockwork Orange* would have been a lot less immersive if he hadn't taken so long.

We should be thankful that today's artists enjoy a similar luxury. Although they can still find new and impressive ways of screwing things up. Can't they, Bono?

---

105. *Daily Atlas*, February 6, 1853.

Chapter Ten

The Undelete-Able File—or, "Wow, I've Got Some Real Lame Shit on My iPod." "Oh, You, Too?"

U2 are playing live when, in between songs, Bono starts solemnly clapping before pronouncing "every time I clap my hands, a child in Africa starves to death." A wag in the crowd shouts "stop f***ing clapping then!"

—Jack Beresford[106]

Sound quality, size, and bragging rights notwithstanding, the best thing about vinyl is nobody can sneak it onto your phone when you're not looking,

Yes, they can "forget" to come back to collect it after "accidentally" leaving it in your kitchen after a party. Yes, they can wrap it up in colored paper and call it a birthday present. Yes, they can just slip it into your record collection when you're not looking, knowing full well that it's been years since you last looked through your latter-day Lance Corporeal LPs.[107]

But it would take a very special, very cunning, and very evil mind indeed to conceive of simply jamming an album onto your cloud service—and not yours alone. Every other person using the same service as you got one as well. And even worse? You can't actually delete the thing. It's there forever.

It's yours, whether you want it or not.

What were you doing on September 9, 2014? Well, if you owned an Apple device—and there were apparently half a billion people around the world who did—you were either listening to, complaining about, or trying fruitlessly to rid yourself of the new U2 album, ironically titled *Songs*

---

106. Jack Beresford, "9 U2 Jokes You Can't Live With or Without," *Irish Post*, June 1, 2018.
107. See appendix A: An Index of Wholly Imaginary Artists.

of Innocence, and which very un-innocently manifested itself overnight in your cloud.

It wasn't entirely unexpected. U2 and Apple had a firm relationship already, with Bono and Apple founder, the late Steve Jobs ("the hardware software Elvis," as the singer dubbed him), having long been friends; U2 featured in an Apple commercial as far back as 2002, and two years later launched a special edition U2 iPod, itself loaded with the band's back catalog. Another innovation in which the band was involved was 2006's special edition iPod nano, raising money for AIDS research.

This latest venture, however, was both band and company's most audacious yet. Speaking at Apple's annual presentation of their latest creations (the iPhone 6 was the headliner), CEO Tim Cook made a special announcement.

"A decade ago, we began a deep collaboration with one of the best bands of all time, and that band is U2." The group had, he explained, "agreed to perform for you today, and we could not be more excited about this. U2 is among the most respected artists in the world, among the best selling, and they've won more Grammy Awards than any single band in history."[108]

What followed, however, bordered on the surreal. A heartfelt rendition of their latest single, "The Miracle of Joey Ramone," was followed by Bono describing its parent album as being "as good as our very best work, as good as the best we've ever done." So good that they wanted it to reach "as many people as possible." Half a billion of them.

Presumably, the Irish rockers thought they were doing us a favor, giving something back to all the people who'd sustained them at the toppermost of the poppermost for thirty years or more. Indeed, it was a mere seventeen years since the first of over twenty-five million people rushed out to buy *The Joshua Tree*, U2's fifth studio album. Imagine how happy they would have been to receive *that* album for no charge whatsoever?

Unfortunately, *Songs of Innocence* was no *The Joshua Tree*, and it was fair to say that even before it was released. Whatever Bono still hadn't

108. Stephen Silver, "The Free U2 Album 'Songs of Innocence' Was a Debacle for Apple Fans on September 9, 2014," Apple Insider, September 9, 2018, https://appleinsider.com/articles/18/09/09/the-free-u2-album-songs-of-innocence-was-a-debacle-for-apple-fans-on-september-9-2018#:~:text=%22A%20decade%20ago%2C%20we%20began,end%20of%20that%20day%27s%20keynote.

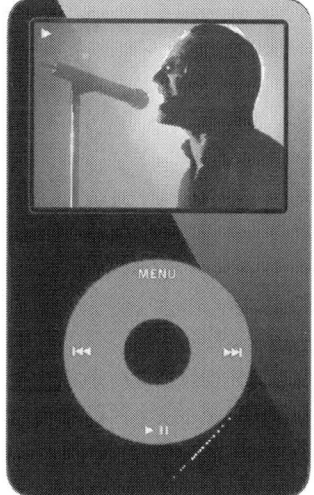

In case you don't have enough U2 on your iPod—here's more.
APPLE PROMO PHOTO.

found that he was looking for back then remained dauntingly elusive. The problem was, not many people now cared whether he found it or not.

In 1987, U2 were skyrocketing higher and higher with every passing single, gig, or Bono interview. By 2014, their last album, *No Line on the Horizon*, was struggling to make five million cash registers sing, suggesting that—far from making that many people happy, the band had lost four times as many would-be purchasers. Purposefully invading half a billion strangers' iPods was not going to bring them back.

In fact, it might as easily drive them away. This "devious giveaway," complained *Wired* magazine, was "worse than spam,"[109] going on to explain, "So long as users wanted to automatically download their media purchases—a reasonable assumption, given that they, you know, purchased them—the album would continue to show up again and again. The only alternative was to disable automatic downloading of iTunes purchases, or to log in to the desktop client and 'hide' the purchase; this wouldn't delete it completely, but you wouldn't see it."

---

109. Vijith Assar, "Apple's Devious U2 Album Giveaway Is Even Worse Than Spam," *Wired*, September 16, 2014.

The Daily Dot declared the giveaway had confirmed U2's status as "the most hated band in America" or, at least, "the new Nickelback."[110] Neither was writer Nico Lang merely voicing his own opinion. He continued, "According to a webpage helpfully titled 'Why U2 Sucks,' the litany of reasons runs the gamut of 'they are pretentious' to 'they are derivative' and 'they just plain suck.' The *Guardian* theorizes, however, that we hate U2 because we hate Bono, while the *New York Observer* thinks they're the Guy Fieri of music, which one assumes means selling bombastic, tacky crap to as wide an audience as possible."

It took Bono a little under a month before he released his first sort-of-apology. "Artists are prone to that kind of thing. Drop of megalomania, touch of generosity, dash of self-promotion and deep fear that these songs that we poured our life into over the last few years might not be heard. There's a lot of noise out there. I guess we got a little noisy ourselves to get through it."

Eight years later, however, he was still saying sorry. As he wrote in his 2022 autobiography,[111] "We didn't just put our bottle of milk at the door but in every fridge in every house in town. In some cases we poured it on to the good people's cornflakes. And some people like to pour their own milk. And others are lactose intolerant."

As one social media wisecracker put it, "Woke up this morning to find Bono in my kitchen, drinking my coffee, wearing my dressing gown, reading my paper." Or, less kind, "The free U2 album is overpriced." Mea culpa.

Okay, bad move, and if the world could simply have deleted the album from its iTunes and moved on, all would be fine. Unfortunately, it couldn't. You could click and click as much as you wanted, but every time you returned to your cloud, there it was again. The undelete-able file, the unflushable turd.

There was a window of time during which deletions were permissible, opening less than a week after the album made its appearance, but closing not too long after. Indeed, as we approach the tenth anniversary of *Songs of Innocence*, we also approach the tenth anniversary of every Apple customer on earth being unable to simply tell their device to shuffle the

110. Nico Lang, "How U2 Became the New Nickelback," *Daily Dot*, May 30, 2021, https://www.dailydot.com/unclick/how-u2-became-the-new-nickelback/.

111. Bono, *Surrender: 40 Songs, One Story* (Alfred A. Knopf, 2022).

library and play through the entire thing. Because sooner or later, it'll hit a U2 song that they never wanted to own in the first place, and what a downer that will be.

Songs of Innocence is unusual. Yes, it was the first album ever to be provided with its own "delete" function, even if it was only for a short period of time. But it was also the first album that, almost literally, was impossible to escape, at least if you were an Apple user. Even more inescapable than U2 themselves were in the mid-1980s, when otherwise sensible critics were describing them as the greatest rock'n'roll band of the age and the world fell in love with Bono because he danced with that lady at Live Aid.[112]

And you do have to pause and wonder for a moment—has there ever been any album, by any artist, that you could deliver to even a fraction of that many people, without irritating a significant portion of them?

Or any act that was so misguided as to imagine that they could?

---

112. It's on YouTube. Check it out if you must.

Chapter Eleven

Butternut Canker Killed the Video Star—or, Promoting the Pants off Garbage

Before he even went onstage his white makeup and dark eyeshadow was calculated to heighten his usual pinched look of being about to die, but with it being streaked and partly washed away with sweat he now looks as though he is going to keel over at any moment.

—*Mick Farren,* The Tale of Willy's Rats[113]

U2's gift to humankind was, and remains, a reprehensible invasion of privacy. But really, was it worse than having to sit through endless advertisements when you click on a video online or try to watch a show on TV?? Being battered around the head with promotions whenever you log onto social media? Plowing through however many un-forward-through-able trailers when you settle down to watch a DVD? Endless promotions on satellite radio? Public television pledge drives?

They're just as inescapable; just as irritating; just as irrelevant. And somewhere out in ad-land, there's some gnomic whizz kid thinking, "It's not a bad idea in theory. I've just got to think of a delivery method that won't piss everybody off."

It's called marketing, and of all the differences between vintage and recent music, perhaps the most radical is the manner in which the music itself is marketed (or, as more corporate minds would probably have it, "the consumer is primed for their journey").

In the past—certainly throughout the last decades of the twentieth century and into the first years of the twenty-first—the principal outlet for new music was radio, with television a reasonably close challenger, at least following the birth of MTV on August 1, 1980.

---

113. Farren Mick, *The Tale of Willy's Rats* (Mayflower Books, 1974).

What, however, was either service besides a ruthlessly choreographed playlist of a few dozen records that—according to which rumors you chose to believe—were either bought, traded, or bribed onto the airwaves. Indeed, even the most cursory look into the history of pop radio in the United States will forever be darkened by the specter of payola—a late 1950s scandal of such voluptuous proportions that it saw some of the biggest names in American radio disgraced for years to come, for the crime of taking payment (in whatever form it was offered) in exchange for favoring certain records.

Yet, like so many of the other supposedly game-changing scandals that have shaken society over the years, the only real consequence was that people worked harder not to get caught next time. That aside, the scandal, and the punishments meted out in its aftermath, amounted to little more than an attempt to treat a severed limb with the last three band-aids in the box. Lowlife went on around it and for as long as radio play and physical sales remained the key indicators of a song's success, the temptation to give both a helping hand was irresistible.

As late as the early 2000s, dark rumor insisted that *this* song was bought into the charts by the record label; *that* artist only got played on air because the DJ was bribed with kinky sex and nose candy; and as for *that other single over there*, you don't even want to know what transpired before it got its first drive time spin.

Many record industry figures of the 1960s and 1970s even acknowledge their part in such malfeasance. Former Beatles associate Joe Flannery told the BBC that manager Brian Epstein "bought 10,000 copies of [their first single] 'Love Me Do,' and that they were kept in his store room in Whitechapel, because I'd seen them, they were there, 10,000 copies."[114] (Popular legend insists that many of these ended up in the River Thames.)

Seven years later, in 1969, David Bowie's first hit "Space Oddity" was allegedly helped on its way by what author Marc Burrows describes as "a shadowy figure called 'Tony Martin' who . . . reckoned that for a mere £300 he could guarantee a top ten placement in . . . the charts."[115]

Nor was "hype" the only weapon at the enterprising record label's disposal. In Britain in the late 1970s, there was a sudden craze for "limited

---

114. BBC documentary, *Love Me Do: The Beatles '62* (2012).
115. Marc Burrows, *The London Boys: David Bowie, Marc Bolan and the 60s Teenage Dream* (Pen and Sword History, 2022).

edition" versions of potential hit singles—so many thousand copies in colored vinyl, for example. So many in a gatefold seven-inch jacket. So many shaped picture discs, and so on, and all pressed with the idea that sufficient people would rush out to snap up these instant rarities that a high chart entry was all but guaranteed.

Today, much the same happens every Record Store Day, the primary difference being that Record Store Day (RSD) records can only be purchased from a tightly supervised network of independent record stores, and they're not targeted anywhere close to the charts. Back then, similarly exclusive limited editions were distributed to every retailer in the land, and if the edition did sell out, said the promotional gubbins, the record would then be repressed in unlimited "conventional" form.

The odd thing is, the black vinyl version was often the hardest one to find, even at the time. Months later, long after a record's chart life had ended, and certainly sales in the tens of thousands beyond anything the

Silly shaped records were around decades before Record Store Day came along. AUTHOR'S COLLECTION.

initial pressing could possibly have catered for, copies of those limited editions were still sitting on the shelves, still priced at their regular retail price. It was the black vinyl pressings that you never saw. The black vinyl ones that, according to some collectors, are many times scarcer than the limited editions. Which, in contrast, are as common as any quarter-million-selling 45 ought to be.

An understanding of these iniquities is essential to any discussion of what, for this book's purpose, we continue to describe as "old" music; the primal truth that the cream very rarely rose to the top without at least a little help from cash, cocaine, and assorted bodily fluids. And it had curdled long before it reached the apex.

Nobody, of course, is so naive as to believe, when we look at the charts today, or inspect a list of the most streamed songs, that there is not a modicum of jiggery pokery involved.

Bots are as capable of signing up to a streaming service as any real live human being, and they probably know how to solve captchas as well. Record labels are free to offer their entire workforce free subscriptions, on the condition that they only stream certain songs; and, sadly, no technology is immune to those miscreants[116] who get their kicks from dynamiting breaches into the defensive barricades that surround our online world and doing wicked things to our facts and figures.

Nevertheless, we can rejoice in the knowledge that when we do peruse the latest list of the most-listened-to songs and artists on any given streaming service, it is likely that they attained that status through fair means more than foul; and they did so in the face of far stiffer opposition than any so-called hit of past generations.

Back then, an act that released a new record, let us say, in August of a given year, would be competing for glory only against whatever other records were released that month, with a handful of older outliers possibly nudging around as well. For they were the only records that were available in the majority of stores.

Again, a handful of "oldies" might linger in stock and, if we're talking about LPs, the classics were usually on hand as well. But in terms of a

---

116. These characters are often referred to as "bad actors." This, however, is a supposition too far. There is no proven link between certain grotesquely inept Hollywood megastars and an international conspiracy to establish a sinister coterie of undeserving stars at the top of every chart, while simultaneously rigging elections and plotting the downfall of civilization.

significant number of people descending upon a store across a specific number of days, the majority sought only the latest releases, and the past was where it ought to be. Out of stock, out of print, out of sight, out of mind. "The Gaping Chasms?[117] Yeah, I *used* to like them but I've not listened to one of their discs in *weeks.*"

Today, even the most prominent stars and the most ginormous artistes are not only up against anyone else who lays claim to such grandiose titles, but also *more or less every other record ever made.*

Think about that. Twenty-five years ago, if you wanted to hear a certain song, you needed to either own it yourself or know someone who did. You couldn't just switch on *Channel 44, Big Hits That Include the Word "Antelope,"* and have a fair chance of hearing it. You couldn't go to the grocery store and catch it floating down the frozen pizza aisle. You couldn't even catch it soundtracking an erectile dysfunction commercial, or bolstering the appeal of a new kind of car. The fact is—again, out of stock, out of print, out of sight, out of mind.

---

117. See appendix A: An Index of Wholly Imaginary Artists..

The Song Remains the Same (or, At Least, Those Three Notes in the Middle and the Use of the Phrase "I Love You" Do)

Of all the perils that lie in wait for the successful songwriter today, the creativity-crushing cancer of plagiarism, real or imagined, is perhaps the one that they most fear: the knowledge that one pair of "try my luck" ears and an avaricious legal eagle is all it can take to tie a songwriter in legal knots for months—even years—struggling to prove beyond doubt that at no time in their entire life did they ever chance to hear an obscure demo recorded by an even more obscure artist, no matter *how many times* the complainant insists that a compatriot sneaked into the superstar's bedroom and surgically implanted the melody into their dreams.

It's an issue that has plagued rock music since at least the early 1970s, when the likes of John Lennon ("Come Together") and George

Harrison ("My Sweet Lord") were forced to pay up for allegedly ripping off songs by Chuck Berry and the Chiffons respectively.

More famously, Spirit guitarist Randy California had been in his grave for over twenty years before a court finally decreed that no, Led Zeppelin did not lift their best-known song from California's composition "Taurus," with even Circuit Judge Margaret McKeown noting, "The trial and appeal process has been a long climb up the 'Stairway to Heaven.'"

And most recently, it sometimes feels like every time Ed Sheeran picks up his guitar, there's some litigious soul waiting to claim he stole the song from *somewhere*, with the first line of attack being a lyric which Sheeran included in "Take It Back," and no doubt wishes that he *could* take back: "Plagiarism is hidden." Although the obvious response would be, "Well, if it's that well-hidden, then how come you spotted it?"

The issue here, of course, is not whether a song is a work of cunningly disguised plagiarism, deliberately crafted to capture the lightning of one in the bottle of the other . . . if it was, there are myriad sixties beat groups who would still be in court, wrestling with whatever multinational corporation now owns the catalogs of sundry long-deceased bluesmen.

The issue is that on those occasions when the complaint is made, how does either side go about proving their case to the satisfaction of everybody concerned?

It's not as if the alleged plagiarist is going to tour the world performing live medleys of the two songs, after all (although Sheeran was accused of doing just that). And it's not as if songwriting is a formulaic exercise—or, at least, it shouldn't be. As Canadian songwriter Kat Goldman mused, there are writers who "have claimed their songs literally fly into their heads out of nowhere. Some dream their songs or wake up with a melody in their head. How does that happen? Do elves whisper to them in their sleep? Are they making contact with other planets? Can you pull out a song like a rabbit from a hat? What about when a song gets written in 15 minutes? How do you explain that? Does it just roll off your tongue into your fingers and onto your page? Does it write itself?"[118]

---

118. Kat Goldman, *Off the Charts: What I Learned from My Almost Fabulous Life in Music* (Sutherland House Books, 2021).

Answer those questions and perhaps both sides of the argument* ("You stole it!" "I didn't") will be on solid ground. Until that happens, however, all across the music industry, songwriters (especially successful ones; there's no point suing someone who doesn't have a few million to spare) live in fear *not* that the critics will dismiss their latest opus as dingy dishwater, *nor* that the public will ignore the new song because some other star has come along, sporting a far more interesting pair of trousers. The fear is that the renowned legal firm of Fabricate, Settle, and Bolte will be firing off an accusation of plagiarism before close of business tonight.

Maybe someone should sue them, for ripping off old lawsuits?

Today, should you want to hear something, it's barely a couple of clicks away, with only predictive text and your own fat fingers likely to delay you by a few seconds more. Sometimes you don't even need to click. Just call across the room. "Embarrassingly Named Personal Assistant. Play . . . *whatever.*" Even as I write, mine is merrily shuffling Bananarama, and it didn't even pretend to misunderstand my request and order up a box of fruit. *It* wanted to hear them as well.[119]

That might be the single most important innovation of all. The death of the middleman. Forget what the critics say, or the deejays play, or the advertisements get wet legs about. *You* are the deejay, *you* are the critic, *you* are the one reaching for a box of tissues, and the artists are free to be artists at last.

For the first time in the history of popular music, the very act of becoming an artist, and creating the narrative that will hopefully propel you to stardom, is in the hands of the artists themselves. As Dale Bozzio, vocalist with eighties superstars Missing Persons, explained, "Nowadays, you design your identity. You're not picked and chosen by the industry or the people; you submit yourself to them and you get a hearing no matter what you are. If you want to be noticed, you will be and that's a pretty phenomenal tool right there."[120]

---

119. Okay, it only played three of their songs, before lurching into a random selection of "artists that are like Bananarama," which certainly isn't the same thing. But it was better than nothing.

120. Author interview, February 2023.

Or as author Edward Stourton observes, apparently with a tinge of regret, "instead of a choice selection of voices on a handful of radio and television channels, we have millions of voices on YouTube, Instagram, TikTok."[121] Is that really such a bad thing? Everybody wins.[122]

---

121. Edward Stourton, *Confessions: Life Re-examined* (Doubleday, 2023).
122. Except for the majority of artists' bank accounts. According to the website of Congresswoman Rashida Tlaib, a vocal opponent of the streaming services' financial model, an artist would need to attract "more than 800,000 monthly streams to equal the wage of a full-time worker earning $15/hour." According to fellow Congressman Jamaal Brown, "To buy an artist a cup of coffee, you would have to stream their song about 1,000 times."
    To buy the Spotify CEO Daniel Ek a cup of coffee, on the other hand . . . naaah. According to *Forbes*, he is currently (November 2022) worth $1.7 billion. He can buy his own coffee. By comparison, Bruce Springsteen—the highest-rated musician on *Forbes'* 2021 rich list—is worth less than one-third as much. Bruce has written and recorded eleven American chart-topping albums over the past half-century. Daniel, who wasn't even born until Springsteen was six albums old, simply lets you listen to them for ten bucks a month.

Chapter Twelve

The Fifteen Filthiest Progressive Rock Beards—or, Are Sales *Really* the Only Barometer You Respect?

Commercial rock'n'roll music is a brutalization of the stream of contemporary Negro church music, an obscene looting of a cultural expression.

—*Ralph Ellison*

The undelete-able file is not the only inescapable album. There are others. Maybe they don't lurk for eternity in the bowels of your personal device, awaiting the moment when you inadvertently press the wrong button, before springing out to wreak their worst. But they are everywhere regardless, and this time it wasn't Bono's fault.

It was ours.

Success and popularity aren't solely predicated by what the critics like and the industry pushes. We, the public, also have a say in it . . . a big say, in fact, because if we don't buy an album, then nobody will.

True, we cannot always be guaranteed to make the right choice, and yes, our tastes can be swayed by outside sources. But then we pause to glance at the top ten bestselling albums of all time, based upon certified sales—that is, the quantity required to receive silver, gold, and platinum discs in different countries around the world—and, for the most part, it's perfectly understandable why these records are up there. Well, sometimes.

Michael Jackson's *Thriller*. Musically unimpeachable, even if it does sometimes feel a little shop-soiled by the allegations that have been leveled against its late creator.

AC/DC's *Back in Black*. Maybe a surprise? But maybe not. Brian Johnson's penchant for sounding like an especially obnoxious toddler throwing a tantrum notwithstanding, this is one of those albums that

Harry Belafonte (1927–2023), the first artist ever to sell a million albums in the United States. CARL VAN VECHTEN, VAN VECHTEN COLLECTION AT LIBRARY OF CONGRESS / WIKIMEDIA COMMONS.

everyone appeared to own at the time, and presumably, they've just kept on buying it.

The soundtrack to the movie *The Bodyguard.* True, it was the six-song serving of Whitney Houston that close to thirty million certified buyers were interested in, rather than the rest of the album. And most of them probably only cared about the opening "I Will Always Love You." But they purchased it all the same.

Pink Floyd's *Dark Side of the Moon.* The oldest album on this list (it was released in 1973), and one which has graduated from first choice on the playlist at a seventies stoner's bong bonanza to the go-to demonstration album at high-end audio component stores; from the soundtrack to countless cocktail parties to the soundtrack of 1980s college life. Or, more bong bonanzas.

In contrast, Shania Twain's *Come On Over* is the most recent release, a stripling born in 1997 and, again contrarily, probably the least known album on the list, at least if you don't own it. And then there's Fleetwood Mac's *Rumours*; the disco-licious soundtrack to *Saturday Night Fever*; Eagles' first greatest hits LP, from 1975, and the same band's *Hotel California*, with one lyric in its title track so apt that it could almost have titled this book. You can indeed check out any time you want. But as far as vintage music is concerned, *you can never leave.*

It wasn't always like this. Again, *Dark Side of the Moon* (and possibly *Rumours* and *Saturday Night Fever*, both of which took a similarly epidemic grip on the culture of the time) notwithstanding, music never used to be as available . . . some might say inescapable . . . as it is today. Regardless of whether you want to keep it on your mental iPod or not.

There was no need for it to be. Movies still relied on original soundtracks; adverts commissioned specific jingles; stores were happy to trade in silence. Elevators might play very light classical; call waiting did the same with added clicking sounds (the sound, it was assumed, of people checking to see if you were still holding on. "Just leave them . . . they're sure to get bored shortly."). You were more likely to be pursued around your weekly errands by people humming their favorite television theme songs than you were by anything rock or pop musical.

Slowly, though, things changed. But if it's difficult to pinpoint precisely when vintage music "ended," it's less of a problem to identify when it "returned." Indeed, the superstitious among us might say that it had been preparing for such a moment for decades; an avenging angel with no purpose whatsoever beyond reminding us of times gone by.

Television commercials were among the first to acknowledge the power of pop as a marketing tool; although it's important to note that the New Seekers' bestselling "I'd Like to Teach the World to Sing" was developed from a Coca-Cola commercial, as opposed to the other way around.

Another soda, Cresta, rolled out a cartoon polar bear with a nice line in Elvis Presley impersonations (he sang "Teddy Bear"—what else?). There was also a mid-1970s British public safety ad, a shockingly graphic warning against drunk driving, which deployed Philip Goodhand Tait's "Jewel" in surely the most uncommercial surroundings imaginable. "I love this song so much. Especially the bit where the passenger flies through the windshield."

It was the 1980s, however, before things really picked up, when the music that accompanied sundry commercials for Levi jeans ignited the careers of Madonna protégé Nick Kamen (stripping down to Marvin Gaye) and "Spaceman" hitmakers Babylon Zoo, and launched Stiltskin singer Ray Wilson on the road to one day replacing Phil Collins in Genesis. The same company's advertisements also sent old-timers Ben E. King, Marvin Gaye, Steve Miller, and the Clash soaring toward the top of the British charts, without the artists themselves needing to raise a finger in support.

And Levi's sales presumably did quite well out of the arrangement as well.

Après lui, le déluge, to the point where the hits and even misses of yesteryear were suddenly interrupting every TV show you watched, including the growing number that grabbed vintage pop songs as their own opening themes.

Iggy Pop's "Lust for Life" clattering through a cruise liner ad. Nick Drake's "Pink Moon" soundtracking a car commercial and precipitating a veritable explosion of interest in an English folkie who'd passed away barely noticed in 1974, *but was now receiving offers to tour!!* Jimi Hendrix's "Purple Haze" pushing a credit card, and a Super Bowl Pepsi ad, too.

The list goes on and it's churlish to criticize (as some "fans" do), or complain that the artist is somehow "selling out" by making some extra cash. Would you turn it down if, for example, a major corporation phoned you up one day, raved about a piece of work you'd done thirty years ago, and asked if they could rent it for a few months?

Yes, the song (but in an alternate universe, it could be a passage from your journal, a drawing of your cat, a photo of a tree, or a particularly nifty piece of outside consultancy work) is selling an unrelated and perhaps even totally contradictory product. But the product is selling an unrelated song, so everyone's a winner.[123] Except for anybody who just fancied a quiet night in by the television, without some mildewed pop song barging in to despoil their evening's viewing. It's hard to tell the nippers to turn their noise down when the ad break's being just as raucous.

We turn for relief to the movies, and I will preface this by agreeing that one would need to be an absolute curmudgeon not to have derived at least a sliver of glee from the so-imaginative appearance of the Cure's "Plainsong" during the fight scene in the first *Ant-Man* movie. Or Led Zeppelin's "The Immigrant Song" in *Thor: Ragnarok*.

Again, oldies pop and Hollywood blockbusters had never been strangers, even if one deliberately overlooks those movies that either starred a moonlighting superstar (Elvis Presley was a serial offender) or utilized aspects of teen nostalgia (*American Graffiti*), youth culture (*Quadrophenia*), or the music business (*Stardust*) as its central theme.

But nothing spoke to *An American Werewolf in London* (1981) better than Sam Cooke's performance of "Blue Moon." Few songs evoke the mood of *The Killing Fields* (1984) more aptly than John Lennon's "Imagine," or the horror of *Apocalypse Now* (1979) than the Doors' "The End" (unless, of course, it's Wagner's "Ride of the Valkyries").

The Rolling Stones' "You Can't Always Get What You Want" echoes over the funeral scene in *The Big Chill* (1983), the Righteous Brothers' "Unchained Melody" haunts *Ghost* (1990), and there are few moviegoers of a certain age who can hear the opening sequence from Mike Oldfield's *Tubular Bells* without being transported back to their first (and possibly last) viewing of *The Exorcist* (1973).

And, finally, there's the song that started the whole thing off in the first place, Bill Haley and the Comets' "Rock Around the Clock," transporting audiences to a wonderland of fight and frenzy before *The Blackboard Jungle* (1954) had even begun! Because that was all it took. One song dropped into a key moment of a movie could sear that scene on your memory forever.

---

123. Especially whoever owns the song's publishing and sold the rights to a faceless megacorp in the first place.

Fourteen Reasons *Not* to Listen to the Classics

In an essay posthumously published in 1986,[124] the brilliant Cuban-Italian playwright Italo Calvino (1923–1985) offered fourteen reasons to read the great classics of literature. All fourteen were faultlessly faithful to his theme; many, however, can ruthlessly be inverted to ours. For example:

1. The classics are those records about which you often hear people saying "I just heard . . . " as opposed to "I'm deliberately listening to . . . " (Calvino 1)
2. A classic is a song which, with every repeat listening, reveals ever vaster expanses of emptiness and hopelessness, not to mention the eternal question "Was that seriously the best rhyme you could come up with?" (Calvino 4)
3. A classic is a song that has utterly exhausted most of its listeners. (Calvino 5)
4. A classic is a song that the more we know about [its] creation and meaning, the less we care. (Calvino 9)
5. A classic is a song which interrupts the music of the present with an incessant background hum. (Calvino 13)

And one can be left all but untouched:

6. A classic is a song which, even when we hear it for the first time, we feel as though we've heard it many times before. (Calvino 9)

---

124. Italo Calvino, "Why Read the Classics?," *New York Review of Books,* October 9, 1986.

But sometimes, they had the opposite effect. There are, for instance, those sensitive souls who cannot even consider watching *Rocky III* for fear of "Eye of the Tiger," while *Almost Famous* is irreparably hamstrung by the prominence given to (and subsequently enjoyed by) Elton John's "Tiny Dancer."

The godfather of stuffing a movie full of pop songs was John Hughes. Indeed, throughout his 1980s pomp, Hughes developed a peerless reputation for soundtracking his movies with the best music of the day—*Pretty in Pink; The Breakfast Club; Ferris Bueller's Day Off; National Lampoon's Vacation; Sixteen Candles; Weird Science; Some Kind of Wonderful; Planes, Trains and Automobiles; She's Having a Baby; The Great Outdoors;* and *Uncle Buck* all enjoyed soundtracks to die for, at least if you were a certain age.

It's true that Yello's teeth-grindingly awful "Oh Yeah" growling in the midst of *Ferris Bueller's Day Off* (1986) proved that even Hughes was not immune to destroying one's appreciation of an entire movie simply by picking the wrong song for a solitary scene. In general, however, he did okay, and because Hughes made it look so easy, now *everybody* was ramming rock into their pictures, song after song after usually irrelevant song jostling for attention, redolent only of a Roadrunner cartoon, with the hapless Wile E. Coyote tumbling headlong off a precipice for the remainder of time.

Who thought that was a good idea? Which movie exec was the first to sit back and think, "Forget carefully crafted and meticulously arranged incidental music and themes. I'm gonna call around a few record labels and see what they'll pay me for some primo product placement."

Whoever it was, the next thing you knew, there was hunky Harry Hulk and luscious Lizzy Lugworm[125] bumping uglies in a war-torn suburb of post-Armageddon Nebraska, while Numbnuts'[126] peculiar brand of third generation grunge-rap bleeds discordant chords over their moanin' and groanin'—sandwiched obsessively between a dozen other songs that have nothing whatsoever to do with what's happening on-screen, but did make for a super-hip soundtrack CD.

Trailers that doubled as music videos. Music videos that doubled as time to put the kettle on. And movie theaters that doubled as a deranged youth club choir practice, with half the audience singing along with the soundtrack, irrespective of how many times the other half shushed them.

The beast was uncaged, and it didn't care who got hurt. Lindsey Buckingham's "Holiday Road" so fatally besmirching *National Lampoon's Christmas Vacation* (1999). The *Nightmare on Elm Street* franchise not being improved one iota by roping in contributions from Sea Hags, the Angels from Angel City, and Love/Hate, a point proven by the fact that

---

125. Imaginary movie stars; no index provided.
126. See appendix A: An Index of Wholly Imaginary Artists.

your first instinct to that sentence was to look for a footnote. Sadly, there is no index for Imaginary Artists That Actually Existed.

Where Hollywood led, television followed. Dramas first (Hurrah! Another law enforcement drama, another Who song over the opening credits), sitcoms later, and the race to the bottom began. Television talent contests abandoned their previous preference for novelty acts, singing dogs, and all-around family entertainers and focused on uncovering the next chart sensations—with great success, it must be confessed. But do you really need to hear Finland's 2018 Eurovision entrant Saara Aaalto disemboweling "The Winner Takes All," Olly Murs defunking "Superstitious," Jamie Archer not only destroying "Get It On" but getting a lyric wrong too?[127] Or Sam Bailey emoting "Candle in the Wind" into submission; James Arthur transforming "Let's Get It On" into something that really sounds quite creepy . . . although it must be confessed that Alex and Sierra did a nice job with their sultry reenvisioning of "I Heard It Through the Grapevine."

Is any of this actually entertainment? Or simply an evening-long commercial for a bunch of singers you really didn't need to listen to in the first place, singing songs you've heard way too often already? When Harry Styles concluded his 2023 Grammy acceptance speech by remarking, "This doesn't happen to people like me very often," and set social media afire with speculation as to precisely whom these "people like me" might be, at least one interpretation mused, "what, winners of *The X Factor*?" In which case, he was very correct.

Oldies crept into elevators, dangling bat-like from the ceiling in readiness to suck the soul from the next unsuspecting passenger. You might think you're heading up to the forty-third floor. But you're really riding the highway to hell.

The sonic miasma of soft rock seeping down the phone while callers wait to be disconnected the moment they reached a human being. Restaurants replacing their live piano player with a loop tape of Billy Joel downloads. Sinus-colored sports cars parked on the corner by your house, their stereos pounding yacht rock classics while the owners practice smiling in the wing mirror. "Oooh, almost got it that time. If only I could lose the serial killer eye glint."

---

127. He sings "dirty and weak," as opposed to the correct "dirty and sweet."

And before you even realize it, it's last Tuesday afternoon and you're browsing the erotic ices shelf in your local Veggie Supermart and some deranged underling in the back room is literally drilling Harry Chapin's "Cat's in the Cradle" into your head and drowning your screams by demanding "wet cleanup on aisle seventeen."

Ars Rock'n'Roll Goetia

Written or (more accurately) compiled by an anonymous mystic around the middle of the seventh century, *Ars Goetia (the Art of Goetia)* is one of the five books comprising the *Lesser Key of Solomon*, one of the most influential works on magic and demonology ever published.[128]

It is, effectively, a very long listicle—that is, an article masquerading as a list (or vice versa), and a device that today is dearly beloved by all those who labor beneath the misapprehension that modern readers need to take a bathroom break after every paragraph.

But what a listicle! It is nothing less than an aspiring practitioner's guide to the seventy-two demons of hell, ranked in order of importance, with a helpful guide, too, to how they might be invoked. A precursor, then, to those lists of the seventy-two Greatest Rock Bands Ever that permeate our online world, and the seventy-two songs that will bring them to delicious life. Or, maybe, drive you screaming from the room at the very thought of having to listen, once more, to the Doors' "Light My Fire."[129]

Before you read any further, you might want to decide which side you're on. Remember, however, for the incantation to really work, you have to play the record sdrawkcab?

AC/DC—"You Shook Me All Night Long"
Aerosmith—"Dream On"
America—"A Horse with No Name," or that one about the "Tin Man"

---

128. The recommended edition is Aleister Crowley's editing of S. L. MacGregor Mather's *The Book of the Goetia of Solomon the King. Translated into the English Tongue by a Dead Hand*, as originally published in 1904.
129. The list as included in *Ars Goetia* appears to have been based on a similar list of sixty-nine demons published in Johan Weyer's *Pseudomonarchia Daemonum* in 1577; however, our anonymous scribe omitted one name from the earlier listing, before adding four further ones. Let this, then, be our Pruflas.

Asia—"Heat of the Moment"
Bachman Turner Overdrive—"You Ain't Seen Nothin' Yet"
Bad Company—"Rock'n'Roll Fantasy"
The Band—"The Weight"
The Beatles—"Ob-La-Di, Ob-La-Da"
Pat Benatar—"Love Is a Battlefield"
Blue Oyster Cult—"(Don't Fear the) Reaper"
Bon Jovi—"You Give Love a Bad Name"
Boston—"More Than a Feeling"
David Bowie—"Modern Love"
The Cars—"Just What I Needed"
Cheap Trick—"I Want You to Want Me"
Eric Clapton—"Wonderful Tonight"
The Clash—"Should I Stay or Should I Go"
Cream—"Sunshine of Your Love"
Creedence Clearwater Revival—"Fortunate Son"
Deep Purple—"Smoke on the Water"
Derek and the Dominos—"Layla"
Doobie Brothers—"Listen to the Music"
Bob Dylan—"Lay Lady Lay"
Eagles—"Hotel California"
Fleetwood Mac—"Dreams"
Foghat—"Slowride"
Foreigner—"Feels Like the First Time"
Grand Funk Railroad—"Some Kind of Wonderful"
The Grateful Dead—"Truckin'"
The Guess Who—"No Sugar Tonight"
Guns N' Roses—"Paradise City"
Sammy Hagar—"Your Love Is Drivin' Me Crazy"
Heart—"Alone"
Jethro Tull—"Locomotive Breath"
Billy Joel—"We Didn't Start the Fire"
Elton John—"Tiny Dancer"
Journey—"Don't Stop Believin'"
Kansas—"Carry On My Wayward Son"
KISS—"Beth"
Led Zeppelin—"Stairway to Heaven"
Loverboy—"Turn Me Loose"

Lynyrd Skynyrd—"Sweet Home Alabama"
John Mellencamp—"Jack and Diane"
Metallica—"Nothing Else Matters"
The Moody Blues—"I'm Just a Singer in a Rock'n'Roll Band"
Pearl Jam—"Even Flow"
Tom Petty and the Heartbreakers—"I Won't Back Down"
Pink Floyd—"Another Brick in the Wall"
Queen—"Bohemian Rhapsody"
Red Hot Chili Peppers—"Californication"
REO Speedwagon—"Keep On Loving You"
Rolling Stones—"Start Me Up"
Rush—"Tom Sawyer"
Santana—"Evil Ways"
The Scorpions—"Rock You Like a Hurricane"
Soundgarden—"Black Hole Sun"
Bruce Springsteen—"Born in the U.S.A."
Starship—"We Built This City"
Steely Dan—"Reelin' in the Years"
Steppenwolf—"Born to Be Wild"
Steve Miller Band—"Abracadabra"
Styx—"Lady"
Survivor—"Eye of the Tiger"
Three Dog Night—"Mama Told Me Not to Come"
Toto—"Africa"
U2—"I Still Haven't Found What I'm Looking For"
Van Halen—"Jump"
The Who—"You Better You Bet"
Yes—"Owner of a Lonely Heart"
Neil Young—"Rockin' in the Free World"
ZZ Top—"Sharp Dressed Man"

Chapter Thirteen

What Tomorrow's Pop Stars Looked Like Last Week (You'll Never Recognize Number Three)—or, A Plague of Oldies

The trick is in what one emphasizes. We either make ourselves miserable, or we make ourselves happy. The amount of work is the same.

—Carlos Castanada

Short of spending all your time listening to geometry podcasts, oldies have always been with us, and they always will be. The classics that populate, for instance, Rod Stewart's *The Great American Songbook*,[130] that doughty feast of song that has been playing (again, Sam) for so many decades that it's difficult to imagine there was ever a time when its contents *weren't* old.

"Stardust," "As Time Goes By," "A Nightingale Sang in Berkeley Square," "Over the Rainbow" . . . many people probably don't even think of them as oldies any longer. They're just the price you pay for living in the twenty-first century.

They are the songs that will outlive the cockroaches and the plastic when the heat death of the universe finally arrives. And they certainly don't qualify as nostalgia, because very few people under the age of a hundred will remember the first time Eric Maschwitz (writing under the pseudonym of Holt Marvell) and Jack Strachey's "These Foolish Things" was aired in public, for a late-night revue on BBC Radio in 1936. But it's now so much a part of the cultural furniture that we don't even trip over it in the dark.

No, "oldies" are the songs that the audience remembers, or wishes it did, the most convenient delivery method for either a second helping of

---

130. A four-album sequence released between 2002 and 2005, with Stewart reaching deep into the pre-rock'n'roll era to sing songs that were old when even he was young.

your own past, or a taste of somebody else's (hence the sudden surge of millennial interest in cocktail parties and men with hats in the wake of the hit show *Mad Men*). That sudden flash of memory as a once-familiar intro kicks in, a time or a place or a person or a kiss. But also, as George Orwell put it while discussing old books (but it's just as apposite for old records): "They form pleasant patches in one's memory, quiet corners where the mind can browse at odd moments, *but they hardly pretend to have anything to do with real life*."[131] A relived life, on the other hand? No wonder people like them.

However, you can have too much of a good tune; and if that seems oxymoronic, spend a day with the average classic rock radio station. That's about how long it takes for it all to start to sound the same. And one cannot help but wonder, who—outside of the visionary who invented the machine that paints straight white lines up the middle of the inter-state—could ever have thought it a good idea to program Journey, Asia, Saga, Foreigner, Toto, Steel Breeze, and REO Meatwagon in one solid block *while their listeners could be driving, or operating heavy machinery*?

Let's play a game. Let's play "Playlist for an afternoon on a classic rock radio station." Or let's skip the playlist and just take another look at the Rock'n'Roll Goetia at the end of the last chapter. Only this time, we won't play all the records backwards, and we will add the caveat that a few performers could receive multiple entries—instead of "Dream On" you might hear "Walk This Way." Instead of "Listen to the Music," you might get "Long Train Running." Instead of being broken on the wheel, you might be offered a session on the rack. Lovely.

We can play the same game with 1980s radio, too, if you'd like? After all, it will inevitably reprise at least a few of the classic rockers: Yes ("Owner of a Lonely Heart"), the Who ("Eminence Front"), Toto (either "Roseanna" or "Africa," but we might slip in "Ninety-Nine," depending upon how badly behaved you've been today), Bruce Springsteen, and ZZ Top. Plus U2 (although nothing from *The Undelete-able File*), REM, and the Cars.

It won't be quite as male-dominated as the classic station, so kudos to Pat Benatar, Joan Jett, Stevie Nicks, Cyndi Lauper, and Madonna for breaking through that glass ceiling. Not quite so white, either—there

---

131. George Orwell, "Good Bad Books," *Tribune*, November 2, 1945.

were a lot of hits on *Thriller,* after all, and a lot of dance and early hip-hop numbers that scream "it's the eighties, mofo" as loudly as any quaintly coiffed English synthesizer band. And not quite so Anglo-American— hello to Nena (Germany), Falco (Austria), A-Ha (Norway), and Taco (Netherlands).

Plus, if you're really lucky there might even be a period DJ, preferably one who spent the intervening years cultivating the kind of lived-in voice that lets you know they spent their entire youth shouting "way to go!" at Huey Lewis gigs, while chain-smoking doobies the size of Connecticut and gargling shards of pulverized vinyl. Okay, *this* is fun.

Now, we do need to make one point very, very clear indeed. I have absolutely *nothing* against any of the artists we've discussed here. Well, most of them. Some of them. A few of them. One or two. Nothing whatsoever. Indeed, anybody who read *I Hate New Music* might recognize a significant number of them from that tome's recommended listening suggestions.

But that list was compiled almost twenty years ago, in an age when— again—these songs weren't oozing out from every place you turned, and there weren't so many options that turned out not to be options at all.

Change the station—aah, "Walk This Way." Switch to a stream—oh, "Walk This Way." Shift to the classic hip-hop channel—*quelle surprise,* "Walk This Way" again, and from there, it's a relatively easy bleed into a subgenre that really cannot be hammered hard enough, that brief period in the early eighties when white acts decided that they should rap, just to prove how down with the kids they were. Adam and the Ants, Wham!, Blondie (the first rap screened on MTV), Rodney Dangerfield (the second rap screened on MTV!) . . . let's change the subject back again.

The point is this. Any song grows stale if you hear it often enough, which might be why so many surviving classic rock acts have such ever-changing lineups. "I'm sorry, but I cannot play that number any longer." Indeed, we can only thank our lucky stars that we are not fellow members of the band, who *are* still having to perform every night, or we are not their road crew, having to hear it every night.

We have a choice, of course. If you don't like rock radio, then turn it off. Or don't turn it on in the first place. Nobody forces anybody to listen to these radio stations, or choose those particular streaming playlists. There's a world of music out there, so get off your ass and explore it.

Rodney Dangerfield—the second rapper ever to appear on MTV.
PRESS PHOTO, WIKIMEDIA COMMONS.

Except . . . you'll always end up hearing those songs regardless. You could spend a year listening to little more than a cappella performances of medieval English folk songs (I know I did),[132] but sooner or later you have to leave the house . . . to visit the butcher (Survivor, Yes, Springsteen), the baker (Bad Company, Tom Petty, ZZ Top), the candlestick maker (Asia, Journey, the Guess Who). Maybe you received an invitation to a presidential inauguration (Fleetwood Mac, James Taylor, Bruce

---

132. During the writing of *An Evolving Tradition: The Child Ballads in Modern Folk and Rock Music* (Backbeat Books, 2023).

Springsteen); and don't even mention that forty minutes on hold with your neighborhood auto dealer.

In other words, don't go shopping, don't keep appointments, don't make phone calls, don't visit the dentist, don't ride elevators, don't attend parties, don't get in anyone else's car. There, problem solved.

Again, it must be stressed that nobody is blaming the artists themselves for this state of affairs. A lot of performers, whether through personal choice (selling one's entire back catalog to a music IP and song management company[133]) or not (being bound by the terms of an existing contract or agreement), have about as much control over the use of their catalog as they do over the weather.

Less, in fact, because at least if it rains, you can put up an umbrella. But if your greatest hit suddenly turns up soundtracking a truly embarrassing cause, there's no way of sheltering from the fallout. Indeed, it is not beyond the realms of possibility that, in years to come, wealthy political action groups might well launch their own Song Funds, albeit under the cover of a few offshore shell companies, purely to subvert the message of their most prominent musical critics by airing them at fundraisers and election-time commercials.

---

133. As of February 2023, the Red Hot Chili Peppers, Journey, Neil Young, Lindsey Buckingham, Blondie, Chrissie Hynde, Justin Bieber, and Bob Dylan are among those to have sold the rights to their catalogs, relinquishing all say over its future usage in exchange for admittedly grand sums of money.

Colorful Characters from Rock's Rich Tapestry No. 3

The Expert

The Expert is rarely the one who initiates a conversation on their chosen field of expertise. No, the Expert is the one who lurks silently to one side, waiting for somebody else to start it. Then they (but they are almost exclusively male) pounce.

Prior to the invention of the internet and, more pertinent, social media, it was a lonely life—a near-mythological one, in fact, in which our hero was forever doomed to wander the earth in the hope of hearing the magic words, the Open Sesame that would enable them to speak.

In musical terms, this tended to restrict their range to record stores, and the scenario never changed. A customer approaches the counter bearing an album—let us say, one of Lance Corporeal's 1980s releases, best remembered for the two minor hit singles and the portrait that resembled a year-old chicken liver sculpture.

The Expert speaks. "Are you sure that's the album you want?"

The customer looks up with surprise. "Well . . ."

And seizing upon that moment of indecision, the Expert begins, "Come with me. If you're getting into Lance [the Expert is always on first-name terms with the artist], there are far better places to start." And then, for ten, fifteen minutes or more, the Expert will hold forth not only on why *these* albums are better, but why *this* one is the worst of all. Often before convincing the customer that the one album he most needs of all is not even in stock at this store. "But I'm on my way to a far better store. They're certain to have it, come with me." And while the store owner stares in disbelief, both customer and Expert are out the front door.

Sometimes, the Expert doesn't even wait for the customer to make a decision. They pounce while the customer is still browsing. And however far away the next record store is, the Expert will still be declaiming specific knowledge (which is mere opinion, of course) when they get there.

And then, along came the internet, and now the Expert can conduct business at home. So many listicles, so many blogs, so many forums, so many naive innocents seeking the truth. Unless, of course, somebody else has made the same observation that the Expert was about to. In which case, "I used to agree with that. But now, for sure, I think . . ."

That, thankfully, is a pangolin that has yet to be petted (at least so far as we know). What is inescapable is the knowledge that, no matter how overplayed certain songs might be today, we are never going to hit saturation point, because a familiar oldie, a song that has already withstood the test of time, is always going to be more popular with advertisers, campaigners, and/or playlist creators than almost anything that could be considered "new."

And one wonders, given the absolute stranglehold that the rock and pop of the sixties, seventies, and eighties still has on popular culture (and the near-deification of so many of that era's stars that has grown up alongside it), will we ever reach a point where some future edition of this book, perhaps titled *I Hate All Music*, will be bemoaning the primacy of today's heroes—Ed and Harry, Dua and Ariana, the Weeknd, and Bad Bunny, at the expense of yet another generation of talent—in the same bewildered terms?

Will classic folk listeners be begging to be spared another London Experimental Ensemble deep cut? Will classic rap lovers despair every time they hear Ice Spice's name? Or will our children's children's children be recharging their jet packs and dodging the pummeling meteorites to the same old strains of Creedence's "Have You Ever Seen the Rain"?

Chapter Fourteen

Super-Harry-Outsells-Beatles, Though-He's-Quite-Atrocious— or, Editorial Bias Not Included

Everyone looks like Bryan Ferry these days, apart from Kevin Row-land who looks like a French cigarette poster. Record bags look like fashion magazines, everything's so blandly visual . . . an' the music's the same. Whatever happened to the mid-seventies . . .

—*Tony Benyon,* Th' Lone Groover, *1982*

This is not the place to polemicize on popular music as the soundtrack to teenaged rebellion. It was once, maybe, although even at the peak of the rock revolution, it remained an extraordinarily tenuous concept as one remembers that the greatest antiwar artists of the Vietnam era were, ultimately, largely employed by the same corporations as the workers manufacturing the equipment used in that war.

Perhaps, yes, they were subverting from within. But when the "within" is controlled by the very people who have the final word over what you can and cannot say on your latest long-player, the subversion begins to look more like mom letting the little'uns stay up late for a party because it will allow them to let off some steam.

If the music has any "purpose" beyond its sheer entertainment value, it is as the soundtrack to teenaged (including preteens and young adults) *identity*, which is a very different creature altogether. There will always be room for those artists whose greatest wish, they sing, is to smash the system and feed The Man to a shiver of sharks, because that's what a lot of their audience dream of doing. Like Alice Cooper sang in "School's Out," "no more pencils, no more books . . ."

But there's also room for those who are quite content with the way things are, and for those who think the system should be stronger, too. One of the most unexpected hit records of the entire Vietnam era, after

The Dead Tree Press. Once upon a time, all blogs looked like this. BAIN NEWS SERVICE, LIBRARY OF CONGRESS CATALOG.

all, was C Company and Terry Nelson's "The Battle Hymn of Lt. Calley," an impassioned defense of the man who led the massacre of Vietnamese civilians in Mai Lai in 1968. And why? Because some people believed he did the right thing. And whether you like it or not, they also had a voice.

Maybe the vast outpouring of antiwar material from across the American psychedelic scene *ultimately* swayed popular opinion to a point where the administration considered reconsidering its stance on the war in Vietnam. But still, seven long years elapsed between the release of the Candlepark Stickmen's[134] seminal "Stop the Fighting in Nam, Man" and the Ford administration announcing the complete withdrawal of American troops from Vietnam. By which time, half the band's lineup were working in the retail sector, one was dead, and the last was allegedly living in a tent.

---

134. See appendix A: An Index of Imaginary Artists.

Having scored a major hit with "Stop the Fighting in Nam, Man," the Candlepark Stickmen made numerous attempts to follow it up with similarly themed 45s. This one dates from 1983. AUTHOR'S COLLECTION.

Likewise, the Three Henchmen[135] were undeniably ahead of their time when they released "Tricky Dickie's Lies Are Sticky," two years before President Richard Nixon told any of the alleged untruths that brought him down in 1974. But so what? The Henchmen, too, had long since broken up and might have forgotten they even wrote the song.

Opinions today are often described as being at least as divided as they were during the Vietnam era, or even the Civil War. It's a state of affairs that can, insist the sociologists, be placed squarely at the door of not only conflicting ideologies and perceived high-level corruption, but also hyperbolic media, and the ghastly public echo chamber that we today

---

135. See appendix A.

know as social media, but which in past times spilled no less vitriol across the opinion columns and letters pages of the daily newspapers.[136]

It is the same in music. We spoke earlier of the overbearing influence that broadcast media had on record sales and chart positions. However, equally potent was the printed media. Only there, the emphasis was as much on shaping a reader's tastes as it was in dictating how they spent their money.

It is difficult, in 2023, to explain just how all-powerful the printed music press once was. Alongside pornography and the ubiquitous pictures of cats, music news and views represent one of the largest corners of the internet, not only in the form of fan blogs and musicians' home pages, but also via dedicated sections in mainstream news sites, the ease with which a simple tweet can place a bored pop star in the headlines, and more besides. And every one serves its own specific purpose, whether it is a die-hard fan showing photographs of every battle-scarred scrap of Wilkins Micawber[137] memorabilia they can lay their hands on, to an in-depth investigation of the multitudinous label variations that can be discovered across the Eclectic Cabbages' 1960s LPs.[138]

There are sites that are dedicated to previewing new releases; there are sites concerned only with re-reviewing old ones. There are online critics who delight in taking a single sacred cow and tearing it to pieces; there are fan boys who, having found their way onto a record label's complimentary mailing list, dare not say a word against any piece of music lest they find their way off the list again—which is a shame because negative commentary represents one of the modern music industry's last remaining links to the world of the ancients.

Adversarial assaults on artistic endeavor are at least as ancient as the written word, and doubtless predate that. The ancient Greek general Epaminondas (ca. 419–362 BC) was famed as both a singer and a dancer, as well as a military titan. But Roman biographer Cornelius Nepos, writing some 250 years later, assured readers that these much-vaunted talents were both "trivial" and "contemptuous." That he arrived at this

---

136. According to Statista.com, the number of daily newspapers published in the United States decreased from a high of 1,748 in 1970, to 1,277 in 2017, or around a quarter. In the same period, the total circulation of those newspapers (both print and online) has declined by more than half, from over 60 million to under 30 million.

137. See appendix A.

138. See appendix A.

conclusion with no means of actually hearing his subject's efforts might seem surprising, until one remembers how many modern reviewers have been caught out commenting upon concerts they didn't even attend.

In fact, musicians as a whole tended to be looked down upon by both the aristocracy and the intelligentsia of Rome. Cicero is one of several critics who argued that the very act of playing music led to men becoming effeminate; while female musicians as a whole were often tarred with the same brush as the *auletridae*, women who were hired to attend ancient Greek symposia, or social gatherings, in the combined roles of musician and sex worker.

Moving forward in time, ballad singers and street musicians were fiercely prosecuted at different times in England, and not only because they were regarded as a public nuisance. Their talents, apparently, often left much to be desired. Even the greats of what we now refer to as classical music were not above a good critical panning on occasion, and some were as capable of giving as good as they received. Tchaikovsky, for example, once wrote of Mussorgsky, "He is a limited individual . . . rough, crude and coarse . . . [who] flaunts his illiteracy and is proud of his ignorance. So he dashes off whatever comes, hit or miss."

Meow.

There again, not everybody enjoys reading lousy reviews, especially when they relate to an act they like. But the internet as a whole more than compensates, either way. There are in-depth interviews and deep-dive histories. There are high gloss photo spreads and low brow gossip columns. There are even some pages (although they are no longer as widespread as they once were) that, whisper it quietly, *give away free downloads of music.*

All of those things—except maybe the last one—were once the province of the music press, and when we discuss the decline in the number of local newspapers over the years, that is nothing compared to the slaughter of the music press.

Throughout the late 1960s to early 1970s, the United Kingdom could boast no less than five established weekly national music papers, plus a handful more that flourished briefly before folding. Today, there are none. The United States generally preferred monthly publications, but the scene was no less vibrant; rife with rivalry and one-upmanship, informed commentary, and brutal criticism, all of the above *plus* you could cut out the pictures and stick them on your wall.

Every magazine had its own style, every one operated within parameters dictated by its writers' own definition of worthwhile music. Each employed a stable of writers, of whom some—Lester Bangs, Greg Tate, Lillian Roxon, Mick Farren, Nick Tosches, Penny Reel, Greg Shaw, Charlie Gillett, Chet Flippo, Paul Williams—became as widely read and followed as many of the artists they championed.

But every magazine (or almost every one—*Rolling Stone* alone now flies the flag for that once vibrant universe, at least in terms of uninterrupted publication) eventually succumbed, and while the individual causes of death often differed, the nature of their decline rarely did. Nobody needed them anymore.

Once, it was the music press that told you about upcoming releases, because there was no place else to find out. Now, the internet ensures you know the release date almost as soon as the artist. In fact, ofttimes, it's the artist who lets you know, cutting out the middleman altogether.

Colorful Characters from Rock's Rich Tapestry No. 4

The Inadvertent Troll

A corollary to the Trivia Fiend, the Inadvertent Troll is the unfortunate soul who, no matter how helpfully they attempt to answer a question or humorously respond to a remark in an internet forum, it will somehow manage to piss off 50 percent of other users and ultimately lead to the thread being locked by the moderators. Unless, of course, they've all been sacked by a megalomaniac new owner.

For example—

Question: "Do you think 7 Deadly Synths had heard Lance Corporeal's 'Pencil in My Eye' when they recorded the backing track to 'No Newts in the Newtown'?"

Answer: "Unlikely. The Synths' song was recorded in April of that year, and performed in a Peel session in early May; whereas Corporeal didn't even start recording until the second week in June."

Inadvertent Troll: "I expect you know what color belly button fluff they had when they were recording it, as well. LOL."

At least, we assume the trolling is inadvertent. They may just be an asshole.

Once, it was the music press that tipped you off about exciting new rockers, then suggested you go out and find them. Now, bloggers do the same thing, and they usually post a video to the same page.

Once, you had to wait a week to discover why Wasp Invasion split and Neitherwhere[139] sacked their bassist. Now, you know within moments of it happening.

And once, you had to pay hard cash for the privilege of wading through pages of ads for gigs you couldn't get to, artists you didn't want to listen to, and album reviews that were clearly written for the same reason that online news sites allow their readers to comment on certain stories. Today, you can scan the screen and then click off to the next page.

Nostalgia devours the darker memories like a smack of gluttonous jellyfish. Looking back upon the golden era, everything about the music press, from the inky fingers you received every time you turned a page, to the regular front page exclusives proclaiming that the Beatles were about to reform or Elvis was going to tour Legoland, seems to speak of a simpler time, a happier time, an age when all was right with the world.

But you can take nostalgia too far, because the sensation itself is a funny thing—warm and fuzzy for some folk, stirring and strident for others, and just one more thing to pick fights over if you happen to be ornery, online, and *kalsarikännit.*[140]

---

139. See appendix A.

140. Pronounced *kal-sari̱ kæn-it,* the closest English equivalent to this beautiful Finnish word would be "getting drunk on your own, clad only in your underwear." Unfortunately, what was once a very enjoyable and very solitary pastime has now been transduced into one more tiresome "lifestyle" commodity, under the pidgin name of "pantsdrunk."

Chapter Fifteen
Meanwhile, on the Forums

If you make customers unhappy in the physical world, they might each tell 6 friends. If you make customers unhappy on the Internet, they can each tell 6,000 friends.

—Jeff Bezos

You have a choice. Another night in playing *Name the Tune They Stole This Song From* with the local eighties radio station? Or hit the online message boards to see what's shaking the trees out there?

ClashCityRocker96: *FFS there's a book out called I Hate Old Music. I've not read it but is it as poorly written, blindly ignorant and completely wrong about everything as I expect it to be?*

Fabfanforever: *I hate xperts spouting their onions about wot they know nothing about.*

Constantreeder: *I have no need to read it. The title told me all I need to know.*

Doobielover: *I listen to the music, I don't read about it.*

Fabfanforever: *Lol like wot u did there.*

Doobielover: 😀

Bluesman673635289: *Same old 💩, boring hack trying to stir up controvasy saying Legend is betta than Lennon or Mayer is better than Mayall.*

IlovetheDead53: *I don't know what Legend and Mayer even are.*

ClashCityRocker96: *ur lucky.*

Fabfanforever: *Dont wwaste yr $$, it's stupid. ive been listning to classic rock for 60 yrs and Im sure he made up half the bands he writes about. Failed riter says hr dosnt even like saxaphones.*

Broooocerules765: *I bet he's never even herd of Clarence Clemons.*

Doobielover: *I heart sexyphone.*

Theseventieslive: *Yr of the 🐱, Backer Street, anything with Bobby Keez*

YachtRockSailor: *I had Baker Street played at my first wedding*

Judasistheonlypriest: *How long did it last?*

YachtRockSailor: *It was the album version.*

Judasistheonlypriest: *I meant the marriage lmao.*

[YachtRockSailor has left the conversation]

Theseventieslive: *Good one, Judas.*

Voiceofreason*: Its a stupid book idea. I can't think of a single record I like made after 1981*

Bluesman673635289*: 1971*

ElvisLivesInMyOuthouse: *1959*

Judasistheonlypriest: *Priest are still making killer albums. So are Purple and Heep.*

MetalismyMaster666: *Metallica!*

IlovetheDead53: *I don't know what Metallica is.*

HereToTrollYa: *[emoji removed pending approval]*

Theseventieslive: *There's no such thing as old music, oNly great music or shit music.*

Fabfanforever: *gr8 music will live forever. Ppl in the 43rd century will still be listening to the Beetels. Not Bleyonciedie and Shed Rearend.*

IlovetheDead53: *I feel sorry for the future, howw long since any act came along that can measure up to the GIANTS of the 60s and 70s?*

MetalismyMaster666: *[moderator has removed this comment]*

MetalismyMaster666: *Punk rox old and I hate that.*

Fabfanforever: *I dont car wot music is doing in the present, what intrests me is wot it did in the past.*

YachtRockSailor: *Sorry, my connection went down.*

Bluesman673635289: *Anything with sin-thesizers.*

Theseventieslive: *lol bluesman*

Broooocerules765: *Yacht rock*

IlovetheDead53: *I don't know what Yacht Rock is*

[YachtRockSailor has left the conversation]

Broooocerules765: *The reason heritage artists hang on is because nothing is Good Enough to re-place them.*

Fabfanforever: *Agrred. manstreem music sux.*

IlovetheDead53: *Manufactured, formulaic, vapid, repetitive, commercial, sexist, childish.*

Broooocerules765: *I don't see anyone who could match the music produced by the groups we talk about here.*

IlovetheDead53: *I saw Clarence play w/the Dead back in 89. What would be the modern equivalebnt of that?*

Broooocerules765: *That must have been some show.*

IlovetheDead53: *Best evr version of Estimated Prophet*

MetalismyMaster666: *I like a bit of Dark Star*

IlovetheDead53: *PM me, I have a 43 min version from Cleveland that will blow your mind.*

Fabfanforever: *I hav Beetels albums shorter than that lol.*

DarcysMomma5: *AIBU to insist my DCs listen only to music that I owned when I was their age?*

Bluesman673635289: *Depends what you lissened to.*

DarcysMomma5: *LOL, gangsta rap, but when I hear the language and themes in modern music they make me sick to my stomach.*

IlovetheDead53: *I took my cats to see the Dead, they loved it and met the band after. Truckin' (3 yr old calico) and Bertha (8, ginger). PM me for photos.*

HereToTrollYa: *Let me tell you what I think!!! Look at me!!!!!! You're all fucking retards and wrong wrong wrong. Look at me!!!!!!!!!*

MetalismyMaster666: *My dad was a Sabbath fan and I was raised on seventies metal. Didn't do me any harm.*

IlovetheDead53: *Only because you got a plea deal LMBO.*

Brooocerules765: *The book quotes Grace Slick saying all rockers should retire at 50.*

IlovetheDead53: *Rubbish. Jerry was still making grate music after 50.*

Fabfanforever: *Macca's over 8T and he can still rok.*

StonedontheStones: *Mick'n'Keef man*

Smoooooothsoundz: *Terry Kath was only 31 when he dyed but he could hav mad magic forever.*

StonedontheStones: *Brian Jones was 27*

Bluesman673635289: ☹ *the 27 Club*

Smoooooothsoundz: *Too many stars died too soon and it's disrespectful to hate their music. Thats why I won't buy this bok..*

DarcysMomma5: *Tupac was 25.*

ElvisLivesInMyOuthouse: *Elvis never died.*

MetalismyMaster666: *You should play him Guns & Roses Heartbreak Hotel. That'll finish him off lol.*

ElvisLivesInMyOuthouse: *Elvis was the first rapper. Listen to "RU Lonesome Tonight."*

DarcysMomma5: 🤦

Broooocerules765: *Sorry, I don't have a trumpet for my wind-up gramophone.*

ClashCityRocker96: *I used to think the 78 setting on my record player was to liven up boring ballads.*

MetalismyMaster666: *And the 16 setting was for making them sound like Sabbath. I bet that doesn't get mentioned in the book.*

ElvisLivesInMyOuthouse: *If the author doesn't like old music, what does he/she like?*

IlovetheDead53: *I don't know what old music is.*

Broooocerules765: *Music's just music, man.*

MetalismyMaster666: *Unless it's crap.*

ElvisLivesInMyOuthouse: *The next book should b called I Hate Crap Music.*

Darcysmomma5: *But hoo decides wot's crap?*

IlovetheDead53: *Everything that*

Broooocerules765: *The members of this*

MetalismyMaster666: *Forum*

ElvisLivesInMyOuthouse: *Don't*

Fabfanforever: *Like.*

StonedontheStones: *Man.*

[HereToTrollYa has left the conversation]

Chapter Sixteen

Lip-Synching, Libido-Quenching, Foul-Tasting, Debilitating, Buzz-Killing, Shit-Talking, Tired-of-Living, Sick-of-Giving, Fool-Appealing—or, That Sinking Feeling

The wretch, concentred all in self,

Living, shall forfeit fair renown,

And, doubly dying, shall go down

To the vile dust, from whence he sprung,

Unwept, unhonored, and unsung.

—*Walter Scott*, The Lay of the Last Minstrel, *1805*

There is a special circle in Classic Rock Hell, and it is full of water. The sun always shines, the boys are made of muscle, and the girls are all beautiful. The tans are water resistant and the toupees are family pets. Every drink comes with its own personalized umbrella, and the grins glint like fairy lights in the warm tropical breeze.

It's called yacht rock, and you are marooned here for eternity. Get used to it.

Of all the terms that have ever been applied to different forms of popular music, and in particular those that were created retroactively, to create a form that nobody knew existed in the first place, is there anything less appealing, less conducive to having a good time . . . less oozing so much sincerity that you know the whole thing's a fraud . . . than "yacht rock"? Okay, yes. "Emo" sucks as well. But yacht rock edges it, because at least the emo crowd had a few nice tunes. Half the yacht rock brigade probably doesn't even own dinghies.

It's a relatively recent phenomenon, this business of coining catchy titles for retroactively delineated musical "genres." The first, dating back

The crown prince of yacht rock, Bobby Goldsboro. FERNSTACHIT, CC BY-SA 4.0.

to the 1980s, was freakbeat, to be applied to that brief period between the end of what the British call the Beat Boom, but America refers to as the Invasion, and the beginning of psychedelia, when a handful of bands were presciently mashing elements of the two phenomena together. The term caught on, and now it's a part of musical history.

Other tags followed, but few stuck around, probably because it was easier to just preface an existing term with either "proto-" (for the forerunners) or "post" (for the aftershocks) and leave it at that. Nico Teen and the Stains were proto-punk, Wasp Invasion were post-punk. Easy.

Such terms are always applied, initially, by writers, and usually to make the kind of point that only the true cognoscenti would feel was required—to explain how, for example, Neitherwhere avoided being classed as either a gothic rock nightmare or a hair metal experience, despite their repertoire spanning both eras.

Yacht rock, on the other hand, was . . . okay, which would you prefer? The "official" creation myth, as documented on *Wikipedia*? Or the unofficial one that I was going to make up before I thought to Google it? The one about dancing to Captain & Tennille on the deck of the *Titanic*?

It doesn't matter. Neither is particularly complimentary and when you look at the kind of music included therein, that will scarcely come as a surprise. But here's the real one.

Writer and director J. D. Ryznar is credited with inventing the term to title an online video series he was making, creating a fictional reality around the lives and careers of the soft rock stars of the 1970s and early 1980s . . . Toto, Steely Dan, the Doobie Brothers, Kenny Loggins, and Michael McDonald.

It was intended as a spoof, albeit a fairly well-intentioned one, and there it might have stayed but for misfortune. As the second decade of the twenty-first century continued to unfurl, bringing with it ever more calamitous cultural, political, and meteorological crises, what journalist Jack Seale[141] described as "the lush, laid-back sound [that created] the perfect soundtrack for listeners trying to ignore Watergate and Vietnam" in the 1970s was reborn to weave its stultifying spell over listeners hoping to sleep through Brexit, Donald Trump, Boris Johnson, January 6, Covid, wildfires, floods, and so on and so on.

Not because they weren't interested in such matters, but because . . . well, enough already! Seriously, how many days can you wake up to another edi-listi-torial detailing "Five Reasons Why Civilization Is Going to End This Afternoon (And *You're* to Blame)"?

All of which sounds . . . well, obviously it depends upon what is played. A little early Hall and Oates? "She's Gone" isn't that bad a song, as such things go. Steely Dan . . . yeah, "Showbiz Kids" was kinda fun. Hand us a playlist, we'll let you know.

---

141. Jack Seale, "I Can Go for That: The Smooth World of Yacht Rock Review—Lushly Comforting," *The Guardian*, June 14, 2019.

It would be so easy, and infinitely preferable, to just turn in another Index of Imaginary Yacht Rockers here and rattle on about Casual Lovin'[142] and the Soft White Undercurrents,[143] and how the latter's cover of Player's "Baby Come Back" sounded even less like the Bee Gees than the original.

Unfortunately, the reality is so much grimmer, a seemingly endless parade of the kind of music that the 1980s would christen "Power Ballads," but without quite so much power. Ryznar named the ringleaders, and any list of yacht rock atrocities will undoubtedly find much to curse them for. But there were more. So many more.

Basically, if a record made you feel as though you'd just stepped in something moist and yielding, and you knew it had ruined your blue suede sneakers, you had probably slipped (literally) into yacht rock land. And a lot of people were slipping, so many that by the mid-2010s the damage was done. Even as listeners continued assigning fresh horrors to the canon, yacht rock was transformed from a random scattering of radioactive turds that it wasn't too hard to avoid into an *Actual Peer-Reviewed Chapter* in the Authorized History of Rock.

The advent, in 2015, of a yacht rock channel on Sirius XM confirmed its supremacy. The broadcast, in June 2019, of the BBC's *I Can Go for That: The Smooth World of Yacht Rock* documentary was a reminder that it wasn't going away. And then there was the emergence of the Yacht Rock Revue, in which sundry yacht rock tribute acts swarm upon defenseless summertime communities to flaunt their ghastly wares. Today, there are even *brand-new acts* reliving yacht rock of their very own. Next, they'll be telling us that punk's not dead, either.

There is the shelf of books that have appeared on the topic. There are 180-gram vinyl reissues of the grisliest grails in the yacht rock canon. And there's a galaxy of pulchritudinous practitioners who have reemerged to flog their sordid memories one more time. The hope, once so vibrant, that it was *all* a hideous nightmare from which one of us, hopefully, would awaken soon, was crushed long ago.

Of course, it's not wholly a bad thing. No longer, for example, do the crate diggers among us need to flip past vast quantities of mid-1970s soft

---

142. See appendix A: An Index of Wholly Imaginary Artists.
143. See appendix A.

Few album titles better encapsulated the 1970s soft rock ethos, and the attendant beachfront fondue parties, than Casual Lovin's Watchin' You, Droolin'.
AUTHOR'S COLLECTION.

rock in pursuit of whatever it is we are searching for. Indeed, used record dealers exalted in the advent of a musical movement that finally cleared their dollar bins of those old Poco albums that had sat untouched for years. Now, the things were flying out of the racks, no matter what price was put on them. Dr Hook, Christopher Cross, Rupert Holmes, Al Jarreau, the Little River Band . . . and the myriad other sad-sack souvenirs of a softer, stalkier time that their original owners could not wait to rid their collections of.

But mentioning a playlist was not an idle threat. If you like yacht rock, you're gonna love . . .

The one about the guy who hasn't seen his girlfriend for a while, so he calls her up and suggests they go somewhere quiet and isolated . . . a windy park, an empty beach, his place to watch TV . . . because none of that sounds at all weird. Oh, and just in case you're still not sure, "I'm not talking 'bout moving in." Yep, the pig just fancies a booty call.

The one about the dog drifting out to sea. Well, it might be a dog. It could be the singer's mother. Either way, she's gone, and not in a nice Hall & Oates, "I love you but I can't stand having your peculiar-looking friend hanging around the house all day as well" kind of way. This is just grim.

The one about the statutory rape of a seventeen-year-old boy as he's walking on the beach.

The one about the clearly depressed young woman whose husband just toddles off every day (probably to see his secret lover) and leaves her alone in an empty house with nothing to do but watch a tree grow. And one day, she falls prey to a marauding gang of motorcyclists. Or does he mean the other kind of Angels? It's hard to be sure.

The one about a mating pair of *Ondatra zibethicus,* and the almost voyeuristic passion with which the observer details their activities.

The one about the guy who wants you to dance with him. And keeps on about it for so long that not only is the song over, but the disc jockey has retired, the club's been closed, and the would-be Lothario is onto his third hip replacement. But he still wants you to dance with him. Most people give up after the first drink is flung in their face.

And the other one (see chapter 5) about the singer's mom dancing with his granddad . . .

The one about the homeless woman hanging around the railroad tracks, presumably considering suicide; and, in the same song, the curious juxtaposition of the words "pushing mama" and the image of an oncoming locomotive.

The one that babbles on about it raining in Africa, which has absolutely nothing to do with the hundred men who keep getting mentioned and who, in turn, have nothing to do with Kilimanjaro rising like Olympus above the Serengeti, which has nothing to do with anything approaching actual African geography.

The one about the down-on-her-luck lady reduced to peddling hard alcohol to lonely sailors in a rundown harbor town. And conversely, the one about the man who rejects a potential fine wife (or perhaps a strong drink) in favor of the sea.

The one about the guy, another problem drinker, taking out personal ads searching for a likeminded woman, so they can get horribly drunk together.

The one that goes on about how you need to listen to the music, heedless of the fact that if they'd just shut up for a bit maybe you could.

The one about the woman who walks out on her family, flies to the Caribbean, gets pregnant by a local she picks up in a bar, and then returns home to sucker her unsuspecting husband into raising the child as his own.

The one that isn't even a song, it's a couple rowing over the fact he's still hanging out with his ex-girlfriend, and slowly it transpires that yes, they probably did do the dirty. But "her life's in disarray," so that makes it okay.

The one that was the theme to that Dudley Moore and Liza Minnelli movie which really wasn't bad, except you daren't watch it again because that song . . . oh, that song.

Anything by Chicago.

And *this* is what took people's minds off Watergate and assorted other half-century-old perturbations? No wonder the rest of the 1970s were so weird.

How Weird Were the 1970s? A Quiz

1. Which recently estranged couple expressed their disdain for one another by including photos of barnyard animals with their latest album?
   a. John and Paul Beatle
   b. Brian and Mike Beach Boy
   c. Glen and Johnny Sex Pistol
2. Which band took their name from the strap-on rubber penis that Mary milks in William Burroughs's *Naked Lunch*?
   a. Hall & Oates
   b. Steely Dan
   c. The Buzzcocks

3. Why did David Bowie sport an eyepatch for television performances of "Rebel Rebel"?
   a. He poked himself in the eye while trimming his eyelashes.
   b. He was suffering from conjunctivitis.
   c. After everything else the guy wore, you want to pick on the eyepatch?

4. How long did the really boring bit in Yes's *Tales from Topographic Oceans* last when they played it live?
   a. Long enough for their keyboard player to eat a full curry.
   b. Long enough for the entire audience to refresh their drinks at the bar.
   c. Long enough for the entire band to go to the bathroom. Including the one who ate the full curry.

5. From whom did Jethro Tull take their name?
   a. A Charles Dickens character . . . well, it worked for Uriah Heep.
   b. A scion of modern British agriculture[144] . . . well, it worked for George Harrison.[145]
   c. Cockney rhyming slang . . . well, it worked for James Blunt.

6. Johnny Cougar made two great rock'n'roll albums in the late 1970s, before changing his name and singing songs about farms. What was his chosen alias?
   a. Melancholy
   b. Melonhead
   c. Mellencamp

7. Which seventies hard rock frontman would you least like to find living in a shredded paper nest in a hole in the wall behind your bed?
   a. Lou Gramm
   b. Steve Perry
   c. Gene Simmons

8. "Doobie" was . . . ?
   a. A slang term for "cool."
   b. A slang term for a marijuana cigarette.
   c. A slang term for an especially persistent bout of flatulence.

---

144. Jethro Tull (1674–1741) was the inventor of the seed drill.
145. George Harrison Shull (1874–1954) is regarded as the father of hybrid corn.

9. Which group was apocryphally named for the amount of semen in the average male ejaculation?
   a. 5,000 Volts
   b. 10cc
   c. The Little River Band
10. Who is the nepo kid?
    a. Deacon Frey
    b. Lester Bowie
    c. Jacob Marley

Answers: 1–a; 2–b; 3–b; 4–a; 5–b; 6–c; 7–a, b, c; 8–b; 9–b; 10–a

If your answers were
Mostly correct—You were there; you already know how weird they were.
Mostly wrong—You weren't there. We'll spare you the macabre details.
Half and half—You were probably there, but wish you weren't.

Soft rock itself is fine. Not every record needs to race by at 3,000 bpm while the guitarist's bleeding fingers short-circuit the amplification and the singer's larynx disintegrates while he's still saying "hello, Cleveland." Plus, there's always room for low lights and romance.

But there's soft . . . and there's positively viscous. And if you thought classic rock had a problem with women, that's because you've not met the whining, wheedling weirdos that populate the average yacht rock playlist, *despite all the warning signs you were offered just a few lines back.*

Oh baby, come back so we can make sweet love like we used to. Oh baby, I'm so lonesome without you and I know you hate me, but let's do it one more time for old time's sake. Oh baby, I know you don't fancy me in the slightest but is a sympathy fuck out of the question?

Half the songs are a stalker's manifesto, half are a loser's secret diary, and the rest (because fractions are a figment of your imagination) are divided between blatant braggadocio, sordid self-flagellation, and frankly creepy insinuation and threat.

No wonder Honey killed herself.

Chapter Seventeen

Parturient Montes, Nascetur Ridiculus Mus—or, A Sickness of Supergroups

The mountains will go into labor. But all they will give birth to is a ridiculous mouse.

Thus spake first-century poet Horace, in his *Ars Poetica* and, completely unwittingly, the most accurate description of rock supergroups ever written was delivered some two thousand years before there were any groups to be considered super.

This is the story of some ridiculous mice.

For many sports fans, the most exciting aspect of the season is the trading (a nice way of saying, of course, buying and selling) of players. Will your team pick up the superstar that everyone else has been drooling over all year long? Or just another bunch of make-weight maybes who could theoretically pay off one day?

Imagine if bands did that. Imagine if, say, the Dental Assassins had decided one day that Bongo was no longer pulling his weight, and they'd be better off letting him go. So they called up another band's management, worked out a deal, had a few days rehearsal, and then unveiled their new star to the world. Clad in his own Assassins T-shirt, while management grinned around him.

How exciting would that be? How thrilling if, every time rumors ramped up about creative differences in this band or that, the gossip columnists came scampering out, all offering their unique take on the hoary "a close source told me" disguise for pure fiction.

It would be expensive. What is the going rate for a flawless drummer, an ace bass man, a superstar singer? And how long before some canny entrepreneur started scheming the creation of a new aggregation from scratch, comprising nobody but superstars?

"Start at the back. We want Beyoncé on drums. Obviously. Bass—Bieber. Bieber on bass. Just slips off your tongue. Guitar—Ryan Adams. No, not Bryan, Ryan. Thank you. Vocals—Katy Kirby . . . yes, Katy. Not Kathy. And on the Kylie Minilogue synth, Ed Zeppelin. What do you mean, I just made him up? You were okay with the last pair. Alright, Ron Butterfly."

It'd cost a fortune in transfer fees, but the payoff would certainly be worth it. Or would it?

Supergroups are the stegosaurus of classic rock, an impressive-looking creature whose brain was nevertheless so disproportionately small in comparison with its body size that paleontologists once believed that Mother Nature had considered adding a second one in the region of its hips.[146]

Colorful Characters from Rock's Rich Tapestry No. 5

The Authority

The Authority is the one who can answer every question with the utmost authority: a walking, talking encyclopedia of rock'n'roll history, the kind of guy (again, they're nearly always guys) who will not only correct the slightest misstatement in a book, magazine, internet posting, or casual conversation, he will then add that correction to a seemingly endless repertoire of "times I was right," which—because nobody ever thinks to ask him about it—he has become adept at introducing into any conversation.

"Hey, so what have you been doing today?"

"Well, I'm expecting a very important e-mail from Backbeat Books, apologizing for an error in *I Hate Old Music*, perpetuating the falsehood that Rocky Biceps recorded 'around 100 songs,' when it was—if you also include a scrapped session with Phil Spector in 1958, *exactly* 100. I cannot believe such shoddy inaccuracies escaped unnoticed throughout the editorial process."

This observation will then be repeated through online book reviews, introduced into fan forums, and, in the more egregious examples, be conflated into full-blown conspiracy theories regarding a shadowy conclave of embittered former rock critics attempting to rewrite the history of music prior to sacrificing humanity to the Lizard Ladies of Magnesia Milk of VII.

---

146. Apparently they don't believe this any longer.

A stegosaurus heading for the first rehearsal. H. N. HUTCHINSON, 1897. WIKIMEDIA COMMONS.

The first acknowledged stego-supergroup was Cream, whose lineup included only one name known to the majority of period pop fans, Eric Clapton—fresh from mid-sixties stints with the Yardbirds and John Mayall's Bluesbreakers. Bandmates Jack Bruce and Ginger Baker, on the other hand, had spent much of the last few years in the Graham Bond Organization, a jazz blues trio that became a lot better known once its rhythm section moved on than it ever was while they were still onboard. Supergroups, then, were clearly in the eye of the beholder.

The ploy worked, however. For two years, before ego clashes caused the entire shebang to disintegrate, Cream—so-named because they were the "cream" of their profession, and not, as has been written elsewhere, to discourage the lactose intolerant from liking them—were one of the top live draws in both the United States and United Kingdom, and that despite a large part of every performance being devoted to a drum solo.

So Cream broke up, but supergroups lived on, a celebration of virtuosity over vrooom, of skill over substance, of talent over tunes. Who cares that the music is positively unlistenable? Just admire the sheer genius of their playing.

Clapton and Baker immediately borrowed Steve Winwood from Traffic and formed Blind Faith. Emerson, Lake & Palmer (ELP), cast from individual members of the Nice, King Crimson, and the Crazy World of

Arthur Brown, ruled the progressive rock roost throughout the first half of the 1970s; just as Crosby (ex-Byrds), Stills (ex-Buffalo Springfield), and Nash (ex-Hollies) dominated the neo-yacht rock scene of sweet harmonies, gentle ballads, and songs that rhymed "house" with "nice house." Occasionally joined by Neil Young,[147] who was already carving out a solo career for himself, their renown (under the cleverly amended name of Crosby, Stills, Nash & Young) only grew greater.

And so things meandered on, to the point where one needed only to bring together a few dudes or dudettes who'd once been in another band and the media was proclaiming a new supergroup was born: Journey, for example, combining talents from Santana, the Steve Miller Band, and the Tubes; Asia, a veritable conurbation compiling random ex-members of King Crimson, Yes, ELP, and—here's the big one—the Buggles. GTR (Genesis, Yes, Marillion); Foreigner (Spooky Tooth, King Crimson, Hunter-Ronson, and Lou Gramm).

And the frankly turgid predictability of much (Sorry, inappropriate attempt at politeness. *All* their music. Every Last Note) of their music notwithstanding, the one thing that all of these groups had in common was the volatility of their lineups. Again, just like sports teams—who's Steve Howe playing with this season? (Answer: Asia, GTR, ABWH, and oh, he's back with Yes again.)

Emerson, Lake & Palmer reformed with Cozy Powell (ex-Rainbow) in place of Palmer—if nothing else, it allowed them to keep their familiar logo intact; but only after Lake had his own stint in Asia, and on convulsed the crazy convolutions until everyone's address book gave up the ghost and the very concept of supergroups had more stray threads than a whodunit written by cats.

Players didn't even need to be "super" anymore, just somehow attached to an act that had accrued a degree of fame in some distant era, even if only for a few minutes. At times, it was as if someone had designed a card deck in which every suit represented a different instrument, and every card an out-of-work exponent. Shuffle the pack, deal the cards—"Wow, two drummers and a singer who hasn't worked since that

---

147. Also ex-Buffalo Springfield, a circumstance that today would probably justify the whole group passing themselves off as BS revival.

unpleasant incident with the antique counterpane. At least we'll have no trouble getting press coverage."

They didn't, either. It is astonishing, looking back, at the pressure that was exerted on the public to actually pay attention to these bands; the depths to which their backers would stoop to prove that this was a genuine supergroup; the insistence that just because Larry McList[148] filled in for a gig when Billy Big Bananas's trombonist got lost on his way to a show, he can now be credibly associated with BBB when adding his achievements to his next band's pedigree.

But did the people who bought these people's records genuinely like them? Or were they so in awe of the table of contents that they felt they *had* to, to further prove their dedication to one or other of the components? Certainly, that is the only way to judge the success enjoyed by so many of these outfits, and thus we should be grateful indeed that so few of them lasted beyond an album or two before at least half the lineup was replaced.

Until, in the end, even the most gullible Wilkins Micawber supporter had figured out that just because one of their roadies would be manning the merchandise stand on a supergroup tour didn't necessarily mean he helped write their latest single.

And so, inevitably, the supergroup "brand" didn't merely lose its luster, it was last seen selling it from a battered suitcase on the corner of the road. The concept, of course, has certainly lingered on, but they tend now to be passing collaborations rather than genuine career moves, and that is a good thing.

Except, of course, on the revival circuit.

---

148. See appendix A: An Index of Wholly Imaginary Artists.

Chapter Eighteen

One More Time for the Fans—or, Don't They Look Young for Their Age?

*I went to some Herman's Hermits shows, and I'd see these fucking
clowns on stage, "ah, here's one we recorded in 1965," and my friends
would have to hold me back. I just wanted to run up there and have
a tantrum, "you didn't record it . . . the only one of you who was even
in the band back then was the drummer, and he never played on any
of the records!*

—*Peter Noone (ex-Herman's Hermits)*

You know that friend you had, the one who no matter what ailment you mentioned not only had it, but had it worse than anyone else? And they believed it so passionately but that they even exhibited the symptoms?

Medically, it's called Munchausen's syndrome. Musically, it's called tribute bands. And out there somewhere, in vaster numbers than you could ever imagine, there are fans of several thousand old combos who have simply transferred their allegiance to several thousand new ones who don't merely walk in their heroes' footsteps. They wear their underwear, too.

Tribute acts started out . . . not as a joke so much as a novelty. The earliest Elvis impersonators, who can be traced back to the 1960s, made no attempt to fully replicate every move, every breath, and every note the Pelvis performed. It was enough to have a voice that could sink to that sexy southern growl and put on an outfit appropriate to the part of his career they wanted to recapture.

It was fun, it was often fun*ny*, and few people took them seriously. We've already mentioned the Elvis impersonator who made the mid-1970s Cresta soft drinks commercial so memorable, and the fact that he was a cartoon polar bear was immaterial. He sounded *just like Elvis.*

A few years later, the Hee Bee Gee Bees cut a clutch of extraordinarily convincing Bee Gees parodies, windswept hair and medallions included.

We pause here, however, to distinguish between tribute acts *per se* and acts that existed—tongue-in-cheek or otherwise—specifically (there's no polite way of saying this) to cash in on the success of another band. The Beatles had barely recovered from conquering the United States before the Buggs emerged with *Beetle Beat*, an album that sounded not wholly unlike its target, but was clearly a parody. And later, of course, there were the Rutles.

In the early 1970s, the then-struggling Thin Lizzy briefly renamed themselves Funky Junction to record "a tribute to Deep Purple," and something called the Hobos made an album titled *Sounds Like Slade.*

These acts never gigged in these guises; they never sat and studied every nuance of their victim, so as to replicate it to the *nth* degree. They simply made some records that sounded "right," then took the money and ran. Nice job, boys.

Then there was the pustulant cancer of the straightforward rip-offs, a once-common sight on the 1960s revival scene as long-sundered bands reappeared with wholly different lineups playing the beloved songs, because whoever owned the rights to the band's name, it wasn't the band themselves. Or sometimes they did own the name, but someone thought they'd give it a go regardless—the fake Fleetwood Mac of 1974 and a duplicitous Deep Purple in 1980 are classic examples.

The 1990s, however, saw something peculiarly stirring. Australia had never been well-served by visiting superstars; the Beatles went there once, in 1964, and it would be 1976 before even one-quarter of the band (Paul McCartney's Wings) returned. The Rolling Stones toured in 1965 and 1966, stayed away until 1973—then waited twenty-two years before coming back. Bruce Springsteen was there in 1985, then absented himself until 1997. Led Zeppelin visited once, in 1972; ABBA likewise, in 1977. Pink Floyd waited until 1988. And so on.

The excuses were largely much as you'd expect. It's a long way to go for a handful of shows, and a long way to travel between different venues. Which made perfect sense to the accounting team, and probably to the musicians, too. But to be an Australian fan of a Western rocker was not simply an exercise in futile devotion, it was akin to spending your entire life in a lazarium.

So the locals took matters into their own hands, reenacting the shows that the country had missed with body doubles replicating the sound of the act, and—as time passed and profits rose—taking a stab at the lighting and special effects, too.

The Australian Pink Floyd Show, the Beatniks, Zeppelin Live . . . there were so many of them, but it was purely an Australasian experience, and it might have stayed that way had one of their number, ABBA tribute band Bjorn Again, not decided to take their show to London, where they disembarked their plane clad in identical costumes to those that ABBA wore on the cover of their *Arrival* album.

The media loved it, the public seemed amused. Bjorn Again even scored a handful of hits, and proved that ABBA themselves were not their only fascination. Their first was a cover of Erasure's "A Little Respect"; others revisited the theme to the movie *Flashdance* and the festive staple "Santa Claus Is Coming to Town," all relayed in perfect ABBA style, but taking it in different directions.

From tiny seeds.

In many ways, the roots of tribute bands *in their modern* context, lie within the early 1990s fascination with "tribute albums," in which a troupe of usually unconnected acts performed the signature hits of the chosen artist.

If you change your mind . . . take a chance on Bjorn Again. ALEX MARSHALL, CC BY-SA 3.0.

The notion was not especially novel. Enrico Caruso's recordings of Ruggero Leoncavallo's opera *Pagliacci* are often cited as the earliest tribute record, and that was released in 1907. By the 1960s, any artist devoting an entire LP to the songs of another—the Supremes' Beatle-centric *A Bit of Liverpool* (1964), *The Hollies Sing Dylan* (1969), etc.—was making a tribute album. Some artists even made tribute albums to themselves, as when Motown songwriters Holland-Dozier-Holland conceived an LP, recorded by the Supremes (again), called . . . *Sing Holland-Dozier-Holland* (1967).

Where it all went wrong . . . horribly, horribly, wrong . . . was when a respectful novelty became a self-perpetuating black hole filled with the barely listenable clatter of so many unknowns hitching a ride on a past giant's coattails, simply because they could. "If you like Eclectic Cabbage, you're going to *adore* the sound of a dozen unsigned Midwestern bar bands playing their greatest hits." And not one of them has a kazoo. What manner of tribute is that?

Because it doesn't matter how vibrant a career said pub rockers might enjoy around the shimmering nighteries of their native cities. Unless you can take a formless three-hour psychedelic jam and translate it into a twenty-stanza mini-opera, why not simply let the original continue moldering in peace? A single straightforward cover is fine. An album's worth, with no one contributor distinguishable whatsoever from another, is a waste of electricity.

Okay, calm down. Let's look at tribute albums from a less splenetic angle.

Some are resoundingly meritorious.

Again, we're back into pre-internet days, when the majority of non-mainstream music spread by word-of-mouth, and there were far more deserving artists essentially dwelling in obscurity than there were living the high life.

In 1990, former 13th Floor Elevators frontman Roky Erickson, after decades of mental health problems and minimal income from his musical career, was the subject of *Where the Pyramid Meets the Eye*, a "big name" tribute album which saw artists of the caliber (we're talking in commercial terms; the quality of their music is for you to decide) of REM, the Jesus and Mary Chain, ZZ Top, and Poi Dog Pondering come together to record an album's worth of his compositions.

The contributors to 1992's punk tribute to Foxy & the Redcoats were unknown then and remain so now. Even appendix A cannot help you.
AUTHOR'S COLLECTION.

The album was a success, and between the songwriting royalties that he (hopefully) accrued and the interest it sparked in his music, Erickson was ultimately able to renew his career. Plus, if you have ever wondered whether REM made even one good record, their version of "I Walked with a Zombie" is probably it.

Three years later, the presence of Lou Reed, Pearl Jam, Michelle Shocked, Lucinda Williams, and Soul Asylum assuredly drew a whole new audience to *Sweet Relief: A Benefit for Victoria Williams*, and welcome funds, too, toward its subject's battle against multiple sclerosis. (The album also brought about the foundation of the Sweet Relief Fund, a charity assisting professional musicians with health care.)

Like the vast benefit concerts that pockmarked the 1980s and 1990s, projects such as this are effectively beyond reproach because at least there's a reason for their existence. As opposed to . . . well, we're back to the Eclectic Cabbage tribute, aren't we?

Ofttimes enjoyable, if only for a single listen (the novelty often wears off after that), are those tributes that take a single artist and throw them to a pack of musicians from an altogether different discipline—the aforementioned three chord slobber into opera approach. A reggae tribute to Bob Dylan was passingly entertaining; a goth tribute to David Bowie likewise; a Spanish language tribute to the Cure; a Morse code tribute to Kraftwerk.

But really, what is the point? Beyond, of course, further perpetuating the stench of the corpulent carcasses that are most frequently deemed deserving of a new tribute album. Precisely how many collections do we need of largely unknown (or, at best, second division) bands rehashing songs that we are probably sick of hearing, anyway? "Oh goody, half a dozen unsigned electronic eccentrics are recording a tribute to the Bunglebears. I think I'll get the electricity cut off."

Of course, tribute albums do at least allow the guilty tributers the opportunity to make their own mark upon the music of the tributee—even if most of them don't even try. But that goal has always been better left to those artists who have made entire careers from singing other people's songs, and that's everyone from Frank Sinatra to Elvis Presley, from Ringo Starr to Britney Spears.

Ten Great Twenty-First-Century Cover Versions

Death by Chocolate—"My Friend Jack" (The Smoke)
Hausfrauen Experiment—"Spirit of the Age" (Hawkwind)
Ilona V—"The Porpoise Song" (the Monkees)
Leningrad Cowboys—"Kashmir" (Led Zeppelin)
Mordecai Smyth—"Institute of Mental Health, Burning" (Peter Hammill)
Murder by Death—"Moonage Daydream" (David Bowie)
Octopus Syng—"Midsummer's Night Scene" (John's Children)
The Unthanks—"Starless" (King Crimson)
The Use of Ashes—"Set the Control for the Heart of the Sun" (Pink Floyd)
Us and Them—"By the Time It Gets Dark" (Sandy Denny)

For their talent, beyond their spectacular voices and performance style, lies in molding that music to their own personalities . . . to the point where they, too, might some day merit a tribute album. Elvis, at least, already has.

Because the only thing worse than making an utter hash of somebody else's song has to be (drumroll, please) making a version that is absolutely indistinguishable.

If tribute albums are largely humdrum, some tribute acts are astonishingly creative—the all-male Madonna tribute Mandonna, for example, and the all-female AC/DShe. Others received national media attention; a Beatles tribute, the Fab Faux, appeared on David Letterman's late-night show in 2007, and the following year the same host devoted an entire week's worth of guest slots to the likes of Purple Reign, the Cold Hard Cash, Mr. Bronstone, Super Diamond, and the Allstarz, respectively, honoring Prince, Johnny Cash, Guns N' Roses, Neil Diamond, and James Brown.

Others attracted the attention of the acts they were paying tribute to—both Ian Paice and Roger Glover of Deep Purple guested with Purpendicular; and by 2005, the Lynyrd Skynyrd tribute Saturday Night Special could boast more original members of the group than the current lineup of Skynyrd itself. Genesis guitarist Steve Hackett, Pink Floyd drummer Nik Mason, and sundry past members of King Crimson are among those who went even further and formed highly rated tribute bands of their own, Genesis Revisited, a Saucerful of Secrets, and 21st Century Schizoid Men.

And whenever another long-abandoned shambles reforms with just one or two original members playing alongside a host of either thrusting young hopefuls, or their very own offspring, it's very easy to write them off as just another tribute band who forgot to slightly alter their name. The difference is, it's the real tribute bands that will give you the show you wished you'd seen forty years ago.

The ex-members might intend to, but they don't fit the costumes any longer, they've lost the slide show, and they can't reach the high notes. Tribute bands can do all that and more. Indeed, the fact that tribute acts now often appear higher up on a festival billing than the original combo ever managed can only be taken as testament to the pleasure they bring so many people.

So what precisely are they? What creative art should the players really be filed under?

Are they musicians, who have subverted all their own creative urges in order to cast perfect replicas of someone else's talent? Or are they actors whose skill lies in their ability to make the characters they play seem wholly believable?

Or am I completely missing the point? The tribute payers' supporters will certainly say I am, because isn't this what classical music's been doing for the past century or more? How many copies of Beethoven's *Fifth* can anyone need to own?

The difference is . . . you *know* what the difference is. When Beethoven wrote his music (and this applies to almost every other composer whom we now describe as "classical") he wrote only what the musicians were *expected* to play. Rarely was it expressly detailed *how* it should be played. That was left wide open, and deliberately so, to the personal interpretation of the conductor, the musicians, the soloists, whomever.

This is why people have their favorite conductors, in the same way that rock fans have their favorite whatevers. You listen to the orchestra under *this* conductor's baton, and their interpretation of a piece will be radically different to *that* conductor. You listen to *this* featured soloist and their solo will be markedly different to *that*. And so on, until even the sousaphone section in the very back row is playing something ever so subtly novel compared to what you've experienced before.

Tribute acts are the exact opposite. Nothing changes, nothing *can* be changed. If there's a mistake in the drum part midway through a particular recording, they will replicate it—which, in itself, is a talent, because the best mistakes are accidents, and how hard it must be for an accident to be deliberately restaged, not only in itself, but also in the immediate reaction of all around it?

But is slavish devotion all that we require? Whether at its blandest and most manufactured, or wildest and most experimental, popular music is about pushing frontiers, developing, and moving on. And if a genre—and we'll pick on classic rock, because that's where the majority of tribute action takes place—refuses to do that, or worse still, is *unable* to do that, then it's nothing more than a pallid ghost story.

With you in the starring role.

Chapter Nineteen

Named and Shamed—Ten Artists Who Claim They Do Remember the 1960s—or, Oops, There Goes Another Vertebrae

And off we go, out onto the highway looking for a little fun. Perhaps a flatbed truck loaded with human cadavers will explode in front of a Star Trek reunion. One can only dream and hope.

—George Carlin

Nothing gets the blood pounding so wildly as a long-splintered legend announcing that they are reforming. And little gets the blood boiling so much as the discovery that the reunion is, in fact, a mere two original members, accompanied by some wildly inappropriate and often decades younger sidemen, playing a set of old songs together because they (perhaps realistically) don't see the point in writing any new ones.

In and around a debate over the honesty of such outings, and the foolishness of those fans who can now happily claim to have "seen" an act that broke up before they were born, it is worth ruminating, too, on the difference between a functioning outfit writing, recording, and performing their music in the heat of "now," with all the personal and cultural influences that might be brought to bear upon it, and a couple of them reenacting it forty years later, ofttimes with the lyrics taped to the microphone stand.

Because even if the founder members were able to press a big red button on the back of their amplifier and transport themselves back to some halcyon age, there would still be one, two, three players missing, and therefore one, two, three vital components of what made the band a band in the first place.

It's not, after all, just one musician who is being replaced by another. For the band, it's effectively a family member; for the audience, it's someone whose contribution to the band's sound and image, regardless of whether it was headline-worthy or not, is unique. A change in faces almost automatically equates to a change in . . . well, maybe not style, but certainly dynamics.

Which is why so many veteran acts, touring today with a lineup that bears little (if any) resemblance to the original combo, rarely offer anything more than a quickly warmed up greatest hits set—and on the increasingly scarce occasions that they *do* release a new record, the audience goes right on baying for the oldies.

Because given the price of concert tickets these days, every minute wasted playing "and here's another one from our latest album" is literally money out of your pocket. You pay $500 to sit halfway back in a sports arena to see what's left of the Beat Lemurs,[149] you want $500 worth of memories. Not a very expensive encore and two hours spent making excuses—"Well, they're not as young as they used to be. They probably can't sing that high/drum that fast/fit into those costumes any longer."

That's why it's such a crapshoot (with the emphasis firmly on the first word) when some departed darlings of your long-ago youth announce a reunion tour, so "our fans can see us one more time." Because you're *not* seeing them one more time.

In their prime—and we'll stick with the Beat Lemurs here, because they are such a diamond example—the musicians were young, stardom was exciting, society was thrilling, inspiration was rife.

But back together fifty years on, you can see it in their eyes—one of them hoping his hip holds out until the final show; another planning how to invest his share of the money they're making from this outing; a third wondering what is the best time of year to plant Aspidistra. And a fourth who might just be self-aware enough to be feeling a wee bit embarrassed about the entire affair.

It's why hologram concerts are becoming so popular. Why spend however many months either rehearsing, gigging, or arguing contemporary politics with the drummer you have just discovered is a rabid anti-disestablishmentarian, when you can sit at home watching true crime reality shows ("Nigel, the vote is in. You will be executed tomorrow at dawn") and let the replicas do all the work.

---

149. See appendix A: An Index of Wholly Imaginary Artists.

Nobody going to see Matterhorn Slender when they regrouped in 2015, after all, truly believed they were going to see the exact same unit that made all those classic prog albums back in the day, no matter how many original members were sprung from the care home to take their place on the stage.

No, it was five men playing five songs (the Slender never recorded anything less than twenty minutes long), and not even pretending to remember when and why they wrote them in the first place. "Here's a slightly out-of-focus photocopy of a song from our second album. And maybe you all can sing the high notes for me, because I could only just do them in the first place."

There are exceptions. Bands that reconvened for reasons other than cash and nostalgia, who picked up, musically, where they left off, and produced sufficient new music in the twenty-first century that they actually added to their original legend, as opposed to merely topping up the pension account with it.

Ten Reunions That Were Worth Waiting For

(By which we mean, new music that was as good as the old.
Or a new vision that improved on the past.)

The Boomtown Rats (2020)
The Chemistry Set (2010)
The Cult (2006)
The Doctors of Madness (2019)
The Fugs (2017)
King Crimson (2014)
The Slits (2005)
Soft Cell (2002, 2023)
The Specials (2019)
Van der Graaf Generator (2005)

—plus honorary mentions for Sparks and the Stones, who have never actually stopped.

We'll pause here for a moment while you make a list of the ones you can think of, and because there's probably a few, clearly, it's not always a con. Sometimes, a long-sundered lineup (or stubbornly still-going act that you remember from your childhood) *can* transform itself into something wholly different, utterly thrilling, a tale you can tell to the grandchildren. Assuming you can distract them from their Personal Matter Transporters long enough to listen.

Or you might just have discovered another reason to hate vintage music. Because, regardless of its makers' age, what you're now experiencing isn't simply new. It's often superior, as well. Life experience counts, even in the self-proclaimed youthful world of rock'n'roll.

That's what it boils down to in the end. Whether you're spending your money on a tribute band, whose entire *raison d'être* is to recreate, as exactly as possible, the look, the costuming, the stage show, and the sound of the Candlepark Stickmen circa 1968, or the aforementioned octogenarians who used to be Matterhorn Slender, you *may* get the songs, you *may* get the light show, you might even get that brief fission of excitement that you always felt when the intro tape boomed out.

But you are not—and we cannot repeat that word enough—not not not not not not NOT—getting an iota of what you would have seen and

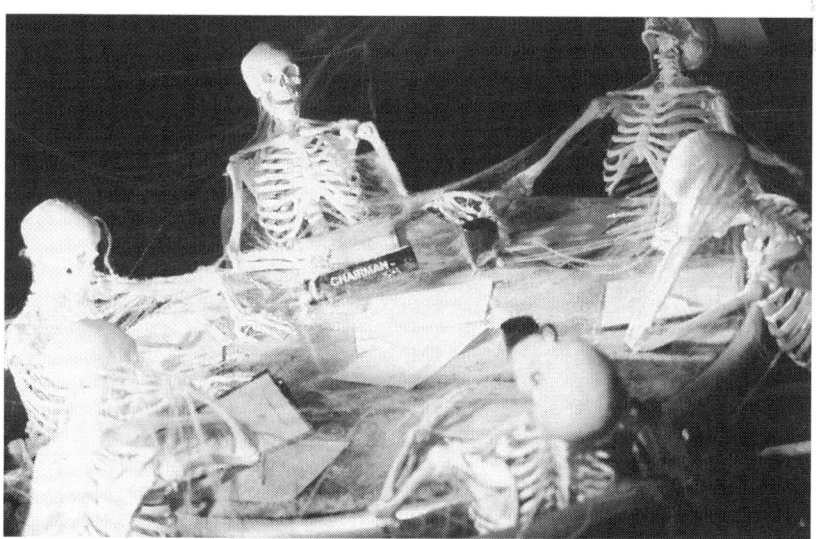

A reformed 1970s band, yesterday. INGRAM PUBLISHING / ALAMY STOCK PHOTO.

heard at the original artists' shows "back in the day" because they are not the same people (which is obvious in the case of the tribute acts, but more of a subjective thing when it comes to original members).

Times have changed, viewpoints have shifted, politics may have twisted. It's only a few years since members of Cat Sandwich were threatening one another with legal action after one of them okayed the use of a song at an antismoking campaign rally, without first ensuring that his bandmates had undergone the same lifestyle conversion as he had. A few months later, though now barely speaking, they were gigging again, and the fans were expected to believe that this was the same tight-knit combo they'd adored half a century before.

So the next time someone comes running up to tell you how great the reformed Nico Teen and the Stains[150] were at Liposuctionpalooza last year, hand them a copy of the band's first live album, taped in a tiny club in 1971, with the blood, sweat, and tears still dripping from the grooves. "That's nice. But I bet they didn't feel like this."

The (all but) final words, however, belong to Charles Dickens, as he wrote in *Little Dorrit* of poor Arthur Clennam's response to meeting again the beautiful girl he had loved and lost twenty-four years before.

"Flora, always tall, had grown to be very broad too, and short of breath; but that was not much. Flora, whom he had left a lily, had become a peony; but that was not much. Flora, who had seemed enchanting in all she said and thought, was diffuse and silly. That was much. Flora, who had been spoiled and artless long ago, was determined to be spoiled and artless now. That was a fatal blow."

Replace Flora with the name of the last reformed band you saw, and then imagine how the group must feel, staring out at the audience. They expect to be greeted, as they always had been, by a sea of fresh-faced youth, starry eyed with devotion and respect.

They receive a room full of people who are the same age as them. And who just happen to be thinking exactly the same thing about the band.

---

150. See appendix A.

Chapter Twenty

The Secret Life of Pants—or, Reviving Vinyl for ~~Fun~~ *Profit* and Profit

The last bar would frequently be prolonged to two or three; and she would sometimes change from C sharp and D, to C natural and D, then warble on these two notes a while, and wind up with a quick chirp on C sharp and D. The distinctness between the semitones was very marked, and easily appreciable to a good ear.

—*Rev. S. Lockwood reviews the song of* Hesperomys cognatus, *the American singing mouse, 1871*[151]

Picture the scene. You're in the schoolyard with your friends. It's 19 ... think of a year. Let's say 1975. And everyone is talking about their favorite pop stars. The Doobie Brothers. The Carpenters. Henry Gross. But you have yet to contribute to the conversation and finally someone asks you. Well?

"Me? I love Eddie Duchin, but Ray Noble's peachy, too. And I have the sheet music to 'Good Ship Lollipop' in my satchel. Would you like to read it?"

It sounds ridiculous. *You* would sound ridiculous. Fifty years have passed since those names were hot ... not even your parents were alive when those records came out.

Today, *apparently*, not so strange. Market research *insists* that teenagers/college students are the biggest market for purchasing new vinyl, while the most recently published sales figures reveal that the biggest selling vinyl releases of the last few years include reissued albums by the Beatles, Fleetwood Mac, and Pink Floyd, and the latest one by ABBA. Names and releases that are themselves fifty (and more) years old.

Therefore—young people *must* be buying old records.

---

151. Quoted in Charles Darwin, *The Descent of Man* (John Murray, 1871).

Yeah. But not for themselves, doofus. When you were a child, what did you give your grandmother for her birthday? Chocolates? Whimsical photo frames? A fragrant spray that was guaranteed to eliminate the smell of boiled cabbage?

Not today. Today's grannies wanna rock. They wore out their copies of *The Wall* while their own offspring were still drawing pictures on one. They exhausted *Tusk* before the little'uns even started to wonder what the title song was really about.[152] And as for *Thriller*, they're of a generation where an artist's work and private life were completely different issues, and their opinion of one has no bearing whatsoever on their opinion of the other. Now, look over there! Shiny new copies of all three!

And before you pooh-pooh that entire idea, Mr. "Looking Good for Sixty-Four," and say there's no grandparent on earth who'd want a pop record for Christmas, take a look at your Endangered Rain Forest wants list and count how many Skull Turnip box sets are listed there.

Besides, if it's young people spending all their money on the oldies, who is purchasing all the new artists' albums? Historically, older generations have always insisted that "young people today have more money than sense," as they reflect upon their own teenaged years of penurious pocket money, a dime a week—and that involved mowing the lawn, washing the car, tidying the bedroom, and creosoting the fence.

But for that single dime, you could attend a gig, buy an album, get drunk on cheap beer, take your significant other to the drive-in, and still have money left over to buy half a bushel of Circus Peanuts.

Not any longer. Given the price of new vinyl today, and the multitude of other must-have purchases that wrestle for the average teen's attention; combined with the fact that music really isn't a must-have purchase any more, at least to the intensity that it once kidded us it was; and, finally, add *that* to the fact that most adult opinions of how young people think are—as they have always been—hopelessly wrong, absurdly skewed, and forever bound up in the bizarre belief that grown-ups know best because . . . what? They start more wars, elect more idiots, and own more novelty dildos than their offspring? Or, as the Liverpool indie band Johnny Boy put it on one of the finest singles of 2006, "You are the Generation That Bought More Shoes and You Get What You Deserve." Whoooopie-doo.

---

152. Erect penises, but you didn't need me to tell you that, did you.

"None of yer new-fangled rock'n roll rubbish here, boys!" Customers at the secondhand gramophone record stall at the flea market in Club Row, Bethnal Green, E1, London, March 1, 1955. TRINITY MIRROR / MIRRORPIX / ALAMY STOCK PHOTO.

Add all those things together and it becomes immediately apparent that . . . just as it always has . . . the market for popular music in 2023 operates to the exact same parameters as it did in 1993, 1983, 1973 . . . 1953, 1923, 1903.

People buy the music they want to buy, and they usually do it on a generational basis. The sixties veterans buy the umpteenth newly remixed reissue of their favorite Dental Assassins albums. The seventies survivors go for Cat Sandwich, the eighties crowd can't get enough Rhubarb, and so forth. Because while market forces can and do influence those purchases as much as they are able, they can't force people to *like* the music as well. In other words, convince me to buy a Granny Massacre Syndrome album once—shame on you. Convince me twice, shame on me.

All of that said, if there is any aspect of the music industry that can claim to have improved beyond all recognition, it is in the marketing of . . . you guessed it . . . the past.

Forget the cultural overkill which engages us elsewhere in these pages. Forget the greasy, leering, patronizing language into which the simple demand "so and so have a new album out. You might want to have a quick listen to it" is now translated.

Forget everything beyond the fact that, if you are a lifelong fan of . . . and we're going to stick with the Dental Assassins, but as always, it could be almost any past-times superstar you like . . . if you're a lifelong fan, you are now living through a golden age of unprecedented bounty.

And why? Because the record companies assume you're going to be dead within the next few decades, and they want to bleed you for as much hard cash as they possibly can in the meantime. Because once your generation is pushing up the daisies, there'll be nobody else they can foist this crap upon.

Ah, but such sweet surrender.

The so-called Vinyl Revival has been one of *the* musical headlines for so long this century that even the cheerleaders are getting a little tired of it. Yes, just like the poltergeists in Tobe Hooper's movie of the same name, vinyl is *baaaaaack*. And not just back in the record stores, and back in the front room after years in your parents' attic; it's back in people's hearts as well, up there alongside internet streaming and the high school hop as *the* principal musical delivery format of the age.

The statistics are definitely remarkable. In early 2016, Forbes.com reported that vinyl records sales in the United States had soared by "an astounding 30 percent" during 2015—the tenth consecutive year of growth for the format. "That figure brought the total number of records sold to just under 12 million [11.92 million to be exact], up from 9.19 million in 2014."[153]

---

153. Hugh McIntyre, "Vinyl Sales Surged 30 Percent in 2015, Led by Adele and Taylor Swift," Forbes.com, January 8, 2016, https://www.forbes.com/sites/hughmcintyre/2016/01/08/vinyl-sales-surged-30-percent-in-2015-led-by-adele-and-taylor-swift/?sh=702725d6d6b4.

Half a decade on, looking back on 2020, the RIAA's annual end-of-year revenue report announced that, even with the coronavirus pandemic raging, vinyl sales had increased by 29.2 percent to $619.6 million, compared to $479.5 million in 2019.[154]

And in early 2023, *Billboard* celebrated "17 Years of Vinyl Growth" with the news that 43.46 million vinyl albums were sold in 2022 (up 4.2 percent from 41.72 million in 2021) . . . the largest year for vinyl album sales since the Luminate data tracking company began keeping tabs in 1991. "Plus, vinyl LP sales posted their single-largest sales week of the

Colorful Characters from Rock's Rich Tapestry No. 6

The Collector

Nothing is good enough for the collector. Tell them the name of your favorite album, they'll demand to know what pressing you have.

Tell them the color of the label, and they'll want to know the relative angle of the labels on either side of the record.

Tell them there's a message scratched in the dead wax, and they'll recommend you send it to a handwriting expert.

Tell them anything whatsoever about the record, and they'll know a version that is of superior value. "Normally I'd lean toward the original Japanese pressing, so long as it was pressed in Yokohama, but in this case, the second Munich, Germany, pressing, with the minuscule (x) 3mm to the left of the copyright information on the label, utilized a 37 percent cleaner stamper, and therefore is the only one to buy, but only if it has the fawn lyric sheet as opposed to the more common tan one, and even then you will need to check the weight of the vinyl . . . Also, make certain that it is still factory sealed."

Then, if you should pass all of these tests, they will ask you what you paid for it, announce that you were seriously ripped off, before carefully studying something on their phone and offering to buy it from you for the same price you paid, to prove that not every rare record hound is a thief.

---

154. Joshua Friedlander, "Year-End 2020 RIAA Revenue Statistics," Recording Industry Association of America, https://www.riaa.com/wp-content/uploads/2021/02/2020-Year-End-Music-Industry-Revenue-Report.pdf.

Luminate era when 2.232 million vinyl albums were sold in the week ending Dec. 22."[155]

No matter that, as the report continued, only half of United States vinyl purchasers actually owned a record player, or that the majority of sales were consumed by the same tiny handful of artists, or even that just eighty-eight different albums sold more than fifty thousand copies on vinyl throughout the past twelve months (up from eighty-seven the previous year). Only fifty-six sold that many on CD.

Regardless of one's feelings about the "vinyl revival," the numbers are impressive, all the more so since they account only for new vinyl sales. Factor in the used market, both on and offline, and who can even guess how many LP records were bought and sold in that one year?

It is more or less precisely forty years since the clanging chimes of doom first rang out for vinyl, tolled by the advent of the compact disc—simple to store, easy to clean, safe to handle—and, apparently, capable of bringing a whole new dimension to the listening experience by virtue of the digital format's ability to preserve an exact accounting of the original recording.

That was the first lie. The format was *capable* of that, for sure. But if you've ever wondered why so many CDs seemed to require successive remastering from this bit-rate to that one, and then to another and another, it's because the technology available in the early 1980s was a lot further from sonic perfection than they ever let on.

The second lie was that you were going to hear the music *exactly* as the artist intended you to. Tinny, tattered, and annoyingly robotic. And what about the presentation? If an artist originally cross-faded songs together, the digital process would insert a gap between each one (the first issue of Queen's *Sheer Heart Attack* is a classic example). If the artist put too many songs on the original album to fit onto a single CD, the reissuing label would simply omit one or two. Usually, the ones they knew could then be applied to the next "best of" collection.[156]

---

155. Keith Caulfield, "U.S. Vinyl Album Sales Rise for 17th Straight Year—But Growth Is Slowing," *Billboard*, January 11, 2023, https://www.billboard.com/pro/vinyl-album-sales-rise-growth-slowing/.

156. At least, this was the cynical response to Stevie Nicks's "Sara" being omitted from the 1987 CD debut of Fleetwood Mac's *Tusk*, only to appear on the following year's *Greatest Hits* CD.

What else? If anything remotely approaching the original master tape was, for whatever reason, unavailable, the CD would be cut from the nearest available alternative, including LPs. (The industry term is "needle drop," but it means the same thing.)

And this is the best one, even if it did take a while to manifest, but if you owned certain CDs manufactured by Philips & Du Pont Optical U.K. Limited (PDO), the clear plastic coating that is intended to protect the CD's digital content proved "unable to withstand the long-term corrosive effects of the sulphur normally found in paper used for CD booklets and inserts."[157] Result—the aluminum oxidized, the laser could no longer read the data, and you were now the proud of owner of a very expensive (CDs weren't cheap in those days, compared to vinyl or cassettes[158]) coaster.

So many disadvantages, so many problems, and so many people didn't care that CD sales soared, vinyl collapsed, and by the end of the 1980s in the United States, and the mid-1990s in Europe, if you wanted to buy a new album (or single), CD was your only choice.

Vinyl did occasionally threaten a fightback of sorts . . . In November 1994, Pearl Jam's *Vitalogy* album was released on vinyl two weeks before its CD counterpart, and immediately breached the top 60. The point being *not* that one of the most eagerly awaited new albums of the year could only debut at no. 55, but that it did so on the strength of a format that was supposedly dead and buried.

It was to no avail. Effectively, the format cleared its desk, packed its belongings in a cardboard box, and skulked out to join all the other forgotten formats of popular culture—wax cylinders, 78s, 8-track cartridges, MiniDiscs, and Pocket Rockers.

A thin trickle of independent vinyl releases and reissues continued to ooze out. By the end of the first decade of the twenty-first century, however, new vinyl accounted for precisely 2,800,000 unit sales in the United States, itself a figure that only reached those heights because of the 2009 reissue of the Beatles' *Abbey Road*, destined to remain the bestselling vinyl record in America for the next four years.

---

157. L. David Lampson, "*CD Bronzing*," Classical.Net, September 1995, http://www.classical.net/music/guide/society/krs/excerpt3.php.

158. Oh, how things change!

But there *was* something going on. In 2011, a million more records were sold in America than in 2010. When 2014 delivered the news that vinyl sales had increased by 260 percent in the past five years,[159] for that aforementioned total in excess of nine million, it was apparent that something was afoot.

How significant was it really, though? In overall terms, vinyl sales still accounted for just 2 percent of total music sales—or, as *Billboard* put it in April 2014, "Vinyl remains a niche part of the market, and no-one is saying the old-school format is the savior of the industry, artists and for entertainment retailers. Consider it a feel-good story in a time when technology and digital streaming models dominate talk on the future of music distribution."[160]

Hard numbers are one thing, however. Anecdote and experience are something else entirely. Keith Jones, whose specialist Fruits de Mer label is one of the collecting sensations of the era (and is stubbornly devoted to vinyl-only releases), told *Goldmine* magazine, "As a vinyl fan, it's got to be good news—amongst all the dull reissues, there are some real gems being released that would otherwise never have seen the light of day.

"Running a small vinyl label, it's tough. The major labels that turned their backs on vinyl are back with a vengeance and they're doing their best to push the small guys to the back of manufacturing and distribution queues that simply didn't exist when we started back in 2008."[161]

Unapologetically, he predicted a day when the current boom becomes a bust, and vinyl—at least as a must-have, must-buy accoutrement to everyday living—falls out of the media spotlight and becomes, again, the province of hardcore collectors, fans, and obsessives. Just like it did in the eighties.

But it hasn't happened yet. True, an awful lot of reissues do seem unnecessary, particularly in those instances where an album is already as common as dirt on the used circuit and can be picked up for a buck or two.

We have to take the bad with the good, however. For every umpteenth go around for the Eclectic Cabbage's debut album, a disc so ubiquitous

159. Lars Brandle, "U.S. Vinyl Album Sales Up by 53% in Q1," *Billboard*, April 17, 2015, https://www.billboard.com/music/music-news/us-vinyl-album-sales-up -by-53-in-q1-6538585/.

160. Brandle, "U.S. Vinyl Album Sales Up by 53% in Q1."

161. Author interview, *Goldmine*, 2015.

that even thrift stores bury them beneath the flowerbed in the parking lot, there are those releases that shine a flashlight into the darkest corners of the archive and occasionally astonish even hardened collectors.

Take mono, for example. For the first fifty years of recorded sound, up to and including the British Invasion era, mono (short for monophonic) was *the* only option for reproduction. It mattered not how many microphones one pointed at the performer, and how many recording machines you had rolling, when it came time to mix the sound together, it would all be crammed into the same little space, as though the entire band/orchestra/whatever was planted smack in the middle of your head.

Experiments in stereo—where the sound could be split into two channels, one for each ear—began in the 1950s, but it was the late 1960s before the music industry as a whole adopted it, a move that coincided with the price of stereo record players (hitherto an expense that was scarcely justified by the number of stereo releases) undergoing a significant drop in price.

Suddenly, it was as if everyone wanted to trade in their once-treasured mono albums and replace them with brand-new stereo ones, and nobody can blame them for that. Who wants to hear their favorite band standing immobile on the spot, when they could be whooshing around every ear they could find, and oh man, you won't believe what it sounds like when you're stoned.

"What, mom's baby aspirin is giving you the collywobbles?"

Suddenly, the used emporiums of the Western world were creaking beneath the weight of so many discarded mono LPs, and the knowledge that many of them, today, comfortably collect three-figure sums when they come up for sale does not change the fact that, at the time, you could buy them used for the price of a new 45.

Today? Today they're pressed on 180-gram vinyl, ofttimes in limited box set editions that serve up the performer's entire catalog at once. No more digging through crates in search of that one elusive, scratched-up nasty. Now—assuming the issuing label didn't cut any corners when pressing the record—you can have it sounding as fresh as it did in nineteen-sixty-whatever. Of course, it takes the fun out of digging through crates, because that's one less treasure you're hoping to find. But no matter. You've got a copy, at last.

Neither is mono alone. Every day, and particularly every Record Store Day, seems to unearth another clutch of albums that sold just a handful in their day and have scarcely been seen outside of museums since then. Now they're just a click away, in pristine, factory-fresh condition.

In fact, we are so double-happy and triple-excited and altogether so breathlessly content that we can barely even sleep at night for imagining what the next treasure to be unlocked might be.

So why is that guy over there looking so glum?

Okay, here's what's wrong with the vinyl revival.

First off, it is inhumanely weighted toward . . . you've got it! . . . vintage music, especially those albums that we could barely wait to throw away when they appeared on CD for the first time.

Yes, new releases are now generally available in both CD and vinyl format and have been since the mid- to late 2010s. But have you ever stopped to think about that quarter of a century's worth of releases that appeared between the final demise of vinyl and its rebirth?

Of the thousands upon thousands of albums dating from the 1990s and 2000s that never felt the pointy kiss of a diamond stylus on their groove,[162] from the most obscure, forgotten indies to the most misjudged of major label signings and onto some of the biggest records of their particular era?

Or even the relatively recent releases that not only don't make it onto vinyl, there's no CD release either. Three years after its release, Paris Jackson's *Wilted*, surely one of the most unexpectedly magnificent albums of 2020, remained stubbornly available only on mp3, almost as though the label (Universal) doesn't actually *want* anyone to own it. And it's not alone.

It would be self-defeating to list every album that someone, somewhere, is still awaiting its vinyl pressing. Any one of them might sneak out at any moment, making a mockery of any specific complaint. But there are online forums that regularly poll their visitors for suggestions of "what album would you most like to see reissued on vinyl?" and once you've waded through the dollar bin regulars that inevitably top the listings, and the RSD exclusives that were pressed in such minuscule

---

162. Contrary to what you may have read in chapter 5, this is not a euphemism.

quantities that the cheapest available online copies are offered at the price of a small car, you'll find a lot of nineties and noughties gems.

Rather than the umpteenth colored vinyl reissue for the overrated mono mix of Swampwitch's second album, how about the jagged glory of Wanda McIntyre's[163] debut?

Yes, it's nice that Lance Corporeal's final words, gasped from her deathbed, included the plea that her former producer remix her second album. (And her third, and her fourth, and her fifth, and so on, until you wonder whether she even had time to actually say goodbye to anyone.) But rather than a twenty-first-century twiddle round a stone cold seventies classic, wouldn't we be better served by a first time pressing for XX the X's[164] still-resonant debut?

And finally, rather than making us wait impatiently for our latest vinyl purchase to arrive, and then wait even longer while the returns process finally unearths a copy that is actually halfway playable, wouldn't it be infinitely cheaper for everyone if new vinyl was pressed and packaged to the same standards than we once took for granted?

From manufacturing defects to mad marketing decisions, the "rebirth" of vinyl remains very much a work in progress. Which would be understandable if it was a brand-new technology, but seems less forgivable being that the humble, long-playing 33rpm album will be three-quarters of a century old in 2025.

And be honest. If an industry hasn't figured out how to make something properly after seventy-five years, is it at all likely that it ever will?

Here's a quick swing through some of the most popular complaints.

1. *How much* did it cost?

Readers of a certain age will remember howling with rage when they discovered that CDs were going to retail at twice the price of the equivalent vinyl. The financial boot is now on the other foot—except that CDs often have twice as much music as their waxen counterpart.

2. Colored vinyl sounds like crap.

"First ever release on a Day-Glo pink swirl margarita-colored picture disc?" Yes, very well done. Very *very* well done. Go you! Now can I have

---

163. See appendix A: An Index of Wholly Imaginary Artists.
164. See appendix A.

a copy that won't sound like the cat has found a paper bag to play in, please?

3. Box sets overkill.

Since when did it become de rigueur to celebrate every conceivable anniversary of an album's release? Twenty-five, thirty, forty, fifty . . . forget the regular reissues and colored vinyl add-ons, there are certain albums that have had so many birthdays now that the least they can do is drive themselves to your house when you buy them. And bring you a slice of cake as well.

That, of course, assumes that you still own a house and haven't mortgaged it in order to keep up with the reissues. All of which you have to own because this one has a surround sound remix, and that one has a bonus disc of B sides, and the latest one has all that, plus that indefinable *something else*.

4. Returns (part one).

As costs soar, standards fall. How many more newly purchased LPs will we need to return before record companies realize they ought to use better quality jackets to prevent the disc from slicing slits into the edges before the buyer has even had the chance to play it?

5. Returns (part two).

And while we're on the subject of quality control, what's with the spindle holes that are too tight to fit the record player's spindle?

6. Returns (part three).

And seriously, if your staff *must* play frisbee with the records they're packing, could you at least ask them to hold them by the edges? I've seen less dabs on a wanted poster than on some of the albums I've bought.

7. Mixed formats.

Another CD box set . . . but wait! It's not *only* CDs!! It's also a *unique* opportunity to pick up matching coasters and a reproduction poster!!! *plus* a *limited edition* half-speed remastered 45rpm *triple vinyl* pressing of a bunch of previously unreleased dodgy outtakes *and* a live recording made in the back row of a crowded venue full of people talking. Well, at least until it's repackaged for some distant Record Store Day.

8. How analogue is it *really*?

It's true, it's not as easy to reproduce music on vinyl as it is on CD. But that's not an excuse not to do it. Simply plopping digital recordings onto vinyl is no more honest than putting a needle drop onto CD. It not only

It's not only vinyl that has been revived. The frailties of the manufacturing process, too, have returned with a vengeance. JASON TONIC.

makes a difference to the sonics, it also negates the purpose of buying the format in the first place. And let's not even get started on "audiophile quality" half-speed remasters taken from the same mp3s that can be downloaded from the net . . .

9. Return of the 8-track.

There is no doubt that an album repressed on 45rpm is going to sound better (not necessarily by a lot, but noticeably) than one pressed at 33. It's also true that converting a single LP into a double, or a double into a triple, will also make a difference to the sonics.

But at what cost?

When Led Zeppelin's *The Song Remains the Same* was expanded thus, the original side-long "Dazed and Confused" suddenly became a side-and-a-half long. Yes folks, it fades out on one side, and then fades in on the other. Just like 8-tracks used to do. And when Bob Dylan's *Desire* was converted to 45 . . . well, remember that thrilling little segue between "Romance in Durango" and "Black Diamond Bay"? Gone. Just like 8-tracks used to do. Which leaves one wondering . . . why not just buy the 8-track?

10. Come upstairs and see my etchings.

Seriously? You really need somebody else to scratch up one side of your latest purchase—and then hand it back to you with all the fanfare of delivering a Picasso to the local art gallery?

If you buy a double album's worth of vinyl (and let's face it, that's what you're paying for), you are not being unreasonable to expect a double album's worth of music. Not three sides of sound, plus a scratchy drawing across side four that you could have done yourself with a ruler and a pointy stick. Or purchased for a fraction of the price from one of those online dealers who sell "near mint" albums that, upon receipt, look like they've spent the last five years in the bottom of a bird cage.

Chapter Twenty-One

We'll Fix It in the Mix— or, Fifty Years Later

My brain burns with hate of you.
I am like a green field swept by scorching wind,
Everything withers.
There is nothing left of promise . . .

—Anna Wickham (1883–1947), Paradox

In one of the final interviews before his passing, in 2016, Greg Lake told *Goldmine* magazine what he really thought about the recent remastering of Emerson, Lake & Palmer's back catalog for what even he agreed was the "umpteenth" time.

"How I feel about it is this. If you take a photograph of a master oil painting, in a way it could be said that some photographs would actually enhance the picture. But others would say it's not original, it's not the way it's meant to be, and it gives a false impression.

"Of course, I produced the original music, but I didn't want to do the remastering myself. Why would I? I gave it everything I had at the time, and I think that was my version of those recordings. I frankly wouldn't have changed an awful lot, because if I'd wanted to, I would have done it back at the time. I acknowledge certain things, with pro-tools you can manipulate, and it's better perhaps, but part of the magic of those original records was, in a way, their imperfections—as it is with all art. Fidelity is not the last word in artistic quality; if you listen to old Motown records, the sound is often dreadful, but the spirit is magnificent."[165]

He was not alone among "classic rock" virtuosos in having a less than positive impression of the art of remastering vintage records . . . or worse.

In October 2022, British producer Mike Batt revealed that he had physically destroyed a number of his original master tapes for one reason

---

165. Author interview, "Greg Lake Discusses the Magic of ELP," *Goldmine*, December 14, 2016, https://www.goldminemag.com/articles/greg-lake-discusses-magic-elp.

only. "I mixed them as I wanted them, not how some corporation or great-grandchild might like to remix them when I'm not around."[166]

In many ways, it was a hollow gesture. Technology has already (or probably will shortly) reached the stage whereby a third-generation mono cassette tape can be remixed into 5.1 surround sound, if only the operator knows which buttons to push. At which point, who will even remember what a master tape was?

If the destruction proves ultimately fruitless in real terms, however, the spirit behind the destruction can only be praised . . . even worshipped. It slaps a massive, neon-lit HANDS OFF across the entire Batt catalog, and if there is a deathly curse attached, too—*abandon hope all ye who fuck with my bass lines*—then all the better.

Sadly, as modern tech advances, and modern media companies search for ever more ruthless methods of ultra-monetizing their back pages, it is more likely that it's the acts whose albums *don't* get remixed who will be left out in the cold. And new artists, too.

It's a little like those grocery items that you've been buying for years, only to one day walk into the supermarket to discover they've doubled in price but have been slapped with a label that screams "new and improved! 50 percent more damp and cloying." But in those instances, it's often true, and the only question is, why didn't they do this in the first place?

Take the same practice into the music marketplace, however, and you cannot help but wonder why anyone would spend their money now on the latest album by nine-time *American Icon* winner Jeff Rotull,[167] when they know if they hang on for a few more decades, there'll be a far superior remix of the same record, and it might even be on colored vinyl.

Seriously. If you'd known that one day five (and counting) of the Eclectic Cabbage's LPs would be reenvisioned by their original producer's son-in-law's first cousin, with artificial intelligence employed to separate individual instruments that were originally simply squished together, just think of how much money you could have saved on . . . well, let's see. Your initial 8-track cartridge. Three or four copies of the vinyl as you wore each one out. The original CD, the better-sounding CD, the remastered

166. Ali Shutler, "Wombles Songwriter Destroys Master Tapes to Avoid the Beatles-Style Remasters," *New Musical Express,* October 10, 2022.

167. See appendix A: An Index of Wholly Imaginary Artists.

The Wombles are just one of the musical supergroups whose master tapes have been destroyed to prevent their being remixed by future generations.
PICTORIAL PRESS LTD. / ALAMY STOCK PHOTO.

CD, the re-remastered CD—and where are they now? All of them gathering dust, rendered utterly irrelevant by twenty-first-century tech.

Which itself, as Beatles remixer Giles Martin told *Variety* magazine, ensures that "when people hear the Beatles . . . it has the same dynamic as the other stuff they're listening to."[168]

But wait! you scream. Do you need to hear the Beatles sharing "the same dynamic" as Billie Eilish and Dua Lipa? Even once?

Probably not, which is why supporters of such shenanigans will hasten to remind you that your original copies are still there to be enjoyed. The remixes and remasters do not *replace* the original album; they complement it and give you an alternate way of listening to the music you know so well. They bring out fresh dimensions and hidden passageways, reemphasizing one thing and de-echoing another. Like walking to a different window in the house and looking out at your garden. Or reading your favorite novel into a mid-1990s speech recognition system and then rereading the printout in a funny voice.

Of course, remixing is one of the oldest tricks on the audio block, at least for as long as it has actually been physically possible. The offspring

---

168. Chris Willman, "Giles Martin Details Beatles' 'Revolve' Deluxe Edition and Remix: In 1966 Sessions, 'You Can Hear Them Unwrapping Their Presents,'" *Variety*, September 7, 2022.

of the marriage between magnetic tape and multitrack recording, which takes us back to the 1950s, the process came into its own during the early 1960s, at a time when the majority of pop artists were still recording in mono, but a growing number of music fans were investing in stereo sound systems.

The earliest attempts to meet this market were less than perfect. As we have already remarked, every new British Invasion album would be delivered to its US label as a mono master. Engineers would then be tasked with creating what the record sleeve proudly proclaimed to be "simulated stereo," a halfway house between true mono and actual stereo, most frequently effected by planting the vocals in one channel and the rest of the performance in the other.

But time passed, technology improved, and more studios acquired stereo recording equipment, until 1967, when the American music industry as a whole decided to abandon mono releases altogether (except for radio purposes) and issue everything in stereo instead. Only to consider beginning the process again, around four years later, when quadraphonic sound enjoyed its brief span in the sun. And again when the twelve-inch single came along around the mid-1970s, and audiences demanded more than the same three minutes for their twice-the-price purchase. And again when . . . and so on.

Until we reach the present day when each of those intermediary steps between "then" and "now" is ripe for reissue and people who seriously *couldn't wait* to dump all their original mono albums and replace them with stereo; or sold off their quad LPs when it became apparent that four ears were not the next step in human evolution; or gave up on disco dancing when the first verrucas appeared. They are all now meteor-like in their haste to be first in line to buy the Foxy and the Redcoats *Mono Masters* collection, or the Cat Sandwich quad box, "because this is how the band intended the music to sound." Huh.

That all of these formats are ultimately just another means of separating collectors from their cash is confirmed by the knowledge that even the best "super deluxe" editions of today will, at some point, be superseded by the "super-duper" edition, and that too will survive only until someone else comes along—the current producer's gardener's brother, for example—and decides they can do it even better. Until finally, but certainly within the lifetime of at least some of this book's readers, there'll be the Ultimate Remix by Some Distant Descendent, which recreates the experience of listening to every classic disc of the sixties on the portable battery-operated record players of the day, and the faithful will champion its radical retro authenticity. Or some such nonsense.

It is, perhaps, important to halt here and point out that remixing, which is the devil's own work, is very different to remastering. In remixing, every note and every instrument on the recording can be . . . shall we say, messed with? Or shall we be mature and say "manipulated"? Your choice. Remastering, on the other hand, takes the recording as a whole and, without interfering with its component parts, gives it the aural equivalent of a nice hot bath. Which occasionally becomes a mud bath, but we will get to that in a moment.

There are a number of reasons for doing this, ranging from the replacement of an existing and perhaps worn or damaged master tape, to fiddling with the frequencies to make the music sound better on whichever media it is intended for. When vinyl gave way to CD in the 1980s, a lot of early releases *weren't* remastered, and can now be lined up on a shelf to laugh uproariously at, as we recall again the new medium's claim to offer superior sound. A lot of them were markedly inferior.

But record companies caught on, and as the capabilities and specifications of both CD and the attendant technology improved, so fresh masters were created, each one offering purchasers a new listening experience, whether it was actually noticeable or not.

There were calumnies, of course, most notably revolving around what are remembered today as "the loudness wars," whereby such impressive-sounding techniques as "dynamic range compression" and "equalization" would be slapped onto a hapless recording to increase its overall volume—at the same time, although they hoped nobody would notice, upping the distortion and the beheading (the technical term is "clipping," but the effect was the same) of the loudest bits in the process.[169]

Overall, however, the industry has been merrily remastering away for years, and when vinyl commenced its comeback in the mid-2010s, there was a whole new palette to play on, even if it did—in the case of so many

---

169. Metallica's 2008 *Death Magnetic* album is the poster child for this process, an album that was *so* heavily manipulated that even people who *don't* think "unlistenable" is Metallica's default position keep well away from it. A version of the album that had not been put through the process was later offered as a free download with the game *Guitar Hero III*. It is, apparently, infinitely preferable.

albums—effectively mean putting everything back to how it sounded in the first place. Except it didn't, because it's a lot quicker, cheaper, and easier to start the process with a digital source, regardless of whether an original analog master exists.

Which can lead to problems.

Colorful Characters from Rock's Rich Tapestry No. 7

The Embittered Critic

The Embittered Critic hates every record made after 1980, and every musician born after 1949. They have interviewed every significant artist of the classic rock era, and every one of them has more talent in a toenail than the past forty years of slop combined could hope to muster. They also have affectionate nicknames for almost every person, place, and drug of note that they have ever encountered.

"I remember sharing a jahoobie with the Bobster and Jimbo right before the Zeppers went onstage at Maddysquared in '73. Kayo and the Lipkid were there, too; they wanted me to hit the studio after the show, to see what I made of their new album. I told them I couldn't make it, so they scrapped the whole thing. Three years of work down the drain, but they knew better than to fuck with the Big I Am."

Their wardrobe comprises eight T-shirts, each an original souvenir of the most crucial concerts in musical history, but they are most often sighted in the one depicting a young man holding an open condom packet and announcing, "worst-tasting bubblegum I've ever had." Apparently, this was considered quite risqué around the office in 1973.

The Embittered Critic does not own any CDs or mp3s, and will argue vehemently that even a scratched and warped, unlistenable "original pressing" sounds better than anything digital sound has yet mustered. They have spent much of the last forty years promising to write a memoir, but claim their lawyers suggested waiting until absolutely everybody mentioned therein is dead, because the story is so sensational.

In truth, unless one has a top-end stereo system, it can be difficult to distinguish between a digital and analog source, especially if one is relying upon something more subjective than the gut feeling in your ears which insists it *can* tell the difference.

Claims that the sound of analog vinyl is warmer, softer, and gentler than its digital counterpart are surely more applicable to a washing powder commercial than a scientific debate over the sonic qualities of a reissue of the third Skull Turnip album. But vinyl possesses a lot of practical advantages, too. Fewer moving parts, fewer nooks and crannies—*plus*, you can watch your music while you listen.

Never trust a medium that hides away while it plays.

But without twisting one's tongue around an entire new technological vocabulary that you are unlikely to employ more than once or twice in your entire life, there are few better ways of putting it.

The curious thing is, there are just as many people who insist that the opposite is true; that CDs offer the most rewarding listening experience. Just as there are those who can sit through the most highly regarded audiophile pressing of Rocky Biceps's greatest hits before declaring that the bootleg 8-track cartridge that their uncle bought at a truck stop in Wisconsin has a more atmospheric and authentic feel.[170]

Either way, it's an argument that, ultimately, nobody can win. He says tomato, she says cauliflower. The only thing the vinyl revival has really succeeded in doing is allow people the opportunity to choose which format they prefer to listen to (because cassettes are allegedly coming back as well) and, hopefully, find the music they want in that format as well.

Except, of course, when the decision is made for them and they end up paying xx times the amount any release is worth, because they're effectively buying umpteen different versions of it in the latest super deluxe box set edition. Here's the music on CD; here it is again on DVD, and here it is yet again on Blu-ray. And just because we love you so much, here it is on vinyl.

Yeah, but I only wanted it for the download card.

---

170. The weird thing is, they might be correct. Deeply unfashionable and hopelessly moribund they might be, but in terms of sonic reproduction, the 8-track is second only to the reel-to-reel tape in terms of reproductive potential. Unfortunately, that is balanced by the fact that they are also highly unreliable and prone to some startlingly imaginative methods of self-destruction.

Chapter Twenty-Two

Twenty Totally Tubular Hits of the 1980s—or, The Wrong Box

Rock and roll might be summed up as monotony tinged with hysteria.

—*Vance Packard*

Box sets are the luxury items of the music industry.

Wander into any well-provisioned record store and you can all but hear the shelving groan beneath the burden of so many boxes, leviathans of sound that might take a day (or longer) to listen through completely and are additionally burdened with sufficient reading material to see you through the entire experience. And so commonplace are these musical treasure troves that it's hard to believe there was ever a time when fans could only dream of such bounty.

But track back to the days when vinyl was *the* primary medium for music and it was a very different picture. A box set release was a major event, be it a collection of an artist's regular albums bound together for a premium price or a specialist celebration for a less-feted star.

Decades before the late Nick Drake was "discovered" on the back of a Volkswagen commercial, for example, he was honored with a box containing almost everything he recorded, and his fans could not have been happier. The few that there were, back then.

There was a Beatles box that rounded up all their albums close to thirty years before another Beatles box that rounded up all their albums. And there were all those fabulous Reader's Digest and Time Life box sets that you can find for mere pennies in any used store in the country, that not only overflowed with "great hits of the fifties (or whatever)," they also allowed you to spread the cost over four monthly installments. Unless, for some reason, you were a certain type of fish.[171]

---

171. Or was I the only viewer who didn't know COD stood for "cash on delivery"?

The advent of the compact disc flushed this history down the drain. For many people, including those who should know better, the first "modern" box set was Bob Dylan's 1985 *Biograph*, a generous package that mixed familiar hits with a clutch of rarities and set the gold standard to which all subsequent boxes needed to aspire, from Led Zeppelin's eponymous 1990 assemblage, to a full accounting of the 1972 Wattstax Festival, spread across twelve CDs (or ten LPs) in 2023.

There were no gimmicks here. For the Dylan box, its release on the still-infant CD format was novelty enough; for Zeppelin, people seemed satisfied with Jimmy Page's assurance that it offered fans the chance to hear the songs in different order.

Others followed, and understandably so. In purely practical terms, the compact disc is the natural home for such packages, and much as fans might dream of a vinyl equivalent of, say, Matterhorn Slender's thirty-four CD *The Complete Mellotron Tune-up Sessions*, it would be both prohibitively costly and impractically heavy—you'd need a forklift truck just to carry it across the room.

In fact, even if we disregard the actual physical format, these packages are things of beauty, greedily anticipated from the moment they're announced, endlessly discussed as the release date approaches, and you know when the first copies reach their purchasers because the internet is suddenly flooded with videos of the boxes (or even single LPs!) being opened, while the proud owner solemnly raises whatever is inside to the camera and portentously informs us what it is.[172]

"Behold. A CD."

And what do collectors do after that? They bitch. If "this" mix of a song is included on the rarities disc, they want "that" one. If this version of an unreleased outtake is featured, they would have much preferred "the other."

Every time a new anthology appears, no matter how thorough it might appear to be, or how specifically its remit is stated, out comes the expert to bemoan the absence of something . . . or even a whole heap of somethings. For Beatles fans, it's "Carnival of Light," a sound experiment that Paul McCartney recorded in 1967, and has kept under lock and key

---

172. Truly, it's astonishing how many people will sit quietly and watch as someone opens up an entire box set. Especially the ones where the camera is situated in such a way that it's impossible to see half of what they're talking about.

ever since. For Stones fans, it's "English Summer," allegedly recorded the year before. For Lance Corporeal fans, it's the demos for the album that she abandoned in 1997 after discovering there was a new species of trip hop she wanted to have a go at.

When Rocky Biceps's *Mono Muscles* box was released a few years back, compiling eighteen albums worth of his original UK singles, B sides, and LPs, the die-hards were upset that his US albums weren't included.

When Foxy and the Redcoats offered a similar gesture several years later, but added the US albums too, people demanded to know why no outtakes were added. But when the band *did* release an outtakes collection, the moaners insisted that the completely wrong songs had been included.

Eighteen LPs plus a generous hardback book and a 40-pound monogrammed barbell ensured purchasers of Rocky Biceps's Mono Muscles box set needed to be fairly fit simply to pick it up. AUTHOR'S COLLECTION.

And all the people who bemoaned the absence of any fun little extras in the early CD box sets . . . they now bemoan their inclusion. Some people just like to complain.

They are disgusted that the box set should insist they buy the music on four different formats as opposed to the one they will actually play. They complain that the modern remix, so painstakingly created by ace-remixer "Twitch" McAllister,[173] either doesn't sound the same as the familiar disc, or otherwise that it does, while also trumpeting their belief that most modern record companies couldn't give a hoot for what the remix actually sounds like because it's just another way of "relaunching" an album whose day passed decades ago by making people believe they're getting something new, as opposed to an irrelevant bauble that they'll play once and then discard because it doesn't have half the charm of the original.

"But you can hear the extra drum pattern that was mixed out of the original." "So fucking what?"

So let's pick holes in one. Or make an unboxing video about it. We won't name it, of course . . . it really doesn't matter. Ultimately, they all contain the same old gubbins in the end.

Here's the original stereo album, lovingly postproduced using modern technology to achieve what the band envisioned all those years ago, utilizing the . . . let's say it's the original master tapes, although it might be a digital copy of them, or it might be some other format altogether. But it's definitely the best quality source we could find. Probably.

Here it is again in mono.

Here's a disc full of previously unreleased outtakes and demos that we certainly did not download from the internet, even though there's absolutely no difference in the quality of the ones you can find for free.

Here's a live recording from the legendary performance blah blah blah, and ditto. We don't even know how to download music from the internet. Plus, it's illegal.

Here's an exclusive-until-next–Record Store Day surround sound remix by "Twitch" McAllister's cousin.

---

173. See appendix A: An Index of Wholly Imaginary Artists.

Here's a hardback book full of photographs and the memories of people who were thereabouts at the time and an essay by a rock critic who wasn't. Here's some photocopied press clippings. Here's the Wikipedia entry with all the funny bits stripped out.

Here's a replica sticker/concert ticket/ephemeral goodie that definitely does not constitute "additional tat to up the price," and cannot in any way be compared to the marbles that Pink Floyd once gave away.[174]

Here's a replica 45 in the seldom-seen picture sleeve prepared for the record's release in a country that doesn't exist any longer.

Here's a poster, personally auto-signed[175] *by the surviving members of the band.*

Here's a big box to keep everything together.[176] *And here's a bill for whatever three figure sum we think you'll be willing to pay.*

Which all looks and feels so callow when it's written down like that, especially in that tone of voice. One man's locust, after all, is another man's grasshopper, and besides, if all the little extras offend you that much, you can always throw them away or donate them to charity.

But no, you won't do that because one day you might want to sell the box set and you need to keep it complete. Just in case. Perhaps you ought to buy two copies while you can still pick them up at retail price, one to reduce to ashes with your withering scorn, and one to store in a hermetically sealed, temperature-controlled vault.

The fact is, people *like* the little extras. They transform what is, after all, the fairly boring routine of opening the box and saying, "Oh look, here's a record" over and over again, into a tactile experience, as a veritable

---

174. In fact, they gave them away three times, with the Immersion box sets for the albums *Dark Side of the Moon*, *Wish You Were Here*, and *The Wall*.

175. Forged celebrity autographs have long been the bane of collectors the world over. In 2022, we learned that automated signatures are likewise despised, as nine hundred fans dropped $599 apiece on allegedly "autographed" copies of Bob Dylan's *Philosophy of Modern Song*, only to discover that the signee had utilized a mechanical autopen, which stored his original signature and then repeated it across the full run. He had, he said, been assured that "this kind of thing is done 'all the time' in the art and literary worlds," but now saw his mistake. "Using a machine was an error in judgment and I want to rectify it immediately." One to remember for the future . . . the federal government will accept an electronic signature. Autograph collectors will not.

176. Which ought to be a no-brainer, but you'd be surprised. When David Bowie's estate released half a dozen live albums in 2020–2021, the accompanying box was sold separately to the music.

treasure chest of oddities spills out. "Oh, look, here's one of those talking fish wall hanging things that sings the chorus to the first hit."

It's funny, too, because people didn't use to complain when, for example, Pink Floyd packed the original *Dark Side of the Moon* with a pair of posters and a couple of stickers, or Paul McCartney's Wings followed suit for *Venus and Mars*. They didn't go "bleaugh" when the Raspberries came out with a strawberry-scented scratch and sniff cover, or the Tom Robinson Band's debut album gave away a cardboard stencil of the band's logo, complete with the warning that you were not to use it to deface public places.

Some people even liked the idea that purchasing a copy of Manfred Mann's Earth Band's *The Good Earth* album granted them ownership of one square foot of land in Llanerchyrfa in Wales.[177]

Yes, they were gimmicks, but gimmicks are fun! They add to the excitement of opening a new album, and if you don't want to use them in the fashion they're intended for—hang the posters, stick the stickers, play with the marbles, deface public places—that's entirely your prerogative.

Just like you didn't *have* to buy multiple copies of Led Zeppelin's *In Through the Out Door* to collect all the sleeve variations, and you didn't *need* to tour a dozen record stores in search of the Rolling Stones' *Their Satanic Majesties Request* with a lenticular sleeve. Goodness, you weren't even compelled at bayonet-point to purchase four copies of Taylor Swift's *Midnights*, simply so you could complete the clock on the back cover.

But if you did . . . good for you. It means you remember what being a fan is all about, and what loving music is all about, as well. Let's hope you're still around to celebrate when *her* career-spanning box set comes out. On CD, cassette, *and* limited edition vinyl for the Record Store Day crowd.

---

177. This is true.

Chapter Twenty-Three

First Time Ever in Limited Edition "Distressed" (Scratchy Warped) Dirty Off-Black Vinyl—or, In Praise of Rip-Off Store Day

Protest is when I say I don't like this. Resistance is when I put an end to what I don't like. Protest is when I say I refuse to go along with this anymore. Resistance is when I make sure everybody else stops going along too.

—Ulrike Meinhof (1934–1976)

It may or may not irradiate the cockles of your heart with glee, but wherever you are, whatever time of year it is, you are never more than six months away from Record Store Day. And you can say what you like about the event itself (seriously, go ahead; we'll wait), but there is no doubt that it has utterly revolutionized the way we collect records in the twenty-first century. And not only because, for the first time in history, it is now possible to drop over $100 on three old LPs and still feel like bragging about it on social media.

For more than fifteen years now, and twice a year latterly, Record Store Day (RSD) is the one (two) day(s) on the calendar when even the most impoverished musical emporium can guarantee a full house.

The one (two) occasion(s) upon which people who might never have set foot in the shop for six months will have been lined up outside since early o'clock, with their wants list in one hand, their wallet in the other, and elbows sharpened to a lethal point in case fellow shoppers don't get out of the way fast enough. Just as their patience will have been honed to a heavy blunt bludgeon after standing in the rain through the coldest night of the year, in the hope that there will still be a copy of the Scam

E-mails,[178] *Live at Whoopsadaisy Funfest 1994* earwax-flavored triple vinyl limited edition.

And all they wanna do is spend, spend, spend.

It's so easy to criticize, isn't it? "Ah, it's just an excuse for the major labels to rip us off," is a common complaint. "Too much product" is another. Or even, "The little labels have all been squeezed out." All of which you will read on the forums before the latest releases have even been announced. Usually contributed, incidentally, by people whose entire wants list comprise major label rip-offs; who are upset that there aren't more releases for them to crave; and who wouldn't know a "little label" if one opened for business in their backyard.

Privately produced Record Store Day posters are sometimes the best thing about the entire day! ART BY BRAD ALMOND, COURTESY RAINBOW RECORDS, NEWARK, DE.

178. See appendix A: An Index of Wholly Imaginary Artists.

True, those are also points that are worth considering. The problem is, they miss the biggest point of all. Record Store Day was designed to breathe life back into the mom-and-pop bricks-and-mortar stores that, back in 2008, were literally an endangered species.

Compact discs, mp3s, piracy, streaming, rapacious landlords, and a veritable shoal of associated vampire squid were gathered on every corner, all with just one aim in mind. "See that store? Shut it."

They appeared to be succeeding, too.

Then Record Store Day came galloping into town, and all it took to save the day were a few dozen slices of brightly colored vinyl, a bunch of 45s by ensembles you've never heard of, and a box set of a label that died before the dinosaurs.

Or, to put it another way, row upon row of major artist archive releases, produced in limited edition quantities that will never satisfy everybody who might want one. Especially if they're shaped like bananas the color of mud, smell like marshmallows, and are packaged in a sleeve partially manufactured from the lead singer's pulped toenail clippings.

With hindsight, the very idea of RSD was genius in its simplicity. By persuading labels and artists to create limited edition releases that would only be available on one single day of the year, it would persuade fans and collectors to arrive early and spend big.

In fact, it's a misnomer that RSD was ever *all* about the indie labels. They've always maintained a presence in the listings, but even at the start, with just ten releases in the maiden 2008 schedule, REM, Stephen Malkmus, and Vampire Weekend were scarcely hapless obscurities. The following year, fellow non-struggling non-bottom-feeders Leonard Cohen, Tom Waits, Bob Dylan, Slayer, and the Stooges were on display.

So what if the major labels treat RSD like several Christmases rolled into one? It just means more exposure (and cash) for the shops that sell their wares, and more muscle for the artists that we're supposed to be adoring. It's no coincidence whatsoever that the vinyl "boom" of the last few years coincides almost precisely with the rise of Record Store Day.

Plus, it would be a bitter soul indeed who does not feel at least a soupçon of excitement when the latest list is published, and six months of "what's coming next time" speculation are finally laid to rest. Usually by the stomach-sinking thud of disappointment and anticlimax, but there's always *something* that *might* be interesting. Several somethings, in fact.

Allegedly featuring former members of Free + REO Speedwagon–Joe Cocker + Cat Stevens + Mountain + The Alan Parsons Project + Blood Sweat & Tears + Three Dog Night + Bryan Adams + Foo Fighters + Manfred Mann + Red Hot Chili Peppers + Asia + UFO + Bon Jovi + The James Gang + J Geils Band + Blue Cheer + Oasis + Mötley Crüe + Uriah Heep + Cheap Trick + The Strawbs + Tommy James and the Shondells + John Mellencamp + Taste + Frankie Valli & the * Seasons + Television + Edgar Winter Group + Toto + Stray Cats–Sly & The Family Stone + Supertramp + The Beastie Boys + Green Day + Queensryche + Kansas– Roxy Music + Steppenwolf + The Black Crowes + Bachman Turner Overdrive + Alan Parsons Project + Soundgarden + Rage Against The Machine + Traffic + Dire Straits + Dave Matthews Band + The Hollies + Alice In Chains + Bill Haley and the Comets + Iron Butterfly + Jeff Beck Group + Thin Lizzy + The Cars + Humble Pie + Charlie Daniels Band + Judas Priest + Styx + The Spencer Davis Group + The Yardbirds + The Amboy Dukes + The Scorpions + Big Brother & the Holding Company + The Guess Who + The Band + The Tragically Hip + The Young Rascals + Journey + The Byrds + The Moody Blues + Marshall Tucker Band + Electric Light Orchestra + The Pretenders + Iggy Pop and The Stooges * Talking Heads + Radiohead + Grand Funk Railroad + ZZ Top–Iron Maiden + Pearl Jam + Metallica + Supertramp + Blue Oyster Cult + Foghat + Crosby, Stills, Nash & Young + Guns N' Roses + Santana + Steve Miller Band + Foreigner + Heart + Fleetwood Mac + The Clash + Deep Purple + Kiss + Cream + Boston + Bad Company + Jefferson Airplane + Def Leppard + * Rush + Chicago + King Crimson + The Beach Boys + Bob Seger + The Doobie Brothers + Genesis–The Police + Steely Dan + Tom Petty & the Heartbreakers + The Eagles + Emerson Lake & Palmer + Jethro Tull + Creedence Clearwater Revival + Lynyrd Skynyrd– + AC/DC + The Doors + Metallica + U2 + Van Halen + Yes * Queen + Aerosmith + The Grateful Dead + The Allman Brothers Band * The Who + Pink Floyd + The Rolling Stones + Led Zeppelin

Incredibly, the debut album by supergroup Harris-Ingman-Thomas-Smith was on the eve of release before anybody questioned the band's first choice of acronym. Restored for a 2019 RSD release, the album sold out immediately.
AUTHOR'S COLLECTION.

Now, you're probably wondering why, if RSD is such a great thing, it is included in a book devoted to hating vintage music, when it clearly pisses off so many vintage music lovers—"why would anyone spend $20 on a Jeff Rotull single when for $150 they could buy a box full of unreleased Beat Lemurs rehearsals?"

Well, (a) because it perpetuates the legend that Beat Lemurs rehearsals are something everybody needs to experience at least once in their life— when, in reality, you are unlikely to play through side one; (b) because producing those boxes (and all the others like it) makes such demands on the vinyl pressing plants of the world that anybody hoping to release something "new" needs to delay their projected release date by months, if not eons;[179] and (c) because there are so many caveats, from both the

---

179. The situation grew so bad that Metallica, in 2023, purchased a plant of their own, Furnace Record Pressing in Alexandria, Virginia.

store owner's point of view and the individual consumer's. Did you know, for example, that stores cannot pick and choose between the offered releases, beyond offering up a hopeful wish list? They receive what they are sent, which is why a lot of people spend almost as long online that evening as they did in line outside the store that morning, looking for the records that their local store wasn't sent. (Or were received in such minute quantities that they'd already been snapped up.)

Did you know that because some releases are a lot more attractive on paper than when they are placed in the store, many stores get stuck with a shelf full of unsaleable junk? But can they return the records that don't move? Are they permitted to sell their unsold stock online? Will no one relieve them of these troublesome platters?

No, no, and, barring consignment to the bargain bin, no.

How about the dealers who *lose* money from RSD? What about the rumors of stores that were actually forced out of business by those losses? What about accusations that the very definition of "independent" record stores seems to have grown ever foggier as RSD has grown bigger? Or that a store in a major market will probably receive more hot ticket items than one in a smaller town?

Well, they're just rumors and tales and accusations, aren't they? And besides, when the stars align, and retailer and customer alike are smiling, Record Store Day is the major labels' answer to dumpster diving, tossing out those treasures that would never, ever have seen the business end of a conventional release because the accountants would never permit it. But bang them out as limited editions, at a higher price than retail could ever normally withstand; round up a captive audience whose only reason for being is to flash some cash . . . now that makes sense for everyone. Allegedly.

What is refreshing, and encouraging, too, is to note that, according to the Discogs record trading marketplace, of the twenty most coveted Record Store Day releases of all time, the vast majority involve artists whose careers began in the twenty-first century, with Green Day and White Stripes making up the remainder.

No wonder the politer queue-ers usually permit granddad to jump in line ahead of them. No way will he want the records that they're after.

Chapter Twenty-Four

The Sound of Tomorrow's Yesterdays Today—or, The Wonder of Eurovision

We have arrived at our own endless present, or Year Zero, where the record, historical and otherwise, is readily falsified.

—Simon Heffer, Daily Telegraph, *February 22, 2023*

The other thing about classic rock, beyond being predominantly white, predominantly male, blah blah blah, is that it was predominantly Anglo-American. No matter that rock'n'roll, by the early 1970s, had spread to every corner of the planet, battling both cultural and political prejudices and prohibitions as it did so. There was American rock, there was British rock, there was a little Canadian rock, the teensiest smidgeon of Australian rock . . . and there was all the other stuff.

A handful of "foreign" acts did occasionally break the barrier. Shocking Blue, Golden Earring, and Focus all imported a taste of the Netherlands to the *Billboard* charts in the early 1970s, with journalists and DJs so dedicated to reminding people of their origins that there might still be people out there who think every group from that country prefaces their name with "The Dutch Band . . ."

German attempts to break the monotony . . . Kraftwerk, Tangerine Dream, Nektar (they were actually English but were based in Germany), and Amon Düül 2 . . . were uniformly described as "Krautrockers" and generally confined to the novelty box, even when (Kraftwerk's "Autobahn," for example) they were in the process of scoring a major hit single.

And then there was the Eurovision Song Contest, an annual gathering that determined which country had the greatest song, and which was possibly the biggest laughing stock of all.

Launched in 1956, the annual quest to find a Song for Europe was born of the same spirit of well-intentioned idealism that simultaneously spawned the European Community (for the best countries on the continent) and soccer's European Cup (for the best teams).

It was pure schlock, a succession of weepy ballads, chirpy ballads, lively ballads, boring ballads. The Swiss won the first competition; the Dutch and the French shared the next four between them; and it would be a full eleven years before any performer remembered by the Anglophone audience walked off with the coveted Grand Prix—barefoot English songstress Sandy Shaw, whose "Puppet on a String" not only beat the best the continent could throw at it, it also set the musical precedent for which Eurovision would be forever renowned.

Given the wide range of styles, fashions, and cultures arrayed in Europe, the idea of one song actually being the "best" is a preposterous one. A brilliant Bavarian oom-pah number will never translate into the bazouki-sodden extremes of the Greek musical mind, while even the French don't really like the sound of accordions.

The most successful Eurovision songs, then, were usually those that exerted the least strain upon its audience's powers of comprehension, and "Puppet on a String" lowered the common denominator so far that even today it rings out of jukeboxes from Lake Geneva to the Finland Station. At the time, the song swept Europe like a plague of singing lice, and when battle was joined the following year, the sonic consequences were apparent from the moment the individual nations' qualifying rounds commenced. An awful lot of songs sounded like "Puppet on a String."

Which means, if you didn't like songs that forced you instinctively to bend your knees in time to the beat, and alternate between holding one syllable for-ever ("Iiiiiiiiiiiii"), then spitting out the next dozen or so like a machine gun ("wonder-if-one-day-*that*-you'll-say-*that*-you-care"), you were not going to enjoy Eurovision.

In terms of youthful viewers, then, the contest was largely viewed as what the television programmers like to describe as "family entertainment," with a catchment area that began with unhip mums and dads, and limped upward from there, a two-hour terror-fest populated by incomprehensible ballads, peculiar pop, national dress, and men with mustaches. Big mustaches, that quivered like overstimulated drain clogs as their owners strained to reach the highest notes in their homeland's chosen entry.

Songs were mostly performed in the native language . . . indeed, between 1966 and 1973, and again from 1977 to 1998, the rules insisted upon it. It was always a very liquid concept, however, giving rise to such masterpieces of linguistic cunning as "Boom Bang a Bang," "Ding a Dong," "La La La," and "Oui Oui Oui Oui" because, let's face it, repetitive nonsense is a lot easier for a multinational audience to comprehend than a song that actually has words.

(That said, the apex of this particular theme was reserved for the 1990s UK sitcom *Gimme Gimme Gimme*, in which the British entry was titled "Dee Do Dee Do Dum Dum."[180] Not to be confused, incidentally, with the Police's "De Doo Doo Doo," which of course was one more masterful piece of deeply meaningful lyrical prowess from the multitalented Mr. Sting.)

Neither was success at Eurovision regarded as a passport to international fame. Most countries sensibly entered artists who were already successful in their homeland (United Kingdom entries over the years included Cliff Richard, the Shadows, Lulu, Sandy Shaw, Olivia Newton-John, and the Brotherhood of Man); and the occasional winning entry *would* make a mark on overseas singles charts—hence, for anybody browsing a book of UK hit singles, one-off entries appear for Gigliola Cinquetti, Séverine, Vicky Leandros, Teach-In, and Izhar Cohen and the Alphabeta.

But launching fresh talent onto the world's stage was never Eurovision's goal. It was all about the songs.

Until, in the midst of all this, ABBA came along and in 1974, with the rule on singing in native tongues temporarily relaxed, gave us the English-language "Waterloo" . . . and they never, ever looked back. Neither, fourteen years later, would Celine Dion, who greeted the world for the first time as the victorious voice of Switzerland in 1988.

Such moments were flukes. Neither success did anything to improve Eurovision's reputation among the hip and the happening. If anything, things got worse, particularly in the wake of ABBA's win. For years thereafter, the Swedes' two-men/two-women lineup became the template for fresh aspirants, all hoping that lightning would strike twice (it did, for the Brotherhood of Man) . . . thrice (it did, for Buck's Fizz) . . . four times? Thankfully, no.

---

180. *Gimme Gimme Gimme* writer Jonathan Harvey went on to write the acclaimed 2023 Eurovision-themed musical *A Thong for Europe*.

The standard of stage performances, on the other hand, soared. No longer was it enough just to stand on the spot and sing your song. Increasingly, and with the insurgent trend in rock videos surely a major influence, entrants put on full performances—eye-catching costuming, convoluted dance routines, death-defying circus acts, quadruple-jointed gymnastic exercises . . . air guitar.

But it also became apparent that, with the visuals often outperforming the songs, several countries were simply losing interest in the whole thing.

For the longest time, for example, the United Kingdom specialized in offal that stood no chance of success. Reflecting upon this sordid past, on the eve of the 2023 event, writer Alexis Petridis chided the nation for feeding Eurovision an almost nonstop diet of "TV talent show runners-up, manufactured pop bands years past their sell-by date, songs so unmemorable it seemed a miracle the benighted souls charged with singing them didn't just forget what they were doing midway through the performance and distractedly wander offstage."[181]

Norway took things even further by collecting zero points twice in four successive contests (1978–1981). Seven years later, Israel's minister of culture threatened to resign after his countrymen elected a pair of comedic Blues Brothers lookalikes, the Lazy Bums, to represent the country with a song about being lazy. And a bum.

The following year, red faces erupted across Cyprus when someone pointed out that the country's chosen entry was a song they'd actually declined to enter four years previous. A few countries stopped competing altogether.

Thus, Eurovision meandered along, sinking ever deeper into a morass of maudlin music and morbid fascination, the audiovisual equivalent of the owner of an abandoned fairground running around pretending to be a ghost, but without even a bunch of meddling kids (and a dog) to witness it.

Then something changed. Several things, in fact.

181. Alexis Petridis, "Mae Muller: I Wrote a Song Review—UK Eurovision Entry Is Far from Douze Points," *The Guardian*, March 9, 2023, https://www.theguardian.com/music/2023/mar/09/mae-muller-i-wrote-a-song-review-uk-eurovision-entry-alexis-petridis.

Croatia's entry for the 2023 Eurovision, long-running punk provocateurs Let3, once appeared live on national television pretending to pop corks out of their buttholes. The performance was cut short. DPA PICTURE ALLIANCE / ALAMY STOCK PHOTO.

Today, over forty nations—twice the number who appeared throughout the earliest years—are eligible to compete for the prize. A single Saturday night of competition has been expanded over two additional evenings of semifinals; and the introduction of public balloting has done much to scourge the contest of the political point-scoring that once characterized the voting.

It's not even a wholly European event any longer. The show is now screened worldwide, with close to two hundred million people tuning in to watch competitors from as far afield as Asia (Israel, Armenia, Georgia, and Azerbaijan are all eligible to compete); north Africa (Morocco, Algeria, Egypt, Libya, and Tunisia likewise); and, since 2015, Australia battle it out with the host continent.[182]

The United States, while never participating, has broadcast the contest live on cable television since 2016,[183] while Eurovision was the subject of Will Farrell's *The Story of Fire Saga*, a 2020 movie that followed the

---

182. Other non-European nations eligible to compete, but thus far absent, include Jordan and Lebanon of western Asia.
183. Intriguingly, PBS aired the 1971 contest.

misadventures of the hapless (fictional) Icelandic duo Fire Saga—and in the real-life contest the following year, Iceland's spokesman referenced the movie's biggest hit, "Ja Ja Ding Dong," in his opening remarks.

So if Eurovision isn't quite a global celebration of song, it is getting close[184] (even China has made overtures about competing), and its reach is enormous. And with that reach there has come both international renown *and* international respect. A tribute, in fact, to the demolition, at last, of rock music's hitherto stubborn xenophobia.

Eurovision itself is not necessarily responsible for this turnaround. That was the work of the electronic dance scene of the 1990s, as a host of European and Asian musicians arose to entertain audiences that frankly didn't care whether they could understand the words (on the occasions that there were any) so long as it was good to dance to.

There was also, during the same decade, an explosion of interest in what was termed World Music, a concerted attempt by a handful of specialist labels to introduce Anglo-American audiences to sounds from further afield than they might ever have experienced before. And the success of that venture can be testified by anybody who recalls wandering into a branch of, for example, Tower Records, to find CDs categorized not by genre or artist, but by nation.

The industrial, darkwave, and metal scenes also played a significant role, again allowing English-speaking audiences to experience the often dramatic sound being pioneered even into the furthest reaches of eastern and northern Europe.

There was no deliberate conjoining of these currents; no single mastermind ever sat down and thought, "Hey, let's create a humongous whole from so many disparate threads." It just happened, a consequence of course of the internet's expanding reach, but also of a modern audience finally tiring of listening to the same-old same-old domestic twaddle that they'd been force-fed for so long and taking it upon itself to actually explore the world.

The Eurovision Song Contest just happened to be poised perfectly to take that audience by their hand and say, "Well, you might not like everything we throw at you. But you're certainly going to hear a lot of

---

184. An all-Asian spinoff has been rumored for several years now, while the United States held its own American Song Contest in 2022.

new music." At the same time, giving itself a much-needed reboot, both musically and culturally.

In 1998, Israeli politics experienced another meltdown when the people's choice (the competition's national qualifying rounds were decided by public vote) turned out to be a trans nightclub singer named Dana International.

Other nations, equally outraged by what they viewed as an assault upon the contest's traditional catchment area, threatened to cut their live feeds while Dana was onstage. The Israel Broadcasting Authority, however, was unbowed, smirkingly declaring, "We checked the body of the song, not the body of the singer," and it was they who had the last laugh. Dana won the competition with a song that wouldn't have been out of place on an early eighties disco dance floor. But it was Dana herself who hit the headlines; as *The Guardian* put it twenty years later, "She led the way for 2014 Austrian winner Conchita Wurst—a Shirley Bassey–type drag queen with a perfectly trimmed beard—and, more broadly, . . . signaled the importance of the fun, free, gregarious culture of Eurovision as an annual LGBTQ-friendly celebration."[185]

More than that, Dana shattered the contest's popular image as something stodgy, boring, and unadventurous. In 2003, Russia was represented at Eurovision by t.A.T.u., a teenaged female duo whose name was supposedly abbreviated from the Russian "Та любит ту" (*ta lyubit tu*), meaning "She loves that"—*that* being the same-sex romance that their performance alluded to even before Lena Katina and Julia Volkova shared the first same-sex kiss ever seen on Eurovision.

Formed in 2000, t.A.T.u. already had a strong homeland presence by the time they came to the attention of producer Trevor Horn. Brought on board initially to help with launching t.A.T.u. in the English-speaking world, Horn would write and coproduce a new version of their debut album, while also composing English lyrics for their now two-year-old debut single, "Ya Soshla S Uma."

The ensuing "All the Things She Said" exploded onto Western dance floors in late 2002, topping charts across Europe, even as its accompanying

---

185. Eve Barlow, "Viva la diva! How Eurovision's Dana International Made Trans Identity Mainstream," *The Guardian*, May 10, 2018, https://www.theguardian.com/music/2018/may/10/viva-la-diva-how-eurovisions-dana-international-made-trans-identity-mainstream.

video was banned and the tabloids screamed about underage gay sex. As the BBC put it, "Comrade Lenin would be spinning in his waxen tomb if he knew that the West had not been conquered by the Red Army—but by a pair of teenage lesbians from Mother Russia."[186]

Russia's entry for Eurovision 2003, t.A.T.u., went on to become one of the contest's biggest international hits since Celine Dion. NATUREBOYMD / WIKIMEDIA COMMONS.

186. Michael Osborn, "More to Tatu Than Shock Tactics," BBC News Online, February 14, 2003, http://news.bbc.co.uk/2/hi/entertainment/2736367.stm.

Twenty-One More Twenty-First-Century Eurovision Bangers

"Allez Ola Olé"—Jessy Matador (France, 2010)

"Boonika Bate Toba"—Zdb Si Zdub (Moldova, 2005)

"Cha Cha Cha"— Käärjä (Finland, 2023)

"Dustin the Turkey"— Irelande Douze Points (Ireland, 2008)

"Et Cetera"—Sinead Mulvey & Black Daisy (Ireland, 2009)

"Euphoria"— Loreen (Sweden, 2012)

"For Real"—Athena (Turkey, 2004)

"Give That Wolf a Banana"—Subwoolfer (Norway, 2022)

"Hatrið Mun Sigra"—Hatari (Iceland, 2019)

"Higher Ground"—Rasmussen (Denmark, 2018)

"In Corpore Sano"—Konstrakta (Serbia, 2022)

"Mata Hari"—Efendi (Azerbaijan, 2021)

"Øve Os På Hinanden"—Fyr & Flamme (Denmark, 2022)

"Nesto Sto Ke Ostane"—Next Time (FYR Macedonia, 2009)

"Rise Up"—Freaky Fortune (Greece, 2014)

"S.A.G.A.P.O"—Michalis Rakintzis (Greece, 2002)

"Salvem El Món"—Anonymous (Andorra, 2007)

"Sister"—Sergio & The Ladies (Belgium, 2002)

"Soarele şi Luna"—Pasha Parfebi (Moldova, 2023)

"Something Better"—Softengine (Finland, 2014)

"Toy"—Netta (Israel, 2018)

"Wolves of the Sea"—Pirates of the Sea (Latvia, 2008)

t.A.T.u. savaged late-night American television, while their outspoken opposition to the then ongoing war in Iraq saw them turn out for Jimmy Kimmel's show wearing "Fuck the War" T-shirts, at least until they were told to change. They appeared instead bearing shirts reading "censored," but apparently still wrote the forbidden words on their host's hand.

Now, it was Eurovision's turn, and "Ne Ver Ne Boysia Ne Prosi" ("Do Not Trust, Do Not Fear, Do Not Ask") was instantly proclaimed one of the most incendiary performances Eurovision had ever hosted, and the fact that the song itself was such a floor-filling banger, all electro beats and thunderous percussion, only emphasized how far the competition had come in a few short years.

t.A.T.u. finished third, and were quick to cry foul when it was revealed that technical problems forced the Irish broadcaster RTÉ to scrap their share of the public vote and use a backup jury instead.[187]

But the genie remained out of the bottle. The 2006 event was won by the Finnish metal band Lordi, all Gwar-grotesque costumes, growled vocals, and pummeling riffs. The contest's support for LGBTQ rights was emphasized once more a year later when Serbia's Marija Šerifović took the top honor, and feminist figurehead Germaine Greer celebrated, "It was wonderful enough that a solid plain girl in glasses won it for Serbia with an old-fashioned torch-song; that she should have sung it in passionate earnest as a lover of her own sex is what made this viewer switch off the iron and start praying that the gods might let her win."[188]

Eurovision has continued shifting ever since, transforming itself from an annual rite of passage that even long-term voyeurs admitted was more of a masochistic compulsion than a pleasurable experience, to an otherworldly cocktail of uber-kitsch glamor, cross-cultural pop, and often scything social awareness, both directly and by proxy—Sweden's 2009 contestant, opera singer Malena Ernman, may have finished a lowly twenty-first on the night, but she became a global name regardless when her daughter Greta Thunberg launched her campaign for climate action.

Traditional Eurovision fare still dominates the annual contest, of course—vast ballads, EDM bangers, rent-a-riff rockers, folk dance flings, and (in another concession to modern tastes), suburban rappers. But the mold is there to be broken, as when Finnish nu-metal rockers Blind Channel took sixth place in 2021.

The same nation's 2013 entry, Krista Siegfrid's "Marry Me," meanwhile, was a bouncing thump of an earworm that called for the legalization of same-sex marriage (although you didn't realize that until the closing moments of the performance); Ukraine's 2016 victor, "1944," was widely seen as commentary on Russia's recent invasion of the Crimea, and was in fact performed in that language; Serbia's 2022 submission, Konstrakta's "In Corpore Sano," was a diatribe against the country's health service.

---

187. RTÉ denied the decision had this effect.
188. Germaine Greer, "Go, Marija! Eurovision's Triumphant Lesbian Gypsy," *The Guardian*, May 21, 2007.

No longer is the contest an ABBA-notwithstanding dead-end street for international success. Duncan Laurence claimed victory for the Netherlands in 2019 with "Arcade," a song that not only ranks among the most-streamed Eurovision songs of all time (as the 2023 contest began, "Arcade" had racked up close to a billion global plays on Spotify alone), it has also been covered by Kelly Clarkson and was the first Eurovision song to enter the American charts this century.

Italy's Måneskin scored the second, with a cover of the Four Seasons' "Beggin'" (but that was only after "Zitti e Buoni" rode to glory at the 2021 contest). Indeed, with forty million physical sales and four billion streams to Måneskin's name by the end of 2022, *Variety* opened 2023 by describing them as "the Biggest Rock Band to Emerge in Years"[189]—a point reinforced when they were also among the best new artist nominees at the 2023 Grammy Awards. They are also the first Eurovision winners ever to open for the Rolling Stones.[190]

The 2023 event, the most recent at the time of writing, was Eurovision's most dramatic and musically varied yet. Staged in the UK after the previous year's victors, Ukraine, were forced by war to relinquish hopes of hosting it themselves, we were sadly deprived of the spectacle of former Sex Pistol John Lydon leading Public Image Limited through "Hawaii" after the song failed to make it through the Irish qualifying contest.

But we saw Sweden's Loreen become the first woman to win the event twice (following her 2012 triumph); Reily becoming the first Faroese performer to compete at the contest (representing Denmark); Australian prog veterans Voyager prefacing the release of their eighth album with a dash of Eurovision; and the similarly long-established German goth-metallurgists Lord of the Lost actually making Lordi look underdressed. Mae Muller finished second-to-last with the most sarcastic UK entry in eons; and Iceland finished second-to-top with a maniacal blend of hard-core techno, thrash metal, and even a taste of K-pop tunefulness.

All of which proves that yes, an old dog can learn new tricks, so much so that exactly the same people who claim there's no great rock'n'roll any longer are now lamenting the loss of a "golden age" of Eurovision, which

---

189. Nick Vivarelli and Jem Aswad, "The Making of Måneskin: How Four Young Italians Became the Biggest Rock Band to Emerge in Years," Variety.com, February 2, 2023, https://variety.com/2023/music/features/the-making-of-maneskin-1235510466/.

190. Las Vegas, November 6, 2021.

itself ended so long ago that you wonder how so many people claimed to hate it at the time. They've certainly changed their minds since then.

Seriously, though. If the Eurovision Song Contest—hitherto regarded among the most hidebound, time-locked, irrelevant institutions in the entire universe of popular music—was able to enter the twenty-first century with a bright smile, a fresh face, and a positively wizard new pair of trousers, then anyone can. Yes, even you.

Chapter Twenty-Five

In Which We Thank the Stars of the Past for Their Service . . . and Tell Them It's Time to Let Go

Nothing is more unpredictable than the mob, nothing more obscure than public opinion, nothing more deceptive than the whole . . . system.

—Suetonius

You know it's time to worry when you start wondering which of your childhood heroes is going to drop dead on stage. It's going to happen—in fact, it already has. The last chords of the night are still ringing out, the Reformed Octogenarians (not, sadly, an imaginary band . . . more of a genre these days) are taking their final bow, and suddenly, "Thank you, Nantucket, you've been a wonderful audiiiiiiiiiiii . . . *splat.*"

Please. We've put up with their voices going flat. We know that the legs are gone. We've seen the oxygen cylinders on the backstage rider. But for pity's sake, spare us twenty thousand camera-wielding gig-goers, each one live-streaming his own seat's view of your final words. Because that's what we'll get, and there's not an algorithm, filter, or unenforceable terms of service agreement that will prevent it.

Nevertheless, we have reached the point in this book (the end) where, one sincerely hopes, we are all very clear on one point. The past is important. It cannot and should not be swept away. But it can, and with equal emphasis, be left alone. Life is for the living, youth is for the young, and popular music is what's popular *now*, not sixty years ago when the grass was greener, the trees were taller, the sky was bluer, and everybody sang together in perfect harmony.

And why is the past important? Because today will be yesterday soon enough. It's important because the past is where your memories and experiences dwell, and it is those, in turn, that shape a person's personality and their interactions with other people. They are also where an artist stores their creativity.

No performer is forged in a vacuum. Whether one accepts or rejects the music of their past, the ability to even make that decision is crucial in the creation of their own music—the so-called Krautrock explosion of rock'n'roll—free electronic music in the early 1970s was, it is said, the result of an entire generation of young Germans rejecting the music, and the culture, of their country's past, both the Nazi regime of World War II *and* the postwar occupation by the victorious Allies. And while that was an extreme example, there are others.

But the opposite can also be true. You don't have to have lived through an era to enjoy the music that was made back then, which is how a teenager in 2023 can make records that sound like they were recorded in 1963; and why recent biopics of Elvis Presley and Freddie Mercury appealed as much to people who weren't born when those stars passed away as to those who lived through their careers at their peak (and can reel off all the mistakes and anachronisms that drive the ridiculous plots).

It's why English punk rockers still make a regular pilgrimage to the site of the Roxy Club, while their elders exchange war stories concerning the venue's notorious bathrooms. It's why grunge lovers still tour the sites of Seattle's most storied venues, and why Paris attracts legions of Edith Piaf and Jim Morrison admirers.

The good old days. The bathroom at the Roxy, London's premier punk venue.
ART BY MIK HESLIN.

Which is the key point here. For all the ranting, raving, ill-tempered asides, and backhanded compliments that you have now waded through as this book barreled on; for all the poorly disguised aliases that disguise unwitting victims, the point is *not* that "old" music sucks, and "new" music is perfect. It's that they are equal. Both have their good moments; both have their bad. Both have their utterly unlistenable. And both are the product of their time.

The fact that those times are themselves very different is immaterial. You're not the same person today as you were when you first heard *She Gets the Fellahs 'Cos Her Fingers Are Yellah* and decided to pledge your heart (and a large portion of your disposable income) to Nico Teen and

The original artwork for Nico Teen and the Stains' second album. The disc has subsequently been released with revised artwork and the simple title of 2.
AUTHOR'S COLLECTION.

the Stains. And the fact that you still listen to their music today, to the exclusion of any music made in the years since they broke up, is the most crystalline evidence of that difference . . . because, back then, you were certainly listening to a lot of other stuff. And unless you were truly obsessive, enjoying some of it as well.

When did that stop? And why? Did you just wake up one morning and think, "That's it. I've heard enough new music for one lifetime?" Did you finally despair after watching MTV (back in the days when the *M* still stood for music) for a month and realizing you no longer cared for whatever sounds were being piped into your house . . . but were maybe too busy to go out and seek new sensations that were more to your taste?

Or did you just give up and allow what was once a key component in your life to wither and die?

You wouldn't be alone in that. But music fans are almost unique in the ease with which they will simply turn off something that used to give them such pleasure—in this case, the very act of discovery—and devote the remainder of their lives to retreading stale ground.

A lifelong book lover doesn't stop reading new novels because "the old ones are better." A dedicated movie buff doesn't stop watching new films because "they don't write them like they used to." Electronic games aficionados didn't stop playing when Pac-Man fell out of fashion, and comic lovers can always find *something* new to excite them, decades after Howard the Duck quacked his last quack.

Why is it so easy for them to keep going, when so many music fans are effectively insisting that they ran into a brick wall however many years ago and they've not been able to find a way around it? So, instead, they spend the rest of their lives tossing their old crap over it and insisting it's superior because . . .

I'll let you finish that sentence yourself.

It's just a matter of reawakening . . . not the kid inside who liked the Dental Assassins a thousand years ago, but the kid who liked music in general, and if the radio and TV weren't scratching the itch for new sounds, then they'd jolly well go out and find something that did.

It's not as if there aren't any places to go, and you don't even have to leave the house anymore. The internet is absolutely lousy with new music screaming out for you to listen to it. Forget what's on the chart or in the papers or grinning out of a forty-foot billboard because they want to share their new product with you. Dig deeper.

Plenty of music websites allow you to search not by artists but by genre. Think of one you like and click the little button. You're not going to enjoy everything you hear, but seriously, did you ever? We talk about "liking seventies music," but what that boils down to is appreciating a very select fraction of what was actually available at any given time, even within realms of the rock you respected. To cite some real artists, for a change, not every British Invasion Beatles fan felt the same way about Freddie & the Dreamers. Not every West Coast Dead disciple was equally excited by HP Lovecraft. Not every Snivelling Shits supporter was so dedicated to the Drones.

Give it a go. Let the algorithms work for you for a change, rather than sitting back while they mine your data to see if you might be a candidate for a revolutionary new treatment for Nasal Hemorrhoid Syndrome.

Remember those sampler albums that labels used to pump out, with titles like *Fill Your Head with Rock* and *You Can All Join In* stuffed full of new releases they hoped you might like? There's one to download at the back of this book.

Remember those lists you used to read in the music press, of bands to watch out for, or records you should hear? There's one of those at the back of this book as well, a twenty-first-century playlist that glides across so many genres that even the people who compiled it don't like everything on it. But they all found something fresh to enjoy, and guess what? Some of them don't like new music, either.

Yes, you can carry on listening to the old stuff as well. It's okay, it won't be jealous. It might even be pleased. "Ah, I wondered what the great grandchildren were up to. Thank you." And if you should succumb to any new band's charms, then file them in with the rest of the collection, and who knows? In a few years' time, Jennifer Dingleberry might be as much a part of your mental landscape as Rocky Biceps.

The difference is, she's still around to make new records.

EPILOGUE
Growing Convictions

1. The fact that it is all but impossible for any act to record more than four "perfect ten" albums, a maxim proven by the fact that even Black Sabbath dropped the ball between their third and fifth.

2. The fact that, if you were to ask people to name their all-time favorite albums, the ones they would take with them to a desert island, the majority would not name more than one or two of the titles we are routinely told are the greatest LPs ever made; and, more likely, would lean toward records that half the other respondents have never even heard of.

3. The fact that not one of the following songs would sound so exciting if it was performed by members of any other profession:
   a. "I'm Just a Plumber in a Firm That Cleans Drains" (but it has to be recorded by the Moody Flues).
   b. "I Wanna Reroof Your House All Night and Grout Your Bathroom Every Day."
   c. "So You Wanna Be a Cable Installation Star."
   d. "Hospital Gift Shops Are Here to Stay."
   e. "It's Still Cosmetic Dentistry to Me"

4. The fact that Grace Slick was correct when she said, "All rock-and-rollers over the age of fifty look stupid and should retire."

5. The fact that people deliberately "mishear" the lyrics to classic rock songs so they can compile amusing listicles about them; when I find myself with Barney Rubble, Wilma Flintstone comes to me. Speaking words of wisdom, no doubt.

6. The fact that, no matter how excruciatingly exciting 1980s metal might have appeared at the time, today it sounds exactly like an overtired toddler throwing a tantrum, while its parents clean the playroom with a leaf blower.

7. The fact that the very same people who spend their days hoping that the next Beat Lemurs' box set will contain every available demo for every song the band ever recorded are the exact same

people who will then describe a similarly comprehensive collection for 7 Deadly Synths as a waste of plastic.

8. The fact that the pandemic saw the delay, or even cancellation, of a host of proposed thirtieth/fortieth/fiftieth anniversary repackagings of classic albums, and there are people out there who think that matters; the fact that they don't believe they already have enough copies of the things.

9. The fact that the majority of classic-era rock stars are infinitely more prolific in death than they ever were in life; the fact that Rest in Peace apparently means something completely different when there are dollar signs attached; the fact that Taylor Swift's "Anti-Hero" video should be required viewing for the grieving relatives of every late pop idol, right before the will is read; the fact that "cats don't even like the beach."

10. The fact that "Serious" music fans mock all the "kids" who buy vinyl today, without even owning a record player, while happily boasting of how many sealed, unplayed copies of such and such an LP they have in their own collection; the fact that it *is* like buying posters of your favorite band when you don't have any walls to hang them from.

11. The fact that the industry tore into the synthesizer musicians of the early 1980s, complaining that their magic boxes full of sounds were putting "real" musicians out of work; the fact that five years later, you couldn't move for "real" musicians faking it with synthesizers of their own.

12. The fact that otherwise perfectly rational people will tell you straight-faced that there is no good music being made anymore, yet when you reply with a list of current acts whose music is very good indeed, they have no interest whatsoever in hearing it; the fact that some will remain convinced that you're just making the names up.

13. The fact that music critics of a certain age will inevitably compare a new band to a veteran one, even when there is absolutely no valid musical reason to do so.

14. The fact that the most insignificant cult psychedelic band of the late 1960s has a better chance of receiving a critically acclaimed

box set than a bestselling album from the early 2000s does of ever reappearing on vinyl.

15. The fact that too many artists don't know when to stop.

16. The fact that way too many seventies-era live albums are rendered unlistenable by the audience's insistence on cheering loudly every time the singer makes a drug reference; the fact that doing so ensured the singer would soon be making another; the fact that those same albums would also be a lot shorter if there were no drum solos.

17. The fact that people still say things like "they don't write songs like that anymore," and everyone else is too polite to reply "thank goodness; it was bad enough the first time around."

18. The fact that nobody has yet invented nicotine-infused dry ice as a way of circumventing the smoking ban at gigs.

19. The fact that people still think it's cool when a band sings about how they're gonna rock'n'roll us all night long, without pointing out that "yes; that's why I bought a ticket to see you."

20. The fact that illegal downloading did not/will not/cannot kill music; the fact that, except in a very select minority of cases, illegal downloaders are not stealing money from the musicians themselves; the fact that, at worst, they are delaying repayment of a usurious record company debt by a few fractions of a cent per song.

21. The fact that the same record companies that spent the 1970s complaining that bootlegs—illegally recorded and released recordings of live shows—were ripping off the fans would have a lot of empty space on their box sets and bonus tracks if the bad guys hadn't been taping all those shows; the fact that a simple "thank you" would be nice.

22. The fact that Bruce Springsteen fans will merrily sit through a three-hour concert, yet will still complain that Taylor Swift's ten-minute rerecording of "All Too Well" goes on too long.

23. The fact that, more than four decades after English astrophysicist Sir Brian Harold May CBE publicly announced that "fat bottom girls make this . . . world go round," not one scientist has yet spoken out against this theory, which is more than can be said for the big bang theory, evolution, and climate change.

24. The fact that a rock star going bald is no longer committing a revolutionary act.

25. The fact that most non-classical outfits whose musicians are classically trained or considered virtuosos are boring.

26. The fact that "Tiny Dancer" is one of the most annoying songs Elton John and Bernie Taupin ever wrote, no matter how "uplifting" (allegedly) that scene from *Almost Famous* may have been.

27. The fact that a veteran artist's longevity is no excuse whatsoever to proclaim their every album "iconic"; the fact that, likewise, not every former member of a veteran band is "legendary."

28. The fact that, if you hadn't threatened to decimate anyone who called multiple LPs "vinyls," they'd probably have stopped long ago, all be it unwillingly; it's fun winding up the Dictionary Police.

29. The fact that a country singer named Garth Brooks once suggested used CD buyers should pay a special tax to compensate artists for the loss of a "new" sale whenever someone bought a previously owned copy of the same disc; the fact that most of his CDs now cost as much as $1 each from online CD sellers; the fact that these two points probably aren't related, but wouldn't it be funny if they were?

30. The fact that buying an album on mp3 is like buying your lunch in ebook format.

31. The fact that CDs used to retail at twice the price of new LPs, but at least they often included more songs; the fact that today, vinyl costs twice as much as CDs and usually has fewer songs; the fact that the industry really ought to make up its mind on the subject.

32. The fact that the only green issues that most major corporations, record companies included, genuinely care about are the ones that fold and fit into a wallet.

33. The fact that suing an ex-lover for leaking your sex tape to the internet does not sound half as awful if it is subsequently revealed that you intended setting it to music and releasing it as your next video.

34. The fact that Pink Floyd's Roger Waters and David Gilmour have now spent longer slagging one another off than they did playing together.

35. The fact that purchasing tickets for a gig . . . for a *gig,* dammit . . . should not involve entering the randomly generated five-digit code that will then be repeatedly refused until you have completed a never-ending sequence of captchas involving traffic lights and bicycles.

36. The fact that, according to *Billboard* magazine, the average length of songs on the Top 100 decreased by one minute and three seconds between 2000 and 2021; the fact that writer Sarah Ditum responded, "If things carry on this way, before the end of this century, the charts will consist of no more than one-second pinpoints of perfectly refined sound;"[191] the fact that this should have started happening fifty years ago.

---

191. Sarah Ditum, "Micro Niche." *The Critic,* May 2023.

APPENDIX A

An Index of Wholly Imaginary Artists

Imaginary artists are old. As old as the talking pictures: 1927's *The Jazz Singer*, starring Al Jolson as Jakie Rabinowitz, was the first ever feature-length "talkie"—and older still: the movie was based on Samson Raphaelson's "The Day of Atonement," a short story that first became a play in 1925. And you can go back further than that: Greek mythology gave us lyrists Apollo, Hermes, and Orpheus; the pipers Daphnes and Pan; harpist Demodocus; aulos (double oboe) virtuosos Marsyas and Eumolpus; lyricist Linus of Thrace; singer Thamyris; and the Sirens vocal group (what a supergroup they would make).

Fictional rock musicians, too, have a history as old as the genre, thanks to such movie pioneers as Jerri Jordan (Jayne Mansfield in *The Girl Can't Help It*, 1956) and Bongo Herbert (Cliff Richard in *Espresso Bongo*, 1959); Stephen Shorter (Paul Jones in *Privilege*, 1967); Jim MacLaine (David Essex in *That'll Be the Day/Stardust*, 1973, 1974); *Bad News* (1983); *Spinal Tap* (1984); Llewyn Davis (Oscar Isaac in *Inside Llewyn Davis*, 2013); and a host of literary equivalents, too—Bobby Sharp (*Teenybopper Idol* by Richard Allen, 1973); Willie's Rats (*The Tale of Willie's Rats* by Mick Farren, 1975) . . . and on to Dürt Würk (*We Sold Our Souls* by Grady Hendryx, 2018) and more.

Comic books have also served up a wealth of talent, from the Archies, in the distant sixties; to grunge idols Leonard the Love Gods (Peter Bagge, *Hate*, 1990–1994), glam rock spaceman Red Rocket 7 (Mike Allred, *Red Rocket 7*, 1997), and Satanic metal heroes Cherry Blackbird (Joseph Schmalke, *Cherry Blackbird*, 2021), and Jack King (Dan Panosian, Dalibor Talajic, Ive Svorcina, *Black Tape*, 2023*)*.

And then, of course, there's Daisy Jones and the Six, who might never have existed but are nevertheless not so imaginary that they aren't the subject of a million-selling book (by Taylor Jenkins Reid), a top-rated television series, and an album of their own, *Aurora*. Aside from all that, though, they're completely make-believe.

Reading and watching all of these adventures, one cannot help but wonder what reality would sound like if these had comprised our actual musical diet and it was real life that was the fiction?

The acts featured in this book make no attempt to match the achievements of the icons of elsewhere. For a start, most of them aren't good enough. But for anybody who cares for the artists who have, throughout this book, deputized for so many of the performers we truly loved/hated/ignored/forgot, these are their stories.

1950s

Rocky Biceps

Emerged from, and swiftly came to dominate, the first wave of American rock'n'rollers for whom the energy of Bill Haley and the Comets' music was wholly undermined by the band members' elderly appearance.

Soft-spoken, deeply religious, and dedicated to his family, Biceps described himself as a cross between "the boy next door and Jack Dellinger," the then-reigning Mr. Universe. His stage act accordingly courted controversy: Biceps tearing off his shirt during his first number and flexing his upper torso and arm muscles in sync with the frenzied rhythm of his music. Appearing on *American Bandstand*, he completely upended traditional television censorship conventions when the show refused to show him from the waist *up*.

Although Biceps never lost interest in music, and continued recording until his death in a still mysterious gymnasium mishap, his profound influence upon the development of rock'n'roll remains rooted in his earliest records.

The Rub-Outs

Pioneering New York doo-wop quintet who became a pioneering New York instrumental act following an outbreak of laryngitis backstage before their 1956 appearance on the *Ed Sullivan Show*. Attempting, upon recovery, to revert to their former guise, the band discovered that the public preferred them when they kept their mouths shut, and over the next three years, the Rub-Outs' unique, tremolo-heavy Coney Island

Sound saw them score multiple hit singles and soundtrack three Hollywood movies.

Breaking up in 1959, the band has been described as a major influence upon guitarists as disparate as Jimi Hendrix, Marty Balin, and Stevie Ray Vaughan, although not, intriguingly, by the guitarists themselves.

1960s

The Beat Lemurs

From southwest England, the Lemurs were prime exponents of Otterbeat, one of several local music scenes that the media named after a nearby river. In the Lemurs' case, however, the ruse did not work and the band's six singles/three LPs output lay undisturbed until the 1980s freak beat movement brought about their rediscovery. Since that time, the legend has grown to the point where a Beat Lemurs reunion tour in 2017 sold out across both Europe and the United States; their self-titled debut album is routinely ranked among the greatest records ever made; and the band are today ranked third in the list of "sixties artists with way too many compilation albums."

Billy Big Bananas

Was first sighted among the ever-changing roster of guitarists underpinning Foxy and the Redcoats (see below), but left in 1967 to drift aimlessly through a handful of supergroups before launching a solo career making jazz-lounge fusion movie soundtracks.

Undeniably one of the greatest guitarists in rock history, Big Bananas is nevertheless frequently criticized for his insistence on writing songs about every unfortunate event to befall him. He is also renowned for espousing unpopular religious, cultural, and political views at the most importune moments, although he has maintained his popularity with award ceremony judges and gambling casino audiences.

The Candlepark Stickmen

San Francisco–based sextet launched in 1968 on a wave of antiwar sentiment and revolt; scored an immediate hit with the still-seminal "Stop the Fighting in 'Nam, Man." Unfortunately, a lack of follow-up material reached its nadir with 1970s, "Stop the Bombing in 'Bodia, Nadia," which even its writers confessed was little more than a callous carbon copy, and the Stickmen broke up the following year—only to reemerge in 1983 ("Stop the Grenades in Grenadie, Sadie"), 1991 ("Stop the Warring in 'Raq, Mac"), 2002 ("Stop the Afghaning in 'Stan, Gran"), and 2022 ("Stop the Bombs Raining in 'Kraine, Jayne"). Reports that they intend to keep doing this until they finally get another hit (or even a single radio play) remain unconfirmed.

The Dental Assassins

The Assassins ruled the sixties like Charlemagne ruled the Holy Roman Empire—wearing pointy hats and long coats. Unstoppable from the moment they emerged from Britain's industrial hinterland in 1962, the Assassins still hold the record for "the most worldwide number ones that people continue to listen to," and at one point occupied so many positions on the *Billboard* chart that they were reported to the Federal Trade Commission for a violation of antitrust laws.

Unapproachable in person, untouchable in musical terms, the Assassins are also unique in that they remain the only significant band of their era not to have been the subject of a parody movie.

Nico Teen and the Stains

The ultimate central Maine garage band, Nico Teen and the Stains existed within so chaotic a maelstrom of sex, drugs, violence, and unrestrained shopping sprees (but not, ironically, cigarette smoking) that it was regarded as miraculous that they even recorded four albums, let alone found a record company dumb enough to release them.

Each sold exponentially fewer copies than its predecessor, with the band's self-titled debut also setting a new record when every single journalist who received a prerelease promo copy mailed it back to the label.

But Lance Corporeal (q.v.) was a dedicated fan, including at least one heavily disguised Scrooges composition on each of her trendsetting glam albums, and—in claiming she wrote them—accepted the blame for them, too.

Several attempts to collaborate failed, but in overseeing a 1992 tribute album, Corporeal was responsible for the Stains being wholly reappraised and, a decade later, the one surviving member, bassist Hans Roller, reformed the band for the Liposuctionpalooza tour of elective surgery offices and has since released a number of solo albums.

The Eclectic Cabbage

The first Bay Area psychedeliacs to break the two-hour limit for playing the same riff over and over, the story of the Eclectic Cabbage is that of a quartet so stoned that they even forgot to break up—thus, they continue playing to this day; in fact, still performing the same riff they started with.

Nevertheless, they have retained the support of an army of loyal followers, and their 1967 "Peachy-Keen-Friday-with-Xtrafries-Please"—the first hit single ever to devour all six sides of a triple album—remains a staple of classic rock radio.

Foxy and the Redcoats

What almost every other band on the planet were to the Beatles, Foxy and the Redcoats were to the Dental Assassins . . . a group that landed sufficient contemporary hits to convince the American media that the two acts were now bitter rivals. Ultimately, it transpired that all five Dental Assassins were on a spiritual retreat in the Siberian capital Novosibirsk, throughout the Redcoats' chart life, and thus had never even heard of them.

Foxy and Co. bounced back, however, eschewing popular success for a career in the emergent fuzzzz rock underground. Guitarist Billy Big Bananas (see above) quit in protest at this new direction, but the Redcoats persevered in their quest for the ultimate obscurity, and by the time they released their final album in 1969, even their own mothers had never heard of them.

Foxy and the Redcoats music was rediscovered in the mid-1980s, with the appearance of a couple of B sides on a low-budget fuzzzz rock compilation album, and the quintet have since enjoyed a record-breaking thirty-four nominations to the Rock and Roll Hall of Fame.

The Three Henchmen

Controversial quartet whose radical politics were so pronounced that it was said FBI agents outnumbered audience members at their concerts, a situation that ultimately saw the band retire from live performance altogether to work instead on what they described as a concept album documenting everything that was wrong with the world and how to fix it.

Unfortunately, just one track, "Tricky Dickie's Lies Are Sticky," was released before vocalist Terence "Smash the" System was found dead in Mysterious Circumstances (a small town in Maine, according to official documentation); the band held auditions for a new singer, but broke up when it transpired that the only applicants were also FBI agents.

1970s

Casual Lovin'

Casual Lovin' was an Anglo-American octet, secretly formed from barely remembered members of sundry seventies staples. Uriah Heep, Jethro Tull, King Crimson, Spooky Tooth, Deep Purple, Foghat, Yes, and Boston are among the acts believed to have awoken one morning to find random components of their lineups missing . . . last seen in a bar talking with a small mustachioed man named Bobby.

All subsequently returned home, claiming to have no memory of the intervening years, but all strangely outfitted in matching suits with platinum disc accessories and claiming co-ownership of a Lear Jet. Their repertoires, too, had expanded to include such soft rock classics as the James Bond–themed "Licentious to Thill," "Soul Divider," and "Love Is a Cattle Field"—fetid wet blankets that are today a staple on yacht rock radio.

Cat Sandwich

Although they had already enjoyed several hits in their native English Midlands, Cat Sandwich came to international attention with the seventy-minute version of their first single, "Hurrumph," as performed at the Woodstock festival. Filmed and released in its entirety as the second feature to the Woodstock movie itself, the success of "Hurrumph" led to their first album, *Songs from the Grand Union Canal Delta*, topping both the British and American charts, an achievement, in turn, which saw mercurial guitarist Alf Smith recruited to Billy Big Bananas's all-star *Who Are Half These People?* jazz jam concept album in 1973.

Ultimately, Cat Sandwich's inability to play anything but extremely long blues rockers lost its appeal to the wider public, and the band broke up in 1976. However, the eighties saw all five former members reappear in a variety of extraordinarily popular but utterly unmemorable album-oriented rock (AOR) supergroups, including . . . I'm Sorry, Who? and I Can't Remember a Single One.

Lance Corporeal

Space rocker, glam rocker, Krautrocker, jam rocker Lance Corporeal did it all, out-chameleoning even the established chameleons of pop by not only changing her image for every album, but changing her face as well.

Thus, the chubby-cheeked blonde of her early hits became the pinch-faced brunette of her mid-period albums; her eye color shifted as fast as her costumes; and she admitted to requiring seven different passport photographs, simply to avoid awkward questions.

A vivid inspiration throughout the seventies (less so in the eighties), but back to something approaching her middling best for the remainder of her career, Corporeal (or at least somebody who didn't look like her) passed away in 2015 and has possibly been fronting Corporeal tribute bands ever since.

The third volume of her bestselling "deathbed requests," *Oh, I've Just Remembered a Few More You Should Remix When I'm Gone*, will be published in 2025.

Darkwater

Early exponents of the all-conquering Philly sound explosion, Dark-water matched exquisite harmonies with loquacious strings and a fuck-me-sideways rhythm, a blend that didn't merely captivate the early seventies dance floor, it took it out on a date and got it drunk on Pernod.

Described by one magazine as "the sultriest, sexiest siren call you'll ever hear in this world," Darkwater's popularity only grew when it was revealed that three of the band were, in fact, genuine mer-people. Unfortunately, this brought them to the attention of the FBI's controversy-ridden Mythical Beings in Music division and Darkwater broke up shortly after President Gerald Ford's much-condemned "Do they even wash between their fins?" remark in 1975.

Larry McList

The original saxophonist with early seventies prog also-rans the Okay, Larry McList was (as the press release gently put it) "excused from further band duties" when it became apparent that every word out of his mouth was a lie, from his insistence on calling up the music press to tell them he wrote all the songs on the band's first album, to the claim that it was he who taught their classically trained bassist how to play, and on to his stock response when these declarations were challenged—"I was misquoted."

Sufficiently gifted that he had little problem breezing through auditions for a subsequent host of other bands, it quickly became apparent that McList had learned nothing from what ought to have been a chastening experience. Thus, a one-off appearance alongside Billy Big Bananas became full-time membership in his band; a few rehearsals with the formative Cat Sandwich became teaching them everything they knew; and a chance meeting with Lance Corporeal as she was taking some new songs to her publisher apparently convinced McList that he'd cowritten them with her.

And so he drifted on, in and out of the spotlight, as he joined, and was then fired from, one band after another, until he finally launched a solo career in the very late seventies—at which point he sacked himself following a succession of public pronouncements that even he didn't believe were misquotations.

McList is currently writing his autobiography. *File under Fiction.*

The Leccylite String Machine

The early seventies were the age of ever-more ambitious experimentation, but few went so far as Birmingham, Alabama's Leccylite String Machine. Initially formed in response to Deep Purple recording an entire album of classically themed pomp with the Royal Philharmonic Orchestra, LSM was an orchestra that added a rock section for an album of fifties hits.

Mocked by critics who regarded it as pretentious drivel and proof positive that rock music should not be merged with any other genre whatsoever, LSM nevertheless found themselves with a major hit and rapidly established themselves among the country's most successful, and spectacular, acts—their 1977 tour, which saw them perform inside a life-size replica of a soulless baseball stadium, was the highest-grossing outing of the decade, despite also being the most expensive to mount.

LSM broke up in 1983, but have since reformed with no original members whatsoever.

Skull Turnip

Formed from the union of the Frantic Fiddle Fiends and the a cappella quartet Aaaah, Skull Turnip turned the UK folk rock world on its head with their electrification of James Taylor's entire back catalog at the 1971 Cambridge Folk Festival. They then pointedly refused to record it for their first album while they pursued, instead, the collection of nineteenth-century English murder ballads released in 1972 as *James Catnatch Fever*.

It proved a sound move. Both album and three accompanying singles were hits, while the group's popularity rose even higher following their ban from British television after they imprisoned a top DJ in the stocks and spent their entire performance pelting him with root vegetables.

Turnipmania reached its peak in 1977, when they joined with punk producer Spit Gobley to record a forty-minute essay titled *Being a Dissertation upon the Similarities between Punk Rock's Dissatisfaction with*

Modern Society, and That Voiced by the Balladeers of the 1830s; the group broke up the following year, torn apart by conflict over the correct pronunciation of several of the medieval instruments deployed on their next album.

The members subsequently regrouped in two bands, Skull and Turnip, but neither was successful, and by the late 1980s, a reformed Skull Turnip were regulars on the European Renaissance Fayre circuit.

Swampwitch

The hitherto unheralded heroes of the 1972 Wattstax festival. Despite being omitted from both the soundtrack and the accompanying movie, word of mouth saw the Detroit-based (not the one in Michigan) funketeers swiftly elevated from the tiny clubs in which they had spent the past four years to stadia across the country.

Renowned for the slinkiest rhythms, the tightest horns, vivacious theatrics, and compulsive choruses, Swampwitch maintained their success into the early disco era but broke up after an ill-advised experiment with Syndrums left their four-man percussion team critically injured.

Wasp Invasion

Forming in 1978 following the demise of two local, south London punk bands, Wasp Invasion adopted their name from the recent arrival on the scene of the Wasp synthesizer, a tiny but extraordinarily versatile synthesizer that marketed for around the price of a midrange guitar but which could do oh so much more, especially if you couldn't play guitar. Frontman Tommy explained, "We were seeing them everywhere and someone said it's like we'd been invaded. And we looked at one another and said that's our name."

With staccato cello, militaristic drums, and the Wasp buzzing around the edges, Wasp Invasion was the sound of permafrost tapping on your brain forever, a chilling, drilling quickstep over which Tommy barked brute force polemics like subpoetic orders.

Beholden to neither melody nor rhythm, Wasp Invasion were a taste that audiences either adored (a minority) or abhorred (the rest), and even at the height of the music press's love affair with them, gigs were more likely to end in a hail of bottles and abuse than a round of applause. "We only ever played one encore, all the time we were together," Tommy later revealed. "It was during a rehearsal and suddenly we heard what sounded like clapping. It was actually the studio cat playing with a stick."

Wilkins Micawber

Early seventies hard rock/progressive act took their name from Charles Dickens, but their musical cues were somewhat easier to spot—*that* organ sound, *that* vocal pitch; *that* disregard for danceable time signatures, *that* level of utter disdain for any audience but their own.

Firmly locked into a landscape poised somewhere between Middle Earth and Gormenghast, with vast gatefold album jackets that reflected the most commonly recognizable elements of each, Wilkins Micawber prided themselves in the disdain of the music press, not only reprinting their own unkindest reviews on their LP jackets, but hijacking those received by other acts as well, crossing out their names and adding their own in purple crayon.

Interviews habitually descended into fist fights, promotional photographs were shot through cracked camera lenses, and relations with their record company soured so often that the band's third album, *Time to Feed the Fish*, was ultimately released in separate installments by five different record labels.

Sadly, tensions within the band were equally fractious, and following the 1976 death of frontman and self-styled peacemaker Hal Burton in a still controversial shampoo accident, the group shattered during auditions for his replacement. Multiple attempts to reform in recent years have ended angrily, often before a single show has been played.

1980s

The Bunglebears

Named for a never-seen (or mentioned) character in the 1970s Boston-area children's television show *Jabberwocky*, the Bunglebears epitomize the One Hit Wonder culture of the 1980s, rising up with one song in which every single note utilized the very latest in musical technology, from the still ubiquitous That Switch Everyone Presses First on the Yamaha DX7, to the Sample That Makes Everyone Go "Whoooah" on the E-mu SP-1200.

Add the distinctive twang of the Robosonics Mark III Triangle Emulator, and 1983's "My Baby's Tattooed Toenails" proved irresistible to everybody who likes to think they're bang up to date in their musical tastes.

The Bunglebears were never able to follow up their first success; however, the band remained active for several years more, recording four albums and a reformed lineup is now a familiar sight on the eighties revival circuit.

Matterhorn Slender

Formed while its seven original members were still at private school in Worcestershire, England, Matterhorn Slender emerged in 1979, a wholly unfashionable outfit steeped deep in the traditions of early seventies progressive rock.

An audience awaited them, however, and as the band's popularity grew, sound investment in vintage tech saw the band's appearance at the 1980 Reading Festival literally transport the entire audience back to 1974, a magical moment that ended only when on-site vendors complained about having to sell their wares at 1974 prices. While wearing 1974 fashions.

Wildly popular in the early to mid-1980s, the acrimonious departure of frontman Walt Rodgers (allegedly over the loan, and nonreturn, of a guitar string at an early rehearsal) in 1986 was succeeded by an ever-revolving lineup which in turn occasioned several unwelcome shifts in the band's signature sound. Nevertheless, Matterhorn Slender still tour and record today, as well as oversee an extravagant "everything including the kitchen sink" approach to archiving releases.

It is unclear exactly how many albums Matterhorn Slender have released. Discographies range between 37 and 186, a consequence of the band having never recorded or performed a song of less than fifteen minutes in duration, thus ensuring that each one consumes at least one entire side of twelve-inch vinyl, regardless of whether it is marketed as an LP or a single. Their most recent release spreads across twenty-four separate discs and that, apparently, was "one of our shorter gigs."

Neitherwhere

One of the plethora of eternal talents spawned by the southern New Jersey Blank Cave scene, Neitherwhere shot to prominence following the death of original vocalist Blackie Blackish in what the coroner described as "the most unusual clove-related misadventure it has ever been my misfortune to comment upon." Media speculation over quite what he meant by this continues to this day.

The arrival of replacement Evan Blacker introduced a dramatic change in direction and Neitherwhere set about bridging the sonic gap between their original gothic art-rock sound and the now-prevalent new wave of American hair metal.

It was an abject failure, and a wholesale shift in personnel saw the band move into the new age–inspired Trappist chant boom, a largely silent medium that nevertheless translated to three platinum-selling albums, *Meditation Tunes*, *More Meditation Tunes*, and returning to their roots, *A Goth Tribute to Tanita Tikaram*.

Rhubarb

Another act who looked to children's television for nomenclatural inspiration, albeit one that swiftly moved in a very different direction. The only English electro duo to make the shortlist for the PMRC's "Filthy Fifteen" (they were cited for encouraging animal cruelty through the lyric "standing on the foot of a pink flamingo"), Rhubarb's hard beats, quizzical lyrics, and decadent taste in stage design saw them rightfully proclaimed figureheads of the gay rights movement of the time, an honor that they repaid by staging a number of high-profile benefits for relevant causes.

Announcing the band's cessation in 1994, the pair subsequently moved into community action and local politics, although they have reunited on several occasions for charitable events.

7 Deadly Synths

This midwestern act took their name from a Brian Eno song, their hairstyles from reruns of *Star Trek*, and were unique among similarly named electropop bands in that they only had five synthesizers, not seven.

Debuting with a single wholly comprising hook line from a dozen popular television commercials, 7 Deadly Synths were one of the first bands to appear on the fledgling MTV and would go on to enjoy a solid three years of massive American hits.

Fiercely dismissed by critics who complained that their every single sounded the same, the Synths later revealed that, in fact, they *were* all the same. They just changed its title and made a new video, and they sold a million every time.

The Soft White Undercurrents

Screaming (or at least making high-pitched noises) out of Puyallup Rock City, the Soft White Undercurrents started life as a Winger covers act before developing their own signature blend of power ballad histrionics and navel-gazing jingle lyrics. Several hits during the late 1980s saw the band poised for fame, but pervasive rumors that they did not appear in their own videos saw the public turn away and it would be thirty years before the Undercurrents returned to American radio, courtesy of the yacht rock boom.

XX the Xth

Rage was palpable when San Diego rapper XX the Xth was omitted from the lineup for Live Aid in 1985, thus ensuring that Run DMC alone would carry the flag for the most vibrant and popular music of the age. XX, whose career to that point had already seen American parents pushed to the brink of despair, responded within days with "How Nice 4 U," a hard-hitting rap that opened with the perfectly enunciated lyric, "How nice for you to play Live Aid and give your talents for free," before demanding to know how many of the participating acts would be equally free with the proceeds of the vast record sales that were already being reported. "And now your record's number one, but the starving are not laughing, indeedy, no . . ."

It was a bold move, tearing apart the benevolent image that the event cast across the music industry, and utterly shattering the complacency of all concerned. And his record company responded, as XX noted in his autobiography, by effectively blackballing him—paying radio DJs *not* to play his music and promotors to spell his name wrong on ads for his gigs, and ultimately removing the Parental Guidance stickers from his entire catalog.

XX retaliated in turn, moving to Silicon Valley and establishing what is now one of the world's most successful music streaming services. He also, unlike many of his rivals, ensures that artists receive the lion's share of the proceeds, up to sixty cents on the dollar. "And then I donate 59.99995 cents from each purchase to charity. Being as they like 'giving back' so much."

1990s

Granny Massacre Syndrome

GMS, as they are widely known, are frequently described as the "ultimate" industrial rock band—and with good reason. On tour, they transformed every venue into a fully operational steel works, their instrumentation ranging from the traditional synthesizers and drums to conveyor belts, motors, cranes, and blast furnaces. In the early days, any items manufactured during the process would be thrown to the audience as keepsakes—GMS reversed this policy after a fan was seriously injured by a newly forged anvil.

Recording three albums before hard-drinking vocalist Bette Bundy perished in what his family described as a "thirsty accident," GMS have maintained their position via an unceasing flow of live recordings and outtakes.

The Scam E-mails

Beloved by many, incomprehensible to more, the Scam E-mails were one of the underground success stories of the 1990s, a band that existed in total opposition to the prevalent currents of grunge, Britpop, and electronic dance music, but who could fill the vastest venue by word of mouth alone.

Five albums released across a twelve-year span remain the Ur-text for any act following in their footsteps; the Scam E-mails also hold the record for the most Record Store Day in-concert box sets released by any one act, a total of fifty-three in just fifteen years, with all selling out on the day of release.

These albums certainly give fans their money's worth, however. No less than the Grateful Dead, Scam E-mails specialized in what felt like endless jams, born out of what—in less adventurous hands—might have remained an innocuous two-minute pop song with a faintly silly title.

Their epic performance of "Seventeen Moonwalkers in Line for Lime Eggnog at 3 a.m. Revisited" at the Mudbath '94 festival is, according to some physicists, still under way today, a full twenty-nine years after the Scam E-mails first tuned up to play it—indeed, there are some who believe that they are *still* tuning up, and the song won't actually commence until the end of this decade. Even more incredibly, not one member of the audience has yet walked out, such is the overall devotion to the band.

Valerie Potsdam

Just seventeen when she cut her first album, Valerie Potsdam was the breakout star of the second Alternative Lilith Fair festival; her harsh confessionals about a childhood spent "making things you can't imagine in the back of my dead poppa's macramé studio" touching chords that few other singer-songwriters had ever dreamed of playing.

Her matter-of-fact delivery and a vocabulary loaded with what Ernest Hemingway once described as "ten-dollar words" captivated millions, even inspiring the formation of support groups and drum circles comprising fellow sufferers.

All came tumbling down, however, when a number of former schoolfriends came forward, casting doubt upon every aspect of Potsdam's professed biography, including her name and her age. She was, in fact, a twenty-seven-year-old housewife from Saskatchewan whose father was not only still alive and well, but didn't think much of macramé, either.

Numbnuts

A bar band performing Glenn Yarborough and Four Freshmen covers around northern California massage parlors, the Numbnuts underwent a complete makeover after hearing "Smells Like Teen Spirit," rewriting their biography (they now claimed to have played Kiss and Boston covers), sacking their organist, and reemerging in regulation lumberjack shirts and boots for an appearance at the 1993 New Music Seminar in New York. A record deal followed and Christmas saw their first single, "My Soul Feels Like Sludge," top the alternative chart, swiftly followed by the album *Tabernacle of the Deputy*.

Headlining several festival dates throughout the following summer, Numbnuts seemed poised to displace the Pacific Northwest as the pumping heart of the grunge movement—only for grunge itself to disavow its very existence, and render Numbnuts . . . and all the little Numbnuts that grew up around them . . . utterly irrelevant.

After breaking up, two Numbnuts returned to the massage circuit; the remainder stayed together as a Nickelback tribute act.

Zonk

Andorran electro quartet Zonk formed in 1997 with the intention of representing their country at the annual Eurovision Song Contest. Foiled in this aim by virtue of Andorra not having actually entered the contest, Zonk turned away from their earlier family friendly dance music with what they described as "the marriage of Wu-Tang and the Prodigy," and a debut album, *The Stasi Stole My Synthesizer*, characterized by such destructive beats and disruptive terminology that a proposed British tour was canceled on the grounds of public safety.

The United States was more welcoming, and Zonk topped the electronic charts for close to three months. However, a four-year wait for their sophomore album, and the band's decision to "go disco," saw their support fall away, and while two subsequent albums saw them return to former pastures, that fourth album would not receive an American release until a Record Store Day reissue in 2018.

The 2000s

"Twitch" McAllister

Launching his musical career on the very tail end of the nineties' ska revival (he played guitar in a series of unknown East Coast bands), McAllister nevertheless insisted that he performed music solely to hone his skills as a producer.

That accomplished, he worked through the early 2000s with a succession of indie landfill bands, many of whom had absolutely no idea how difficult life would become once online search machines replaced word of mouth for info-seeking fans—CIM, Scat, Squirt, Watersports, and the Prick Teasing Hussies from Hell all faded from view after just an album or two.

In 2007, McAllister was commissioned to remix a series of classic jazz albums for a modern audience, a project that revealed his laudable subtlety of touch and sensitivity to the original artist's intentions, even as he proved bold enough to pull the most unexpected moments out of the mix to establish them in the heart of a song. By the end of the decade, McAllister was being offered remixes across the musical spectrum, before hitting "the big time" with his multi-award-winning remix of the Soft White Undercurrents' fourth album.

Since that time, McAllister has established himself as *the* go-to guy for music so wet that you literally could float a yacht in it, while he has also released several solo albums of similar sounds.

Mark Syllabub

Young, good-looking, and tough as nails, Mark Syllabub (real name Gregory Syllabub) emerged seemingly from nowhere (a basement flat in Peoria) with what is still hailed as the most perfectly formed debut album of the century, a dozen songs that nobody doubted were just the opening shot in a career that would last a lifetime. Sadly, twelve songs were all he had—and ever would have. A sophomore set so disappointing that nobody even remembers what it was called, literally vanished without a trace, and Syllabub followed it into obscurity.

Wanda (McIntyre)

One of the era's most potent songwriters, former DJ and dance music aficionado Wanda was already approaching thirty when her debut album, *About Bloody Time*, was released to unanimously positive reviews. Three successive singles found their way not only into the charts, but were also co-opted for a variety of television shows, video games, and movie soundtracks. A four-year gap preceding her second album, however, saw what had once been a tidal wave of anticipation reduce to a trickle, and the disc itself proved tragically underwhelming. A third album was even further delayed (and even less interesting), and Wanda appears now to have abandoned recording altogether. *About Bloody Time*, however, created one of the decade's most indelible musical marks, a suite of songs that—though intensely personal to Wanda herself—reached out to millions of lost souls around the world.

The 2010s

The Bleeding Goblins

Formed in 1972 but completely unknown until reinventing themselves (for the fourteenth time) as fearless purveyors of what they described as nu–Death Metal, there is little to say about the Goblins that has not already been written about a host of other bog-awful clattering noise merchants. They are mentioned here wholly out of spite.

The Gaping Chasms

Emerging unexpectedly as winners of the 2015 erotic reality show *The XXX Factor*, the Gaping Chasms—who soundtracked the series, as well as appearing in it—abandoned the sax and wah-wah-heavy sounds of their breakthrough to deliver instead an album of eleven sharp, jagged instrumental pop songs, each titled for one of the erogenous zones.

It was already on course for a top ten berth when a second album, with the songs now featuring lyrics, was released; while the Black Friday Record Store Day delivered a limited edition double album comprising both discs on colored vinyl, plus a third featuring music from *The XXX Factor* soundtrack.

Further *XXX Factor* material was made available at Christmas, following a unique linkup between the Gaping Chasms and bespoke English vintner Abbey Wines—every bottle included a download code engraved into its cork, each redeemable for one of ten available tracks. In addition, a so-called golden cork entered the winner into a prize draw for one of a hundred vinyl pressings of an album comprising nine of the songs.

A fresh Gaping Chasms album was scheduled for release in 2020. Unfortunately, although a new single was issued, entering the UK chart at number three, the album was ultimately delayed—first by the pandemic, and then by the band's decision to scrap it and begin again. However, downloads of individual tracks from the abandoned album are currently being offered as an alternative to cash prizes in a series of branded scratch cards.

The 2020s

Jennifer Dingleberry

The daughter of the husband-and-wife speedway champions Joe and Marilyn Dingleberry, Jennifer is oft regarded as the Queen of American Nepo-rock. Behind her carefully crafted, deliberately drafted pop confectionary hits, however, is a voice so unique that even autotune cannot improve it, while her genius for seeking out fresh collaborators from across the worldwide grime, indie, and anime scenes has seen her score hits in five different languages, including braille, emoji, and medieval heraldic symbols.

Jeff Rotull

Another Gen Z unfortunate whose parents thought it would be hilarious to *almost* name him after a famous rock performer; but he got the last laugh by becoming one.

Identifying as Hippopotomonstrosesquipedaliasexual, Rotull was the dominant force on the last series of *American Icon* before production was shut down by the pandemic (that's what they said, anyway, although there are alternate rumors). In its wake, Rotull's debut album, 2021's *Seventeen-Syllable Words for Snow*, sold so many copies that the RIAA was forced to invent a whole new precious metal to press his award in.

Two years later, the release of the first song from his still-upcoming sophomore set, *My Mother Made the Tea for the Donaudampfschiffahrtselektrizitäten-hauptbetriebswerkbauunterbeamtengesellschaft,* was responsible for blackouts across the western seaboard as all available power was diverted to the servers that hosted the stream.

APPENDIX B
Twenty-First-Century Playlist

Midway through the writing of this book, I came across an attempt I made at cataloging my very-early-twenties' record collection and the total of three hundred or so different so-called rock, pop, and related artists whose music I had purchased throughout my first decade of record collecting.

My tastes at that time were surprisingly (to me) catholic, extending from a handful of Elvis Presley and Cliff Richard singles dating from years before I was born, to the latest by the Boomtown Rats, the Specials, Soft Cell, and TV Smith. But there was a quarter of a century's worth of records on the list, taking in the entire "rock'n'roll era" so far. And I wondered, if I was that age today, could I find as many artists whose music I have purchased—and kept—if rock'n'roll had been born in 2000? The answer, it appears, is yes.

I then attempted a similar list of equally worthwhile music released this century by artists whose careers predated that cutoff point. It took a while, but I reached a dozen, including the latest by the Boomtown Rats, the Specials, Soft Cell, and TV Smith. Old habits clearly die hard. Coincidentally, there were around the same number of performers in my original list who commenced their recording careers prior to 1955.

What does this prove? Beyond a certain consistency in my buying habits, not much. Or maybe it does.

The history of popular music—whether it is actually genuinely popular or not—cannot be sliced up into neat chronological pieces. Yes, one can look at the multitude of musical styles that have become popular with certain sections of the audience, and which history now records as specific eras: the original insurgence of rock'n'roll itself (1955–1958), the British Invasion (1964–1966), psychedelia (1967–1968), glam rock (1972–1974), punk rock (1977–1979), grunge (1991–1994), and so forth to the present day, from emo to EDM, from grime to wyrd folk.

But so what? At the end of the day, it's all pop music and what follows, then, is a gentle easing into the modern equivalent of that very same world, and a reminder that "new music"—which of course you disdain because it isn't "old music"—does not altogether comprise the acts that you see on television, or read about in the Sunday funnies, with their tempestuous love lives and their aversion to shaving, their peculiar clothing, and their omni-bludgeoning dance beats.

Nor does it wholly comprise that funny little chap whose every song seems to sound exactly the same as something else, but with (allegedly) just enough of his personal something to get away with it every time.

Rather, it's a playlist of suggestions to set you on your way the next time someone asks who your favorite new acts are and the best you can muster are the Chemistry Set (formed 1988), Tricky (1993), Sigur Rós (1994), and Garbage (1995).

True, "new" is in the eye of the beholder (several bands on this list have already outlived the Beatles almost three times over), but the rule of thumb is simple. If their first release predates the end of the last century, they're out—even if they are, like the aforementioned Chemistry Set, currently making the best music of their lives.

As with the remainder of this book, there is little rap, reggae, or R&B on this list, nor funk and jazz, and not much folk, and the reason for that is simple if you really want to think about it. They're not the genres that are continually rubbing their past in our faces, saying, "Look! You tapped a toe to Cat Sandwich. That *proves* old music is better than new."

Oh, please.

Neither are they the genres whose cheerleaders insist that music is dead, and everything new is steaming (or streaming) horse droppings. Indeed, for a century that too many rock music fans will tell you has produced nothing of note, its maiden quarter has produced some genuinely invigorating sounds.

What follows, then, is a wholly subjective but—for once in this book—a reasonably democratic[192] stab at pinpointing those acts to have emerged since the dawn of this century that (say it quietly) you may find yourself enjoying. And then, because who has the time to listen to the entire catalogs of 300-odd bands we might never have heard of, there's a single recommended track from a single recommended album.

---

192. I asked a bunch of friends for their suggestions, too. Journalists, ex-journalists, musicians, ex-musicians, record store owners, record label owners, whoever came to mind.

There's a lot of new music out there that you probably wish you had missed. This list suggests some you might wish you'd heard. This is the sound of the twenty-first century . . . at least into mid-2023.

62 Miles from Space—"Time Shifts" (EP *Time Shifts*)

The Advisory Circle—"Winter Hours" (album *From Out Here*)

Air France—"Collapsing at Your Doorstep" (single)

Airbag—"Sounds That I Hear" (album *Identity)*

The AKAs—"Shout Out Loud" (album *White Doves & Smoking Guns*)

The Aliens—"I Am the Unknown" (album *Astronomy for Dogs*)

All My Faith Lost—"Because Your Voice" (album *Chamber Music*)

Aloe Blacc—"The Man" (album *Lift Your Spirit*)

Amanda Votta & the Spectral Light—"I Am the Moon" (album *Secrets to the Sea*)

Amyl & the Sniffers—"Some Mutts (Can't Be Muzzled)" (album *Amyl & The Sniffers*)

Anaïs Mitchell & Jefferson Hamer—"Riddles Wisely Expounded" (album *Child Ballads*)

Angeline Morrison—"Black John" (album *The Sorrow Songs: Folk Songs of the Black British Experience*)

Animal Collective—"My Girls" (album *Merriweather Post Pavilion*)

Annie—"Heartbeat" (single)

Apse—"From the North" (album *Spirit*)

Arlo Parks—"For Violet" (album *Collapsed in Sunbeams*)

Art Brut—"Formed a Band" (album *Bang Bang Rock'n'Roll*)

Assemble Head in Sunburst Sound—"The Slumbering Ones" (album *When Sweet Sleep Returned*)

Audiobooks—"Hot Salt" (album *Now! [In a Minute]*)

Authority Zero—"Revolution" (album *Andiamo*)

Autumn's Grey Solace—"Within the Depths of a Darkened Forest" (album *Within the Depths of a Darkened Forest*)

Babyshambles—"Fuck Forever" (album *Down in Albion*)

Band of Horses—"The Funeral" (album *Everything All the Time*)

Bang Gang—"Everytime I Look in Your Eyes" (album *Ghosts from the Past*)

Bat for Lashes—"What's a Girl to Do" (album *Fur and Gold*)

Battles—"Atlas" (album *Mirrored*)

Baxter Dury—"Love in the Garden" (single)

Beach Bunny—"Colourblind" (album *Honeymoon*)

Beatrice Dillon—"Workaround One" (album *Workaround*)

Beaulieu Porch—"View from Gainsborough Point" (album *Beaulieu Porch*)

Beautify Junkyards—"Tomorrow's Children" (album *The Beast Shouted Love*)

Beirut—"Postcards from Italy" (album *Gulag Orkestar*)

Belbury Poly—"The Willows" (album *The Willows*)

Bitter Ruin—"Chewing Gum" (album *Hung, Drawn & Quartered*)

Black Country—"Science Fair" (album *New Roads—For the First Time*)

Black Pumas—"Touch the Sky" (album *Black Pumas*)

Blue Giant Zeta Puppies—"The Magician" (various artists album *The Darkest Voyage*)

Bon Iver—"Creature Fear" (album *For Emma, Forever Ago*)

Bones U.K.—"Filthy Freaks" (album *Bones U.K.*)

Booka Shade—"Mandarine Girl" (EP)

Brigitte—"Coeur de Chewing Gum" (album *Et Vous, Tu M'Aimes?*)

Broadcast—"Black Cat" (album *Tender Buttons*)

Broken Bells—"The High Road" (album *Broken Bells*)

Broken Social Scene—"Cause = Time" (album *You Forgot It in People*)

Bruiser Wolf—"Whip Test" (album *Dope Game Stupid*)

Burial—"Archangel" (album *Untrue*)

Califone—"The Orchids" (album *Roots & Crowns*)

Candy Claws—"Into the Deep Time (One Sun)" (album *Ceres & Calypso in the Deep Time*)

Carolina Chocolate Drops—"Cornbread and Butter Beans" (album *Genuine Negro Jig*)

Casino—"Love Go On" (single)

Cate Lebon—"Me Oh My" (album *Me Oh My*)

Charlotte Gainsbourg—"Deadly Valentine" (album *Rest*)

Charming Disaster—"Grimoire" (album *Super Natural Tales*)

Chloe X Halle—"The Kids Are Alright" (album *The Kids Are Alright*)

Christine & the Queens—"Comme Si on S'aimait" (album *Chris*)

Cigarettes After Sex—"Touch" (album *Cigarettes After Sex*)

The Civil Wars—"20 Years" (album *Barton Hollow*)

Clinic—"Distortions" (album *Internal Wrangler*)

The Coral—"Dreaming of You" (album *The Coral*)

Coralie Clément—"L'Enfer" (album *Bye Bye Beauté*)

The Courettes—"Misfits and Freaks" (album *Back in Mono*)

Courtney Barnett—"Pedestrian at Best" (album *Sometimes I Sit and Think, and Sometimes I Just Sit*)

Cranium Pie—"This Was Now/Awakening of the Birds" (album *Mechanisms Pt 1*)

Crystal Jacqueline—"By the Way" (album *Sun Arise*)

Custard Flux—"The Hit Parade" (album *Helium*)

Cut Copy—"Hearts on Fire" (album *In Ghost Colours*)

Cut Off Your Hands—"Oh Girl" (album *You and I*)

Dan Deacon—"The Crystal Cat" (album *Spiderman of the Rings*)

Danielle Ponder—"Some of Us Are Brave" (album *Some of Us Are Brave*)

Dead Sea Apes—"Sixth Side of the Pentagon" (album *Spectral Domain*)

The Dead South—"Banjo Odyssey" (album *Good Company*)

The Deadfly Ensemble—"Flight of the Invisible Siamese Three-Year-Olds" (album *An Entire Wardrobe of Doubt and Uncertainty*)

Death by Chocolate—"The Salvador Dali Murder Mystery" (album *Death by Chocolate*)

Death from Above 1979—"Romantic Rights" (album *You're a Woman, I'm a Machine*)

Deerhunter—"Nothing Ever Happened" (album *Microcastle / Weird Era Continued*)

Dirty Projectors—"Stillness Is the Move" (album *Bitte Orca*)

Dltzk—"Goldfish" (album *Frailty*)

Dodson & Fogg—"Crinkle Drive" (album *Dodson & Fogg*)

Doomsdale High—"Another Scream, Queen" (single)

Dry Cleaning—"Her Hippo" (album *New Long Leg*)

Duel—"Hey, Tu Ne Me Manqueras Plus" (album *Gunnn Express*)

The Duel—"Better Bombs, Better Drugs" (album *Let's Finish What We Started*)

Earthling Society—"The Halloween Tree" (album *Stations of the Ghost*)

Eccentronic Research Council—"The Hangman's Song" (album *1612 Underture*)

Eivør Pálsdóttir—"Í Tokuni" (album *Slør*)

Elfin Bow—"The Wisdom" (single)

Ellie Bryan—"Sheath and Knife" (album *Am I Born to Die*)

Embertides—"A Thousand Dead Stars" (single)

Emily Jones—"Hermagant and Maladine" (album *Autumn Eye*)

Emma-Jean Thackray—"Spectre" (album *Yellow*)

Emmy Lazarus and the Recently Deceased—"Get Haunted" (album *Get Haunted*)

Ethel Cain—"Family Tree" (album *Preacher's Daughter*)

Every Cloud Has a Silver Lining—"A Stolen Life" (album *Every Cloud Has a Silver Lining*)

Fallen—"Ravenhand" (album *Secrets of the Moon*)

Faun—"Walpurgisnacht" (album *Luna* 2014)

Feist—"Borrow Trouble" (album *Multitudes*)

The Field—"Over the Ice" (album *From Here We Go Sublime*)

The Focus Group—"Reflected Message" (album *Hey Let Loose Your Love*)

Fontaines D.C.—"Boys in the Better Land" (album *Dogrel*)

Freelance Hellraiser—"A Stroke of Genius" (single)

Future Virgins—"No Echo (album *Western Problems*)

Gabriels—"To the Moon and Back" (album *Angels & Queens Part I*)

Gang of Youths—"Benevolence Riots" (single)

Geese—"Disco" (album *Projector*)

Genesis Owusu—"The Other Black Dog" (album *Smiling with No Teeth*)

Girl Band—"Paul" (album *Holding Hands with Jamie*)

Girl Talk—"Smash Your Head" (album *Night Ripper*)

Glass Animals—"Gooey" (album *ZABA*)

The Go! Team—"Huddle Formation" (album *Thunder, Lightning, Strike*)

Goat Girl—"Cracker Drool" (album *Goat Girl*)

Gogol Bordello— "Not a Crime" (album *Gypsy Punks*)

Grails—"Space Prophet Dogon" (album *The Burden of Hope*)

Greanvine—"Child Among the Weeds" (album *Mark You That & Noat You Wel*)

Green Question Mark—"Pegasus" (single)

Grizzly Bear—"Deep Sea Diver" (album *Horn of Plenty*)

Guillemots—"Trains to Brazil" (album *From the Cliffs*)

Gwenno—"Chwyldro" (album *Y Dydd Olaf*)

Haken—"Sleeping Thoughts Wake" (album *Enter the 5th Dimension*)

Halsey—"Ghost" (album *Badlands*)

Hanford Reach—"Shifting Patterns" (EP *Canyons*)

Hannah Hu—"Secrets" (EP *Prisoner of Love*)

Hannah Peel—"Don't Kiss the Broken One" (album *The Broken Wave)*

Hare and the Moon—"Bard of Eve" (album *Wood Witch*)

Hausfrauen Experiment—"Spirit of the Age" (EP *Baby's on Fire*)

The Headless Prince of Zolpidem—"Nothingness" (album *Somnambulant*)

The Heart Attacks—"Widowmaking" (album *Hellbound and Heartless*)

The Heavy—"Set Me Free" (album *Great Vengeance and Furious Fire*)

Heilung—"Anoana" (album *Drif)*

Hercules and Love Affair—"Blind" (album *Hercules and Love Affair*)

Hold Steady—"Stay Positive" (album *Stay Positive*)

The Honey Pot—"Walking on Eggshells" (album *Inside the Whale*)

Horsegirl—"Dirtbag Transformation (Still Dirty)" (album *Versions of Modern Performance*)

Hot Chip—"Over and Over" (album *The Warning*)

Icarus Peel—"The River" (album *Tea at My Gaffe*)

Idles—"Well Done" (album *Brutalism*)

Ilona V—"Universe Arms" (single)

International Noise Conspiracy—"Smash It Up" (album *Survival Sickness*)

Interpol—"Obstacle 1" (album *Turn on the Bright Lights*)

Iris Aneas—"Chemtrails en el Aire" (album *Por La Verdad Libre*)

Jace Everett—"Bad Things" (album *Jace Everett*)

Jain—"Heads Up" (album *Zanaka*)

Jamie Lidell—"Multiply" (album *Multiply*)

Jeffrey Koepper—"Interlogic" (album *telelektra*)

Jem—"24" (album *Finally Woken*)

Jens Lekman—"Black Cab" (album *Oh You're So Silent Jens*)

Jesse Ware—"Running" (album *Devotion*)

Jessy Wilson—"Stay Cool" (album *Phase*)

Joanna Newsom—"Peach, Plum, Pear" (album *The Milk-Eyed Mender*)

Jockstrap—"Greatest Hits" (album *I Love You Jennifer B*)

Jóhaan Jóhaansson—"Ég heyrði allt án þess að hlusta" (album *Englabörn*)

Johnny Boy— "You Are the Generation That Bought More Shoes and You Get What You Deserve" (album *Johnny Boy*)

Johnny Flynn and the Sussex Wit—"Detectorists" (album *Live at the Roundhouse*)

Jovian Tea—"Strange World" (single)

JT & the Clouds—"Scattered Leaves" (album *Delilah*)

Junior Senior—"Move Your Feet" (album *D-D-Don't Don't Stop the Beat*)

Jupiter Hollow—"Deep in Space" (EP *Odyssey*)

Justice—"D.A.N.C.E." (album *A Cross the Universe*)

Kaelen Milka—"Yndisdráttur" (album *Glimmer and Aska*)

Kalevauva.fi—"Espoo" (album *Kaupunkilaulut Vol. 1*)

Karnivool—"Mauseum" (album *Themata*)

Katy Kirby—"Cool Dry Place" (album *Cool Dry Place*)

Katzenjammer Kabarett—"Gemini Girly Song" (album *Katzenjammer Kabaret*)

King Gizzard & the Lizard Wizard—"Big Fig Wasp" (album *Nonagan Infinity*)

Klaxons—"Four Horsemen of 2012" (album *Myths of the Near Future*)

The Knife—"Heartbeats" (single)

The Kooks—"Seaside" (album *Inside In/Inside Out*)

Kurt Vile—"Pretty Pimpin" (album *B'lieve I'm Goin Down*)

La Femme—"Amour Dans Le Motu" (album *Psycho Tropical Berlin*)

LA Priest—"Beginning" (album *Ini*)

LA Witch—"Get Lost" (album *LA Witch*)

Ladytron—"Destroy Everything You Touch" (album *Witching Hour*)

Lafille—"Dans Mon Apartment" (album *Tout Attaché(E)*)

Lara Jones, Saxophone—"Look" (album *Fig*)

Large Plants—"The Carrier" (album *The Carrier*)

Laura Cortese & the Dance Cards—"Lay Me Low" (album *Into the Dark*)

Lava La Rue—"Magpie" (single)

Leathers—"Fascination" (single)

Left Alone—"Monday Morning" (album *Lonely Starts and Broken Hearts*)

Len Price 3—"Chatham Town Spawns Devils" (album *Chinese Burn*)

Leprous—"Bilateral" (album *Bilateral)*

Les Pommes de Lune—"Une Fleur" (single)

Let's Eat Grandma—"Eat Shiitake Mushrooms" (album *I, Gemini*)

The Liars—"The Other Side of Mt. Heart Attack" (album *Drum's Not Dead*)

The Libertines—"Up the Bracket" (album *Up the Bracket*)

Life Without Buildings—"The Leanover" (album *Any Other City*)

Lindstrøm—"I Feel Space" (single)

Lisa Hammer—"Be Not Afraid" (album *Dakini*)

Locksley—"Don't Make Me Wait" (album *Don't Make Me Wait*)

London Experimental Ensemble—"The Elfin Knight" (*Child Ballads*)

Lounge Bar Orchestra—"Wake Up to Craft" (album *Pilot Episodes*)

Love Is All—"Make Out Fall Out Make Up" (album *Nine Times That Same Song*)

Love Spirals—"Windblown Kiss" (album *Windblown Kiss*)

Luke Haines—"Lou Reed Lou Reed" (album *New York in the 70s*)

Luomo—"Tessio" (album *Vocalcity*)

Mad Painter—"Illusion" (album *Splashed*)

The Mae Shi—"Run to Your Grave" (album *HLLLYH*)

Maisy Grace—"Until We Meet Again" (single)

Makaras Penn—"Promises" (album *Makaras Penn*)

Måneskin—"I Wanna Be Your Slave" (*Teatro D'Ira—Volume I*)

Mark and The Clouds—"You and Me in Space" (album *Waves*)

The Mars Volta—"Roulette Dares (The Haunt Of)" (album *De-loused in the Comatorium*)

Mclusky—"To Hell with Good Intentions" (album *Mclusky Do Dallas*)

Me and My Kites—"Porcelain" (album *Is It Real or Is It Made?*)

Melody's Echo Chamber—"Snowcapped Andes Crash" (album *Melody's Echo Chamber*)

Mercury's Antenna—"A Waking Ghost Inside" (album *A Waking Ghost Inside*)

MGMT—"Time to Pretend" (album *Oracular Spectacular*)

M.I.A.—"Amazon" (album *Arular*)

Midwich Youth Club—"Has Motorik Been Overdone?" (Album *Lapis Lazuli*)

Miles Kane—"First of My Kind" (album *Don't Forget Who You Are*)

Mira—"Space" (album *Space*)

Mirablis—"Undercurrent" (album *Sub Rosa*)

Miss Derringer—"Click Click (Bang Bang)" (album *Winter Hill*)

Monica Richards—"Death Is the Ultimate Woman" (album *Kindred*)

Moor Mother—"Made a Circle" (album *Black Encyclopedia of the Air*)

Mordecai Smyth—"Billywitch" (album *The Mayor of Toytown Is Dead*)

The Mortlake Book Club—"Live Deliciously" (EP *The Exquisite Corpse*)

The Naked and Famous—"The Sun" (album *Passive Me, Aggressive You*)

Nathan Hall and the Sinister Locals—"Green Goblin Blues" (album *Golden Fleece*)

Nation of Language—"Serene" (EP *Nation of Language*)

Naxatras—"Proximi Centauri" (album *Naxatras*)

Neighborhood Strange—"Wytches Sky" (single)

Neon Kittens—"I Dreamt of Being a Teenage Stripper" (single)

Nicole Reynolds—"When We Meet Again" (album *This Arduous Alchemy*)

No Age—"Teen Creeps" (album *Nouns*)

Noir Désir—"Le Vent Nous Portera" (album *Des Visages des Figures*)

Octopus Syng—"Cuckoo Clock Mystery" (album *Reverberating Garden #7*)

One-Eyed Doll—"The Ghosts of Gallows Hill" (album *Witches*)

The Owl Service—"The Dorset Hanging Oak" (album *A Garland of Song*)

Paolo Sala—"Stone Mermaid" (album *Foam*)

Paris Jackson—"Repair" (album *Wilted*)

The Pattern Forms— "Black Rain" (album *Peel Away the Ivy*)

Paulina Fawe—"Lullaby" (album *The Secret Language of Trees*)

Permanent Clear Light—"Higher Than the Sun" (album *Beyond These Things*)

Pete Doherty—"Broken Lovesong" (album *Brace/Wastelands*)

Peter Bjorn and John, with Victoria Bergsman—"Young Folks" (album *Writer's Block*)

Phoebe Bridgers—"Motion Sickness" (album *Stranger in the Alps*)

Phoenix—"Long Distance Call" (album *It's Never Been Like That*)

Pigs Pigs Pigs Pigs Pigs Pigs Pigs—"Sweet Relief" (album *Feed the Rats*)

The Pipettes—"Pull Shapes" (album *We Are the Pipettes*)

Polly Paulusma—"Give It Back" (album *Scissors in My Pocket*)

The Polyphonic Spree—"Section 11 (A Long Day Continues/We Sound Amazed)" (album *Together We're Heavy*)

Pom Pom Squad—"Drunk Voicemail" (album *Death of a Cheerleader*)

The Postal Service—"Such Great Heights" (album *Give Up*)

Prana Crafter—"Holy Tempel of Flow" (album *Bodhi Cheetah's Choice*)

The Premonitions—"Some Strange Lust" (single)

Prisoner of Mars—"Super Duper" (album *Gestalt*)

Public Service Broadcasting—"Go" (album *The Race for Space*)

Pussy Riot—"Chaika" (single)

Pye Audio Corner—"Gathering" (album *Black Mill Tapes Volume 1*)

Radiant Children—"Go Left" (EP *Tryin'*)

Red Birds—"River" (album *Fanks*)

Revuee Noir—"She Is the Madman" (album *Anthology Archive*)

Rob Clarke & the Wooltones—"Statue at the Pier Head" (album *Putting the L in Wootones*)

Rosalia—"Día 14 de Abril" (album *Los Ángeles*)

Rowan Amber Mill—"Face of Flowers (Woodcut)" (album *Harvest the Ears*)

Rowan-Morrison—"We Rode the Horses" (album *Bury the Forests*)

Roxanne de Bastion—"Buckle Up" (single)

Saffiyah Khan/The Specials—"Ten Commandments" (album *Encore*)

Sendelica—"The Hedge Witch" (album *Anima Mundi*)

The Seventh Ring of Saturn—"Mountain of the Moon" (single)

Sexwitch— "Kassidat El Hakka" (album *Sexwitch*)

She Rocola—"Molly Leigh of the Mother Town" (single)

Sidewalk Society—"Venus, Saturn and the Crescent Moon" (album *Venus, Saturn and the Crescent Moon*)

Silver Moth—"Mother Tongue" (album *Black Bay*)

Sky Ferreira—"Boys" (album *Night Time, My Time*)

Sky Picnic—"Most of a Box of Winter" (album *Her Dawn Wardrobe*)

Soccer Mommy—"Hudson River / Swollen Bloody Knuckles" (album *Songs for the Recently Sad*)

Soriah with Ashkelon Sain—"Xiuhcoatl" (various artists album *XiX*)

The Soulless Party—"The Watcher from the Village" (album *Tales from the Black Meadow*)

The Soundcarriers—"Volcano" (album *Harmonium*)

The Soundflowers—"Notes on a Ghost" (EP *Soundflowers*)

Special Interest—"Young, Gifted, Black, in Leather" (album *Spiraling*)

Spoek Mathambo—"Let Them Talk" (single)

Sproatly Smith—"Blackthorn Winter" (album *The Minstrel's Grave*)

Squid—"Documentary Filmmaker" (album *Bright Green Field*)

Stay—"Mersey Dream" (EP *Mersey Dream*)

Stephen Prince—"Night Wraiths (1878)" (album *The Corn Mother*)

Stone Foundation—"That's the Way I Want to Live My Life" (album *To the Spirit*)

The Strays—"Future Primitives" (album *Le Futur Noir*)

Street Dogs—"Modern Day Labor Anthem"(album *Savin Hill*)

Striped Bananas—"Silver Heels" (album *Dreams Upon the Mast*)

Stylus—"Pluen Eira (Snowflake)" (single)

Subsonica—"Livido Amniotico" (album *Controllo del Livello di Rombo*)

Sun Kil Moon—"Track Number Eight" (album *Among the Leaves*)

Switches—"Step Kids in Love" (*Heart Tuned to D.E.A.D.*)

SZA—"Drew Barrymore" (album *Ctrl*)

t.A.T.u.—"Ya Soshla S Uma" ("All The Things She Said") (album *200 Po Vstrechnoy*)

Tearwave—"Shattered Fairytale" (album *Different Shade of Beauty*)

Ted Leo and the Pharmacists—"Where Have All the Rude Boys Gone?" (album *Hearts of Oak*)

The Teskey Brothers—"Crying Shame" (album *Half Mile Harvest*)

Tess Parks—"Suzy & Sally's Eternal Return" (album *And Those Who Were Seen Dancing*)

Thee Oh Sees—"Drone Number One" (album *The Cool Death of Island Raiders*)

Titus Andronicus—"Joset of Nazareth's Blues" (album *The Airing of Grievances*)

Tor-Peders—"Incident Vid Domsten" (album *Brev Från Ederstorp*)

Total Control—"Carpet Rash" (album *Henge Beat*)

The Tough Alliance—"Silly Crimes" (album *New Wave*)

Towers of London—"Kill the Pop Scene" (album *Blood and Towers*)

Trappist Afterland—"Lucifer Mosquito" (album *Afterlander)*

Tropical Fuck Storm—"You Let My Tires Down" (album *A Laughing Death in Meatspac*e)

Turnstile—"Holiday" (album *Glow On*)

TV on the Radio—"Staring at the Sun" (album *Desperate Youth, Blood Thirsty Babes*)

Ty Segall—"When I Met My Parents Part One" (album *First Taste*)

United Bible Studies—"The Blackened Fields" (album *Doineann*)

The Unthanks—"My Laddie Sits Ower Late Up" (album *Last*)

Us and Them—"Fogwalking" (album . . . *And I Observed the Blue Sky*)

Vanity Fairy—"He Can Be Your Lady" (album *Lust for Dust*)

Vespero—"Rito" (album *Rito*)

Vibravoid—"Creepy People" (album *Void Vibration)*

Vitalic—"La Rock 01" (album *OK Cowboy*)

The Walkmen—"The Rat" (album *Bows + Arrows*)

Wasted Arrows— "Russian Dance" (album *Wharfman's Blues*)

Weep—"Lay There and Drown" (album *Never Ever*)

Wet Leg—"Wet Dream" (album *Wet Leg*)

The Whip—"Trash" (album *X Marks Destination*)

White Boy Scream—"Thou" (album *Remains*)

White Lies—"To Lose My Life" (album *To Lose My Life*)

White Sails—"Departed" (album *White Sails*)

Widows Weeds—"A Whisper in the Woods" (album *Revenant)*

Wolf Parade—"I'll Believe in Anything" (album *Apologies to the Queen Mary*)

Working for a Nuclear Free City—"The Tree" (album *Businessmen & Ghosts*)

Xiu Xiu—"I Luv the Valley OH!" (Album *Fabulous Muscles*)

The XX—"Crystalised" (album *The XX*)

Yard Act—"Quarantine the Sticks" (album *The Overload*)

The Young Fathers—"Soon Come Soon" (single)

The Young Punx—"You've Got To . . . " (album *Your Music Is Killing Me*)

Zeitkratzer & Carsten Nicolai—"Synchron Bitwave" (album *Electronics*)

Zombie Picnic—"Democracy Cannot Survive" (album *Rise of a New Ideology*)

Plus . . .

Benevolent Antenna Records was launched in 2022 by Schizo Fun Addict's Jet Wintzer, with a focus on "artists who have a long history of passionate work behind them to which the greater outside world is sadly unaware." Three super-limited-edition lathe-cut singles have already been and gone, but they have now been collected, alongside further material, on the label's first sampler album—available to readers of this book via this QR code.

Bellavista—"Shelter Shock"

The Bordellos—"Blank Letter"

Discount Sunset—"Slippery"

Schizo Fun Addict—"Activate"

Bellavista—"The Northwest Room"

Novio Electrico—"Metralettaa"

Schizo Fun Addict—"Outrun"

Lounge Bar Orchestra—"BALM"

The Soft Hearted Scientists—"What Grows in the Garden"

BIBLIOGRAPHY

Books

Bono. *Surrender: 40 Songs, One Story.* Alfred A. Knopf, 2022.

Burrows, Marc. *The London Boys: David Bowie, Marc Bolan and the 60s Teenage Dream.* Pen and Sword History, 2022.

Cohn, Nik. *Awopbopaloobop Alopbamboom: The Golden Age of Rock.* Paladin Books, 1970.

Connolly, Ray. *Stardust.* Fontana Books, 1974.

Elborough, Travis. *The Vinyl Countdown—The Album from LP to iPod and Back Again.* Soft Skull Press, 2009.

Farren, Mick. *The Tale of Willy's Rats.* Mayflower Books, 1974.

Goldman, Kat. *Off the Charts: What I Learned from My Almost Fabulous Life in Music.* Sutherland House Books, 2021.

Goodman, Lizzy. *Meet Me in the Bathroom: Rebirth and Rock and Roll in New York City 2001–2011.* Dey Street Books, 2017.

Gore, Tipper. *Raising PG Kids in an X-Rated Society.* Abingdon Press, 1987.

Guralnick, Peter. *Last Train to Memphis—The Rise of Elvis Presley.* Little, Brown Book Group, 1994.

Hardy, Phil. *Download! How the Internet Transformed the Record Business: How Digital Destroyed the Record Business.* Omnibus Press, 2012.

Jones, Lesley Ann. *Mercury: An Intimate Biography of Freddie Mercury.* Touchstone Reprint Edition, 2012.

Kozinn, Allan, and Adrian Sinclair. *The McCartney Legacy: Volume 1: 1969–73.* Day Street Books, 2022.

Levitin, Daniel J. *This Is Your Brain on Music: The Science of a Human Obsession.* Dutton, 2007.

Lewisohn, Mark. *The Complete Beatles Recording Sessions.* Harmony Books, 1988.

Martin, Linda, and Kerry Segrave. *Anti-Rock—The Opposition to Rock'n'Roll.* Da Capo Press, 1993.

Rubin, Jerry. *Do It!* Simon and Schuster, 1970.

Slonimsky, Nicolas. *Lexicon of Musical Invective.* University of Washington Press, 1965.

Stourton, Edward. *Confessions: Life Re-examined.* Doubleday, 2023.

Magazines

Assar, Vijith. "Apple's Devious U2 Album Giveaway Is Even Worse Than Spam." *Wired*. September 16, 2014.

Barlow, Eve. "Viva la Diva! How Eurovision's Dana International Made Trans Identity Mainstream." *The Guardian*. May 10, 2018.

Beaumont-Thomas, Ben. "'Tours Are No Longer Fun': Neil Young Lambasts Ticketmaster for Ripping Off Fans." *The Guardian*. March 24, 2023.

Beresford, Jack. "9 U2 Jokes You Can't Live With or Without." *Irish Post*. June 1, 2018.

Brandle, Lars. "U.S. Vinyl Album Sales Up by 53% in Q1." *Billboard*. April 17, 2015.

Brown, Craig. "Here There and Everywhere." *The Oldie*. Spring 2002.

Calvino, Italo. "Why Read the Classics?" *New York Review of Books*. October 9, 1986.

Clash, Jim. "Grace Slick: 'Rock Is Like Sports—You Have a Certain Run, Then Get Out.'" Forbes.com. December 11, 2015.

Ditum, Sarah. "Micro Niche." *The Critic*. May 2023.

"The 500 Greatest Albums of All Time." *Rolling Stone*. May 31, 2012.

Garr, Gillian. "Crossing Paths: When Elvis Met the Beatles." *Goldmine*. 2009.

"Gee, Thanks Dad." Forbes.com. October 18, 2004.

Green, Andy. "50 Genuinely Horrible Albums by Brilliant Artists." *Rolling Stone*. February 15, 2023.

Greer, Germaine. "Go, Marija! Eurovision's Triumphant Lesbian Gypsy." *The Guardian*. May 21, 2007.

Harrington, Linda M., and Tribune Staff Writer. "On Capitol Hill, a Real Rap Session." *Chicago Tribune*. February 24, 1994.

Hilburn, Robert. "McCartney's Absence Sparks Rancor at Rock Hall." *Los Angeles Times*. January 22, 1988.

Iverson, Ethan. "The End of the Music Business." *The Nation*. April 17/24, 2023.

Leimkuehler, Matthew. "Dolly Parton Removes Herself from Rock & Roll Hall of Fame Consideration." *The Tennessean*. March 14, 2022.

May, Lizzie. "'He's Not Worthy of Shining His Shoes': David Bowie's Producing Partner Tony Visconti Hits Out at Claims That Harry Styles Is the 'New Bowie' after Winning Album of the Year at the Grammys." Mail Online. February 7, 2023.

McCombs, Phil. "Watt Outlaws Rock on Mall for July 4." *Washington Post*. April 6, 1983.

McIntyre, Hugh. "Vinyl Sales Surged 30 Percent in 2015, Led by Adele and Taylor Swift." Forbes.com. January 8, 2016.

Michaels, Sean. "Guns N' Roses Lead Rock and Roll Hall of Fame Inductions." *The Guardian.* April 16, 2012.

Orwell, George. "Good Bad Books." *Tribune.* 1945.

Petridis, Alexis. "Mae Muller: I Wrote a Song Review—U.K. Eurovision Entry Is Far from Douze Points." *The Guardian.* March 9, 2023.

Seale, Jack. "I Can Go for That: The Smooth World of Yacht Rock Review—Lushly Comforting." *The Guardian.* June 14, 2019.

Shutler, Ali. "Wombles Songwriter Destroys Master Tapes to Avoid the Beatles-Style Remasters." *New Musical Express.* October 10, 2022.

Sprague, David. "Sex Pistols Flip Off Hall of Fame." *Rolling Stone.* February 24, 2006.

Swenson, John. "Frank Zappa Talks Music, Money and Steve Vai. . . . " *Guitar World.* March 1982.

Tapper, James. "Are Bands Dead? How Solo Stars Took Over the Charts." *The Guardian.* January 29, 2023.

Uhelszki, Jaan. "Ozzy Says 'No Thanks' to Hall of Fame." *Rolling Stone.* October 5, 1999.

Vivarelli, Nick, and Aswad, Jim. "The Making of Måneskin: How Four Young Italians Became the Biggest Rock Band to Emerge in Years." *Variety.* February 2, 2023.

Willman, Chris. "Giles Martin Details Beatles' 'Revolver' Deluxe Edition and Remix: In 1966 Sessions, 'You Can Hear Them Unwrapping Their Presents.'" *Variety.* September 7, 2022.

Zucchino, David. "Rock Censorship: Big Brother Meets Twisted Sister." *Rolling Stone.* November 7, 1985.

ACKNOWLEDGMENTS

Thanks first and foremost to Mike Edison, both for his dynamite foreword and for conceiving and commissioning this book's predecessor, *I Hate New Music*, back in the misty recesses of time. His enthusiasm for that book was partially responsible for this one, too.

To Amy, for living through the writing of this, and for never complaining as any number of grotesque ditties seeped out of the stereo; to Jo-Ann Greene, who waded through my initial notes, tweaking and twisting them into ever new shapes and offering up some wizard suggestions, too.

To Chris Haug, Todd and Miranda Brewer (International Groove Records), Stephen Stannard, Icarus Peel, Crystal Jacqueline, Brian Bordello, Keith Jones, Duncan Shepherd, Alex Gitlin, Grey Malkin, and Anders Håkanson for joining Amy, Jo-Ann, and me in compiling the playlist at the end.

To everyone at Backbeat for making this book a reality.

And to Rainbow Records, Mik Heslin, Karen and Todd, Tanya, Jen, Kateypoos, Dennis and Frankie, Trevor and George, snails and fish, Mrs. Beast and Geoff Monmouth for often unwittingly adding their own tuppence-worth to the trough.

ABOUT THE AUTHOR

Dave Thompson has been a professional writer and author for forty years and, despite what you might read elsewhere (ummm . . .) he has loved almost every minute of it, except those spent listening to certain songs and artists.

Specializing in rock, soul, reggae, and folk music, he can be read across a wide variety of publications, books, magazines, and online resources, including the Library of Congress's National Registry of Songs.

He is author of some two hundred books, including co-written auto-biographies with Motown songwriters Eddie and Brian Holland, the New York Dolls' Sylvain Sylvain, Walter Lure of Johnny Thunders Heartbreakers, Yardbirds/British Invasion legend Jim McCarty, Nik Turner of Hawkwind, and Fairport Convention founder member Judy Dyble. In addition, he has written biographies of numerous artists—including David Bowie, Patti Smith, Kurt Cobain, Roger Waters, Genesis, and Joan Jett—and a number of encyclopedias and reference books.

He is currently researching a semi-authorized biography of the Dental Assassins.